A History of English Architecture

A History of English Architecture

Part I

by

PETER KIDSON

Conway Librarian Courtauld Institute of Art

Part II

by

PETER MURRAY

Witt Librarian Courtauld Institute of Art

George G. Harrap & Co. Ltd

London Toronto Wellington Sydney

First published in Great Britain 1962
by GEORGE G. HARRAP & CO. LTD
182 High Holborn, London, W.C.1

Composed in Baskerville type and printed
by Jarrold and Sons Ltd, Norwich
Made in Great Britain

Acknowledgments

'he authors wish to thank Dr Margaret Whinney, who read one whole :ction of the book in typescript, and who made a large number of nprovements, which are most gratefully acknowledged. We further 'ish to thank Miss J. Allday, Miss M. Mount, Mr G. McIntosh, and 1r H. Murray, who read the proofs, and Miss S. Pavry, who compiled ie Glossary.

Permission to reproduce the illustrations in this book has been given y the following: T. and R. Annan and Sons, Ltd, 114; Architectural ress, 81; Barber Institute of Fine Arts and Dr K. Downes, 102; J. Bony, 1; Brentford and Chiswick Public Libraries, 91; Brighton Corporation,)4; Bristol Public Library, 110; Central Press Photos, Ltd, 49; Country ife, Ltd, 92, 95, 96, 98, 100; Courtauld Institute of Art, 8, 10, 12, 18, 2, 23, 27, 28, 29, 31, 32, 33, 35, 38, 42, 51, 66, 67, 68, 72, 74, 75, 76, 77,), 83, 84, 88, 94, 99, 101, 103, 105, 108, 109, 112; Coventry Cathedral econstruction, 115; F. H. Crossley, 7, 13, 15, 16, 25, 36, 37, 40; Her [ajesty's Stationery Office (Crown Copyright), 52, 61, 62, 82, 90; . F. Kersting, 19, 34, 39, 44, 86, 93; National Buildings Record, 3, 4, 9, , 17, 21, 26, 43, 45, 46, 56, 79, 106, 107, 111, 113; Nottingham City orporation, 54; Penguin Books Ltd (from *Architecture in Britain 1530–30*, by Sir John Summerson), 50, 53, 55, 57, 63; Photo Precision, Ltd, , 73; Royal Archaeological Institute of Great Britain and Ireland, 6; oyal Commission on Historical Monuments (England), 60, 64, 65, 69, , 71; Mrs J. P. Sumner, 41; Times Picture Library, 89; Valentine and ns, Ltd, 78; Victoria and Albert Museum (Crown Copyright), 59, 87, .

Contents

PART I

PART II

Illustrations

Map

Famous British Buildings

1
2
3
4
5
6
7
8
9
10
11
12
13
14
15
16
17
18
19
20
21
22
23
24
25
26
27
28
29
30
31
32
33
34
35
36
37
38
39
40
41
43
44
45
46
47
48
49
50
51
52
53
54
55
56
57
58
59
60
61
62
63
64
65
66
67
68
69
70
71
72
73
74
75
76
77
78
79
80
81
82
83
84
85
86
87
88
89
90
91
92
93
94
95
96
97
99
100
101
102
103
104
105
106
107
108
109
110
111
112
113
114
115
116
117
118
119
120
121
122
123
124
125
126
127
128
129
130
131
132
133
134
135
AJS.

KEY

Edinburgh
Seaton Delaval: Seaton Delaval Hall
Ruthwell: runic cross
Bewcastle: runic cross
Hexham: abbey
Jarrow: monastery
Monkwearmouth: monastery
Durham
Bishop Auckland: Bishop Pudsey's Hall
Escomb: church
Whitby: abbey
Richmond: castle
Rievaulx: abbey
Byland: abbey
Barrow-in-Furness: Furness Abbey
Castle Howard
Ripon: Fountains Abbey
York
Beverley
Hull: parish church
Leeds: Kirkstall Abbey
Liverpool: St George's Hall
Maltby: Roche Abbey
Sheffield
Lincoln
Anglesey: Menai Strait Bridge, Britannia Bridge
Chesterfield: Hardwick Hall
Conway: castle
Tattershall: castle
Caernarvon: castle
Boston: church
Southwell
South Wingfield: manor-house
Holkham: Holkham Hall
Binham: priory
Nottingham: Wollaton Hall
Stamford: Burghley House
Derby: Kedleston Hall
North Elham: church
Oakham: castle
Houghton: Houghton Hall
Norwich
Peterborough
Repton: church

45. Breedon-on-the-Hill: church
46. Ramsey: abbey
47. Gretton: Kirby Hall
48. Ely
49. Lichfield
50. Acton Burnell: Acton Burnell Hall
51. Much Wenlock: Wenlock Abbey
52. Earls Barton: church
53. Birmingham: Aston Hall
54. Lamport: Lamport Hall
55. Stokesay Castle
56. Bury St Edmunds: abbey
57. Cambridge
58. Coventry
59. Brixworth: church
60. Kenilworth: castle
61. Worcester
62. Hereford
63. Pershore: abbey
64. Evesham: abbey
65. Abbey Dore: abbey
66. Kilpeck: church
67. Lavenham: wool church
68. Tewkesbury: abbey
69. Deerhurst: priory
70. Sezincote: Sezincote House
71. Colchester
72. Saffron Walden: Audley End House
73. St David's
74. Gloucester
75. Winchcomb: church
76. Layer Marney: Layer Marney Hall
77. Woodstock: Blenheim Palace
78. Bradwell: church
79. Hatfield: Hatfield House
80. St Albans
81. Oxford
82. Cirencester
83. Coleshill: Coleshill House
84. Ealing: Pitzhanger Manor
85. London
86. Ockwells Manor
87. Osterley: Osterley Park House
88. Brentford: Syon House
89. Thornbury: castle
90. Greenwich
91. Margam: abbey
92. Malmesbury: abbey
93. Windsor: St George's Chapel
94. Twickenham: Strawberry Hill
95. Chiswick: Chiswick Villa
96. Eton
97. Eltham: Eltham Palace, Eltham Lodge
98. Reculver: church
99. Rochester: castle
100. Hampton Court Palace
101. Reading: abbey
102. Bristol
103. Canterbury
104. Chertsey: abbey
105. Bath
106. Mereworth: Mereworth Castle
107. Chevening: Chevening Place
108. Silchester
109. Bradford-on-Avon: church
110. Basing: Basing House
111. Lyminge: church
112. Sevenoaks: Knole
113. Old Sarum
114. Woking: Sutton Place
115. Wells
116. Warminster: Longleat House
117. Wilton: Wilton House
118. Stonehenge
119. Norton St Philip: George Inn
120. Waverley: abbey
121. Salisbury
122. Winchester
123. Bodiam: castle
124. Penshurst: Penshurst Place
125. Glastonbury
126. Romsey: abbey
127. Tisbury: Wardour Castle
128. Battle: abbey
129. Herstmonceaux: castle
130. Sompting: church
131. Brighton
132. Chichester
133. Sherborne
134. Exeter
135. Lewes: priory

A Note to the Reader

It should be pointed out that in many cases a single date has been assigned to a building with an obscure and often complicated history of construction. This date is not intended to do more than indicate when the design was likely to have been made. In the case of some of the later houses a date is actually found on the building itself, and this is often the only date we possess for its construction.

Part I

CHAPTER I

The Anglo-Saxon Period

OR the purposes of this book architecture in England is the architecture f the English people. No doubt if one wished to be really thorough it ould be argued that there has been something which deserved to be alled architecture of a sort in England at least as far back as Stone-enge, for the great circles of upright stones joined overhead by orizontal lintels use a constructional technique well-known in Iycenean Greece. Or, if Stonehenge seems too isolated and remote, ne could still very well begin with the buildings of Roman Britain. At ath, St Albans, Colchester, along Hadrian's Wall, and elsewhere iere is still abundant evidence of building activity which, though iodest by the standard of Roman achievements elsewhere in Europe, ertainly reveals a higher level of competence than anything to be ound in the country for centuries afterwards.

All the same, there are good reasons for beginning with the Anglo-axon invaders who settled in England during the fifth and sixth enturies. Not only were they to form the nucleus of the permanent opulation of the country, which means that they can provide the ecessary element of continuity that gives meaning to any study of hanging and developing forms, but from a strictly architectural point f view there is the added convenience that they made what virtually mounts to a fresh start. Whatever their reactions may have been to omano-British buildings, they were certainly indifferent to them as n architectural inheritance. It is true that here and there Roman cities ich as York, Lincoln, Canterbury, and London appear to have sur-ived in some form or other to become the local capitals of Anglo-axon kingdoms; but in terms of actual buildings this does not mean ery much. During the early stages of the occupation the amount of ieer destruction must have been considerable, and nearly all those estiges of the comparatively highly organized way of life in Roman ritain which were not destroyed outright seem to have been treated by the newcomers with the disdain of incomprehension. Buildings such a baths, temples, basilicas, and theatres lay wholly beyond the range o their experience. Moreover, the pattern of settlement changed over th entire country. Many Roman towns and nearly all the Roman countr villas were totally abandoned; so that from the Anglo-Saxon point o view perhaps the most important aspect of Roman buildings was th facility with which they could be exploited for building material.

It is now almost impossible to say with any accuracy how much us there was for buildings other than dwelling-houses in Anglo-Saxo society. They were certainly among the least civilized of the Teutoni peoples who partitioned among themselves the Western provinces o the Roman Empire; and if one had to commit oneself to an opinion would perhaps be prudent to stress their backwardness, and th simplicity of their way of life, rather than their sophistication. Yet w know from *Beowulf* and Bede that their chieftains held court with the retainers in great communal halls, and more than once Bede alludes t pagan temples which were destroyed by Christian proselytes in th zeal of conversion. Their skill in purely decorative work is known t have been formidable. So it would be unwise to dismiss their capacit for construction out of hand. The communal halls in particular must b accounted the ultimate ancestors of the great dwelling-houses of late times. But the one important thing that needs to be said about th earliest Anglo-Saxon buildings is that once they aspired beyond th level of mud, wattle, and thatch they must have been made of woo not stone. By origin, and perhaps by inclination, the English wer forest-dwellers, and the handling of wood came as easily to them a brick, stone, and concrete did to the more civilized peoples of th Mediterranean. Timber was their natural building material; masonr was something which they had to learn about from abroad. Even whe they acquired proficiency in masonry timber continued to be used on large scale, and throughout the Middle Ages the virtuosity of Englis woodwork was one of the most remarkable and distinctive features o English architecture.

Building in stone came to England with the first Christian mis sionaries, led by St Augustine, who arrived from Rome at the end o the sixth century. The provision of church buildings adequate to serv the needs of the cult was an obvious, if not always an immediate, ai of the Christian bishops and clergy. It is true that in the early stages o the conversion many congregations were compelled to assemble in th open around great crosses, which were set up in public places becau the means were not available for the building of churches; and it also true that in many cases where churches were built they were ood. But the desire for permanent buildings, and even more the desire or imposing buildings, proved a constant inducement for church esigners to master and exploit the technique of masonry construction. he conversion therefore deserves to be regarded as the most decisive vent in the creation of what we can recognize as English architecture. rom the beginnings of Christianity—about 600 until the Reformation n the sixteenth century—*i.e.*, for a period of more than 900 years— hurch-building continued to offer by far the most numerous and lavish pportunities for the exercise of architectural talents. No doubt the olume of building for secular purposes was always large and became teadily larger, especially toward the end of this period; but it was set onsistently at a lower pitch of ingenuity and skill. The view that nglish architecture before the Reformation was fundamentally an cclesiastical architecture cannot seriously be disputed. After the Refor- nation this was no longer so. That is why this book divides there, and vhy the first half of it is so overwhelmingly concerned with churches.

Anglo-Saxon architecture falls very definitely into two periods. The irst of these extends from the conversion to the Danish invasions of the inth century. The second may perhaps be said to have begun with the fforts made by King Alfred to restore English society, at the end of he ninth century, although it hardly got under way before the middle of he tenth. The impetus with which it began had virtually spent itself efore the Conquest. For neither period have we anything like enough vidence for a fair assessment. The great buildings such as cathedrals nd abbeys, which set the pace and showed what could be done, have ll been rebuilt many times. Occasionally we have descriptions of nportant buildings by people who saw them; but these accounts are o notoriously vague that they seldom add anything more than con- usion to our ignorance. Apart from these, there is Brixworth Church, Vorthamptonshire, the one really substantial and impressive Anglo- axon building that has come down to us. But for the rest all we have o go on are a few mutilated fragments, ruins, and excavated founda- ions which, although of absorbing antiquarian interest in so far as ome of them can be identified with buildings mentioned in surviving exts, and because their similarities prove that there were definite types f church-design in vogue at certain times, hardly deserve to be taken ery seriously as architecture. No one could infer the splendours of Gothic cathedrals from the modest parish churches which were con- emporary with them; and, in the same way, although the parallel is ot exact, it would be unwise for us to judge Anglo-Saxon architecture nerely by what is left of it for us to see.

According to Bede, when St Augustine arrived in England there wer at least two Roman churches in the vicinity of Canterbury that wer still capable of being put into a state of repair. One of these, St Martin's was already being used as a private chapel by the Christian Queen c Kent. The other stood inside the city, and when it had been patched u it became the first cathedral of Canterbury (602). Quite a number c Christian churches must have existed in Britain during Roman time Three British bishops, including those of York and London, attended Council of the Church at Arles, in 314. These must have had churche of some kind. The foundations of another have actually come to ligh among the ruins of the Roman city of Silchester. It is doubtful whethe many of these Romano-British churches were in a fit state to influenc their Anglo-Saxon successors, but the case of Canterbury provides a least two exceptions. We have a description of the cathedral by a certai Edmer the Singer, who had seen it before it was burnt down in 1067 Edmer says that it was "arranged in some parts in imitation of th church of the blessed Prince of the Apostles Peter"—*i.e.*, old St Peter's at Rome. It would be a mistake to read too much into medieval state ments of this kind, for similarities between buildings were not always or even often, thought of in terms of appearances. In this instance w know that what really impressed Edmer was the fact that the cathedra of Canterbury possessed a 'confessio,' or crypt, similar to that of ol St Peter's. In other respects the analogy may not have been very close We have no means of telling how much restoration was carried out b Augustine, or how much of what Edmer saw was the work of late archbishops. But there is no reason to doubt Bede's word that it wa originally a Roman building, or Edmer's that it had an apse at the eas end, and a nave flanked with side aisles, like the earliest Christia churches of Rome itself. The fact that it was taken over by a body c Roman missionaries, sent direct from Rome, where they had bee familiar with the early Roman churches, seems to suggest that, so fa as he was able, Augustine wished to reproduce in England the tradi tional type of Roman church-building along with all the other aspect of Roman Christianity.

But this was not the only church with which Augustine was con cerned. Bede also tells us that he persuaded Ethelbert, the King c Kent, to build another near the monastery which he had founde outside the city walls. It was dedicated to SS Peter and Paul, and i became the church of the Benedictine Abbey of St Augustine. Unlik the cathedral, this seems to have been an entirely new building, an although only the lower parts of the walls can still be seen, it is clea that it must have been a much less grandiose affair, and of quite lifferent design. Instead of the usual arrangement of nave and aisles, t consisted of a series of compartments, or chambers, of varying sizes, vith a large one in the centre, and the rest grouped round it, and pening from it. With one exception, all the other early churches in Kent about which anything is known conformed to this type of plan in reference to that of the cathedral. Two others were at Canterbury; nother formed the first cathedral at Rochester; another was at yminge, also in Kent; and most impressive, as well as the latest of the roup, was Reculver on the Kentish coast (*c.* 669). The only differences re to be found in the number and arrangement of the subsidiary ooms.

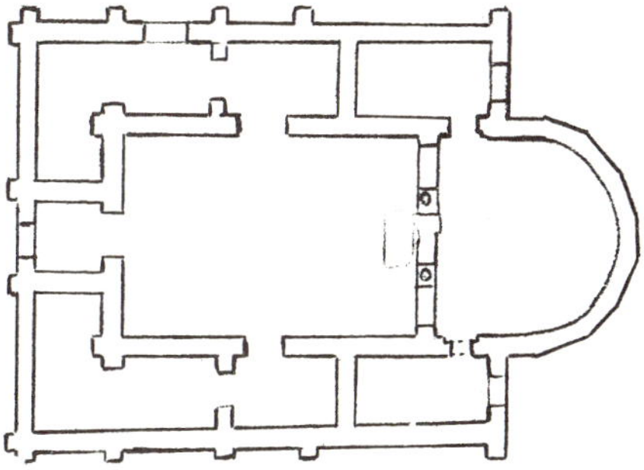

1. PLAN OF RECULVER CHURCH

The most important questions that can be asked about this Kentish roup of churches are: Who built them? How was the design arrived t? The mere fact that the competence of the masonry was of a high rder rules out the possibility that Augustine used local Kentish workien. Nor is it likely that he brought masons with him all the way from taly. The case of SS Peter and Paul suggests the most plausible xplanation. When churches were needed they were provided by the King of Kent himself. He made available the sites on which they were uilt, and, according to Teutonic custom, he retained a proprietary iterest in the fabric of the church. The men who actually did the work ould have been recruited by him; and there can be little doubt that e borrowed their services from his kinsmen in the Frankish royal amily just across the Channel. It is a great pity that nothing is known f the typical church buildings of Northern France in those times, and cholars have been forced to look farther afield for illuminating comarisons. It has always been urged that the polygonal-apse form, which ppears in Kent instead of the more familiar semicircular variety, was erived directly from Ravenna, in Italy. This may have been the case, lthough polygonal apses of a slightly different form were certainly known north and west of the Alps as well—for instance, at St Mauric d'Agaune, in Switzerland, and St-Bertrand-de-Comminges, in th South of France. But the crucial matter, and the one most urgentl in need of a satisfactory explanation, is the use of the subsidiar chambers, or 'porticus,' as they are called.

The earliest porticus seem to have made their appearance in th eastern Mediterranean to serve the special needs of the clergy and th cult. Something of the kind was known in Italy in the fifth century, fc we hear of chambers flanking the nave of a church built at Nola soo after 400, and again at Como at the end of the fifth century. St Bertranc de-Comminges also had them. At Nola they were reserved for privat devotions, and as memorials for the dead. In this connexion it is wort noting that in SS Peter and Paul, at Canterbury, two porticus wer used as burial-chambers, one on the north side for the early arch bishops of Canterbury, and the other on the south for the Kentis royal family. Others were apparently used as porches.

But to know the uses to which they were put offers only a parti explanation. Certain purely architectural exigencies were also involve One way of describing churches of the kind found in Kent is to sa that the porticus have taken the place of side aisles. Another way putting the same point would be to say that as far as possible they we built without columns and arches. The column with its carefully turne and tapered shaft, sometimes fluted, sometimes smooth, surmounted b a well-carved capital, and standing on a moulded base, is a mo evocative symbol, not only of the balanced calm and dignity of Roma architecture, but also of the precision and craftsmanship which mac that architecture possible. Except in the monumental structures, whic were made of concrete, rows of columns were a traditional feature Roman public buildings; and the earliest churches which were bui after Christianity was officially recognized were all raised upon suc rows, which served to divide the aisles from the nave as well as support the upper parts of the nave. When the Roman Empire in th West went into decline, one of the symptoms of its decadence was th gradual disappearance of the skill which in earlier times had produce these columns, and they tended to become scarce. One solution of th difficulty was to use again old columns from buildings that were n longer required, such as pagan temples. But this was a restricted an uncertain source of supply, especially in the more remote and le developed parts of the Empire; and in the end the inevitable result w that buildings had to be designed without columns. Sometimes maso felt competent to put piers of masonry in their place; but more ofte than not they were content with walls unbroken except for occasion oors and windows. Where churches were involved, this meant either bandoning side aisles altogether, or else turning them into self-ontained compartments which were, in effect, porticus. All these ideas ere tried in all parts of Western Europe including Italy itself, and it ould probably be a mistake to attempt to associate any one solution ith a particular region. Instead, it would be better to think of all 'estern European architecture during the centuries which we call the ark Ages as being in varying degrees a debased survival of Roman rovincial styles. Occasionally, where conditions were propitious, a uilding might be produced which approximated in form and even uality to the archetypes in Rome. But at the other extreme a crude isticity prevailed, in which architecture was little more than the aking of walls.

In such a hierarchy the Kentish group of churches must have :cupied a lowly place. Yet even here we find traces of an awareness of e finer points of architecture. At Lyminge and Reculver, at Bradwell, Essex, and at Brixworth, we know that pairs of columns were used to rry a triple arcade between the nave and the chancel or apse. Those om Reculver can still be seen in the crypt of Canterbury Cathedral, gether with fragments of a great stone cross which stood between em. In their original setting columns and cross must have made an iposing sight, in sharp contrast to the bare walls which converged oon them.

The extent to which Canterbury Cathedral was distinguished from e Kentish group of churches is something that cannot now be etermined. It is reasonable to suppose that it was put in order by the me workmen who built SS Peter and Paul, but we cannot say whether had columns or piers, or whether it had an upper storey. It seems to ave had porticus as well as side aisles, but the mere fact that it had sles puts it further up the scale than the little churches with only orticus.

When we turn to the other group of early Anglo-Saxon churches hich were built in the North of England toward the end of the seventh ntury these distinctions can be handled with more precision. In the st third of the seventh century, and at the beginning of the eighth, orthumbria witnessed a remarkable efflorescence in literature and the ts. The early history of Christianity in the North was hardly affected Augustine's mission. In 625 Paulinus left Canterbury on his specta-ılar journey to the King of Northumbria, which resulted in the ilding of a temporary wooden church at York, in 627, and its replace-ent by a permanent building a few years later. This was still un-iished when the pagan reaction of 632 put an end to further progress for a time. Paulinus is also known to have used a church at Lincol which may or may not have been a survival from Roman times. Tl pagan reaction in Northumbria lasted only two years, but as a resu the whole course of Christian expansion in the North was deflected in a new channel. The new Christian King, Oswald, had imbibed h religion, not from Paulinus, but from Irish monks at Iona; and as soc as he was in power he gave his support and protection to an Iri mission from Iona, led by St Aidan. This operated from Lindisfarn and for the next twenty years or so the Irish applied themselves to tl work of conversion with a zeal that made the activities of the Southe church seem tepid by comparison. But so far as architecture w

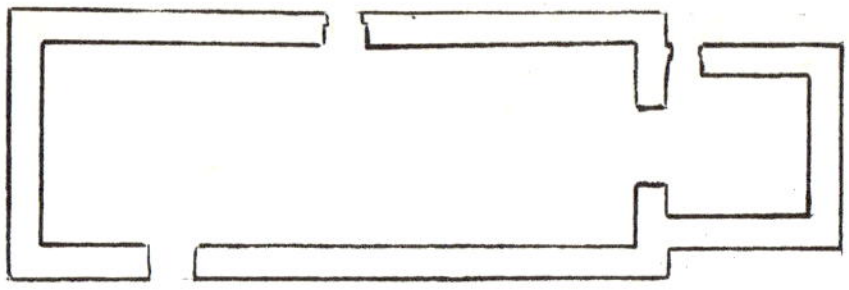

2. Plan of Escomb Church

concerned, their influence was retrogressive. The extreme asceticisr which the Irish prized as the highest religious virtue, was satisfied wi very small, crude, and simple buildings. The church at Lindisfar was of wood and only roughly thatched. Sometimes they used dr stone walling, but even when this was handled with the virtuosi which we can still admire in the Oratory of Gallerus, in County Kerr Ireland, the scale remained of necessity small. The result is that Engli architecture, unlike the decorative arts, owes hardly anything to Iri influence. The long and extremely narrow nave of Escomb Church, County Durham, may perhaps owe its shape to an earlier Irish buildin but at Bradwell Church, which is known to have been built by tl Irish-trained St Cedd, there are no recognizable Irish features. C the contrary, it was built in the corner of an old Roman fort, and h to be accounted an outlier of the Kentish group.

The impact of Roman Christianity in the North was therefo delayed until after the Synod of Whitby, in 663, which settled ou standing differences between the Irish and the Roman missions favour of the latter. Soon afterwards, the arrival from Rome of a ne Archbishop of Canterbury, Theodore of Tarsus, infused new life in the English church; but although Canterbury remained undisputed the ecclesiastical capital, all the great achievements took place Northumbria, where the political centre of gravity lay. Caedmor verses and Bede's *Historia Ecclesiastica Gentis Anglorum* were the gre

:erary landmarks of this age; the crosses at Ruthwell, in Dumfries-
ıire, and Bewcastle, Cumberland, and elsewhere testify to the vigour
' its sculpture; and the Lindisfarne Gospels preserve a wonderful
pertoire of its decorative art. Its architecture was no less interesting.
.ere the evidence allows us to divide the buildings very clearly into two
.ain groups. On the one hand were the comparatively ambitious
ıurches that were built by Bishop Wilfrid of York. According to
/ilfrid's biographer, he built a church at Hexham, Northumberland,
hich had aisles, and columns between the nave and aisles, and galleries
/er the aisles. The description is not profuse, but it is clear from these
cts alone that it was fairly closely modelled on the galleried churches
' Rome itself, which had been built during the previous century.
/ilfrid's crypt at Hexham still survives, along with other fragments of
undation walls, and it confirms the Roman affiliation. Wilfrid knew
ome well. He went there several times in connexion with lawsuits that
·ose out of the numerous ecclesiastical appointments which he held.
.e was precisely the kind of churchman whose conception of clerical
.gnity found expression in fine buildings, and, not satisfied with his
ıurch at Hexham, he provided two more, at Ripon and York. The
·ypt at Ripon survives to suggest that the whole church was similar
› Hexham. About York nothing whatever is known, although when
rchbishop Albert rebuilt his cathedral round about 770 "it was
ıpported on columns and arches, and surrounded by porticus; it had
great number of upper apartments with separate roofs, and had as
.any as thirty altars"; all of which suggests that whether or not
/ilfrid's York had aisles and galleries the tradition which he intro-
ıced, and patronized so lavishly elsewhere, lasted for a long time after
.s death. Wilfrid is also known to have built a centrally planned
ıurch at Hexham, which again implies a source of inspiration close to
oman works of this kind.

Over against Wilfrid's group can be set the much less ambitious
ıurches of Benedict Biscop, a contemporary and colleague of Wilfrid,
ho founded monasteries at Jarrow and Monkwearmouth, in County
urham. According to Bede, Benedict brought over to England masons
om Gaul who were to build a monastery "after the manner of the
omans." Presumably the reference is to one of his own monasteries,
ıt the remark is confusing because fragments of churches at both
aces have survived, and it is clear that neither was the least bit
oman in the sense that Wilfrid's were. Bede may have meant no more
.an that the churches were built of re-used Roman masonry from the
:ar-by Roman Wall, and that the only place where masons were to
: found capable of handling such material was southern Gaul, which

still preserved something of its old classical character. Certainly if v are to judge their work by what is left at Monkwearmouth and Jarro they deserved their reputation, for the masonry is of a high qualit But their skill does not seem to have extended further. The windows Jarrow and the door in the north side of the related church at Escon are almost pathetically primitive; while the crudely turned balusters the porch at Monkwearmouth are very little better.

In plan these surviving Northumbrian churches were simpler tha those of the Kentish group. They made little use of the porticu although the nave at Jarrow (which was once a separate church) had row of four down each side. The others, however, were long, high, ar narrow buildings, with small flat-ended chancels projecting eastwa from the naves. In spite of their simplicity, or perhaps because of buildings of this kind seem to have been erected well into the eigh century, for the type appears in Germany, where English missionari were active at that time. The first church at Paderborn (777), Wes phalia, is a case in point.

In the absence of Wilfrid's churches it would be unfair to jud Northumbrian architecture by those of Benedict Biscop, which probab represent the least enterprising level of contemporary Gallic wor Much more impressive in every way is Brixworth, the only survivi early Anglo-Saxon church which gives us some idea of what could produced on a more ambitious plane. Brixworth was founded abo 670 by monks from Peterborough, and there is no reason to suppo that it was particularly outstanding among the churches of its tim Yet the scale is unexpectedly monumental. It consisted of a nave of fo great arches which have since been walled up but which original opened into porticus arranged like those in the larger church Jarrow. Beyond this was a chancel, and beyond that a polygonal aps Between the nave and the chancel was a triple arcade, all trace which has been removed. The really important thing about Brixwort by comparison with the other surviving Anglo-Saxon churches, is t fact that the masons were prepared to use arches systematically, and a large scale. Columns were either not available or, more probably, t designer preferred to rest his arches on great rectangular masses masonry. Sir Alfred Clapham considered that this masonry w sufficiently defective to be regarded as the work of native Angl Saxons; but if this was the case, then paradoxically the enterprise mu be rated even more ambitious.

In the third region of England, the West Country, the origins Christianity were traced in Glastonbury legends to a time long befo the coming of the Saxons. But the conversion of the invaders only beg

3. Brixworth Church

earnest during the second half of the seventh century. Of the first ıportant ecclesiastical figures, one, Agilbert, the first Bishop of orchester on Thames, was a Frank by birth; while the other, Wine, e first Bishop of Winchester, received his education across the hannel. No doubt their notions of church architecture were likewise rived from Gaul.

The nearest counterpart in Wessex to Wilfrid in the North was St dhelm, who founded churches at Malmesbury in Wiltshire, Sherrne in Dorset, and Bradford-on-Avon, Wiltshire. At Bradford a xon church still remains, but in the form that it has come down to us hardly represents the style of Aldhelm's time. The earliest church in essex of which we have archaeological information is that built by ing Ine *c.* 700, at Glastonbury, Somerset. This was of the porticus pe. We know that Aldhelm received his education at Canterbury, d this sort of link could easily account for the appearance of the entish type in the West. Another church, however, dating from *c.* 680, e first monastic church at Abingdon, in Berkshire, seems to have en much more original in form. We know of it only from a later description, but this states unambiguously that it was "round at bo ends," which almost certainly means that it had two apses. If this w the case, then it anticipated the famous example of this arrangeme at Fulda, in Hessen, by more than a century.

It is a great pity that we cannot follow the fortunes of this fi English architecture in stone, once it was established. In particular cannot say for certain when the first symptoms of insularity began show. The period of two hundred years between the middle of t eighth century and the great monastic revival of the second half of t tenth century is the most obscure in the whole history of Engli architecture. The lead which had already passed from Kent to No thumbria no doubt passed later, along with the political supremac to Mercia and Wessex. Brixworth remains to show that Merci architecture had an auspicious beginning; but of the first Midla cathedrals and abbeys, such as Worcester, Lichfield, Peterborough, Ely, nothing remains that will afford us any notion of their scale a form. The great age of Mercian prosperity came at the end of t eighth century when its King, Offa, was recognized as overlo throughout England. At this time across the Channel Charlemagne w bringing the kingdom of the Franks to the zenith of its power, a relations between the two countries, both in learning and commerc were close enough for us to speculate on the possibility that Offa tri to emulate the building activities of his great contemporary. The s called Carolingian Revival was a crucial epoch in the development European architecture, and many historians have detected referenc to Carolingian works in later Anglo-Saxon buildings. The time of O is when we should expect this new wave of Continental influences begin, but if anything of the kind happened, then all traces have be thoroughly effaced. The key building was Offa's own abbey at Albans, but we know nothing whatever about its appearance. T only positive clues are to be found in the field of decorative sculptu In the church at Breedon-on-the-Hill, in Leicestershire, there are to seen built into the present walls an angel and friezes which are distinct Carolingian in type, and which seem to date from this period. B although evidence of this kind suggests that Carolingian art began exercise its influence in England during, or soon after, the reign Offa; and although we can infer from records and surviving traces th certain Carolingian architectural ideas were belatedly used in Engla during the tenth and eleventh centuries; it is necessary to resist t temptation to bracket later Anglo-Saxon architecture wholehearted with that of the Carolingian Empire or its immediate successors. The is no evidence of any building in England that could ever have be iously mistaken for a Carolingian construction. On the contrary, as shall see, everything suggests that later Anglo-Saxon architecture farther and farther behind the most ambitious Continental works, d that it developed idiosyncracies which imply separation from, her than contact with, Europe. This insularity was by far its most portant characteristic, and it is this which distinguishes later from lier Anglo-Saxon architecture.

The Danish invasions of the ninth century destroyed the precocious tural life of Northumbria, and played havoc with organized religion oughout the country. Monastic communities living under strict e virtually disappeared. It was not until Dunstan became Abbot of astonbury, in 943 or 944, that a serious and permanent improvement the quality of English religious life took place. Once started, however, nstan's reform movement acquired considerable momentum. ingdon was revived in 954 by one of his disciples, Ethelwold, who er became Bishop of Winchester. Dunstan himself became Arch-hop of Canterbury in 960, and another follower, Oswald, was made hop of Worcester in 961. Although they were bishops, the primary n of these men was to restore monastic life according to the full rigour he Rule of St Benedict, and it is through the foundation of a veritable te of new monasteries, or the restoration of old ones more or less ribund, that they left their mark on the history of English architec-e. More than thirty monasteries and at least six nunneries came o being between the middle of the tenth century and the beginning he eleventh. Each of the leaders was responsible for a group of these ndations. Thus Malmesbury, Bath, and Westminster owed their ival to Dunstan. Ethelwold brought monks from Abingdon to nchester, and refounded both Ely and Peterborough. Oswald's ef foundation was at Ramsey, in Huntingdonshire, but the main d of his activities was in the West Country, where houses were ablished by him at Pershore and Evesham, in Worcestershire, and Winchcomb, and probably Deerhurst, in Gloucestershire. He also roduced monks at Worcester; and later, when he was made Arch-hop of York, his attention turned to the North as well.

This monastic reform movement was directly inspired by similar vements on the Continent. All the leaders spent periods at European nasteries such as Ghent and St-Benoît-sur-Loire, so they were iliar with architecture there. One would have expected the new glish monasteries to have been modelled on appropriate Continental mples. Perhaps they were; but so little on either side of the Channel survived that the extent and precise nature of such relations cannot investigated. On the whole, however, the main wave of activity in

England came rather too early to benefit from the enterprising arc tectural experiments which were conducted under the general influe of the European reform movements toward the end of the tenth centu So far as we can tell, this new English monastic architecture tended be conservative. Some of the features known to have appeared in church designs undoubtedly came from the Carolingian tradition. I instance, at Durham, *c.* 999, and at Ramsey, we hear of churches t had towers at either end; and in one case—Canterbury Cathedra a western choir seems to have been added to the original buildi during this period. Both of these ideas imply the Carolingian notion a 'double-ended' church. But if this means anything at all in the te and eleventh centuries it is symptomatic of insularity rather than new Continental inspiration. In two cases where we can study l Saxon churches of cathedral or monastic rank—North Elmham, Norfolk, and Deerhurst—we are confronted by architectural rema of an extremely modest, not to say retarded, character. Admitte neither foundation commanded great resources. All the same, when find that neither was built with side aisles it is clear that we are dealing with the Carolingian notion of a great church, but with sort of thing represented by the lesser buildings of the early Ang Saxon period. It is not just the absence of columns or piers that gi this impression. In plan both were frankly archaic. Deerhurst s adhered to the porticus type, while North Elmham went back s farther to the Early Christian T transept and simple apse. It is t that some German churches of the same period shared these char teristics of North Elmham; but there the scale and articulation w infinitely more developed. The bare walls of Deerhurst, which seem have been built not long before the Conquest, suggest an almost to incapacity to think of masonry in any other terms except flat surfac and if anything was done to make them interesting to look at it m have been by means of painted decoration. This brings us back to t contrast between the strictly architectural conception and the embelli ment of Anglo-Saxon buildings which was mentioned earlier.

All the evidence suggests that the Anglo-Saxons were far m interested in decorating their buildings than in giving them impos structural forms. The best-known instance of their taste for surf ornament is undoubtedly the early eleventh-century tower at E Barton, Northamptonshire, which is plastered with little strips a arches. At Earls Barton the effect is harmless if bizarre. But in a w like the crypt at Repton, Derbyshire, we find it assuming a sligh more disturbing aspect. At Repton there are columns which have b roughly but deliberately shaped to give the impression that they w

4. The Crypt, Repton Church

made of an elastic, instead of a rigid, material. This is done by spir
thongs which are, as it were, wound round the shafts to produce
series of slight bulges. The motive on which this pattern was bas
came ultimately from Roman sources, and no doubt it was intended
simulate the twisted columns which stood around St Peter's shrine,
Rome. But at Rome the columns were purely decorative, whereas he

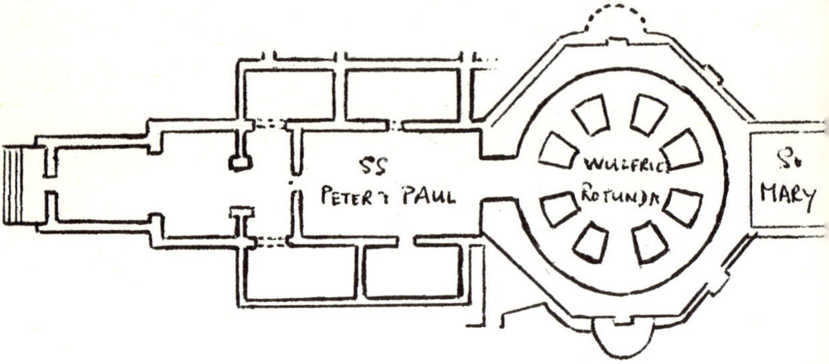

5. PLAN OF THE SAXON ABBEY OF ST AUGUSTINE, CANTERBURY, SHOWING WULFRIC'S ROTUNDA

they have a definite structural function to perform. The incongruity handling a supporting member as if it were no more than an elem in the decoration of a building tells us a great deal about the attitu of the Anglo-Saxons toward architecture at this time. It was not much a case of their being out of touch with Europe as of their caring. Where money was plentiful it was spent, not on masonry, b on precious objects such as gold and silver reliquaries, crosses a plate, rich vestments and sumptuous books, such as were showe upon the abbey of Peterborough by its last Anglo-Saxon Abb Leofric.

Even before the Norman Conquest there were signs that this sularity was coming to an end. At Sompting, in Sussex, Norm capitals and a German type of tower-spire made their appearance i late Saxon church. Two much more important building operati during the reign of Edward the Confessor must have convinced a lo Englishmen that what was happening across the Channel deser their attention. One was the rotunda which was started at St Aug tine's Canterbury soon after the return of its abbot from the Cour of Reims, in 1049. This was clearly inspired by the rotunda of Bénigne, at Dijon. The other was the Confessor's own church Westminster Abbey. Although it has completely disappeared, we kn at it was modelled on the abbey of Jumièges, in Normandy, which ıs then the most up-to-date building in the Duchy. The Confessor's ste for all things Norman is notorious; but in this case we may be rtain that he had good reason for his preference. The implied iticism of the native tradition is highly significant. There is something ghly symbolic in the fact that the last Saxon king should have built ıat was in effect the first Norman church in England.

CHAPTER 2

Norman Church Architecture

AFTER the Norman Conquest of 1066 the lack of evidence in the sha of surviving monuments, which drastically curtails our ability to ma a just assessment of Saxon architecture, and tends to reduce nearly our statements about it to the level of tentative guesses, is no long quite such a serious problem. From this point onward we are in position to base our opinions on buildings of a kind which set t standards instead of following them at a considerable distance—that the great cathedrals and abbey-churches. Many of the Norm buildings in this category are still standing, even though they a seldom to be found in their original form. It would be idle to prete that we know all we should like to know about these greater Norm churches. As we shall see, there are several problems outstanding whi are simply due to the fact that some of them have disappeared witho a trace. But the handicaps are no longer crippling.

A problem of another kind arises from the fact that whereas we kn what many of these greater Norman churches looked like, we do n in the case of their Saxon counterparts. This means that we have try and measure the significance of the change from Saxon to Norm without being able to make a true comparison between the beginni and end of the process. As the Normans themselves were chie responsible for the effacement of the larger Saxon churches, it see fairly safe to say that whatever else may be involved in the change, t Normans had such a poor opinion of the buildings they found England when they arrived that they set about replacing them wi buildings of a quality to which they were accustomed as soon possible. This tends to give the impression that Norman architectu in England was transplanted bodily from Normandy, and that involved a total repudiation of everything the Saxons had achieve But although there may be a good deal of truth in this view, it needs be hedged around by numerous qualifications.

The contempt which the Normans felt for English church buildings as only a part of their wider contempt for almost everything connected ith the religious life of the country. This attitude was not merely an xpression of their natural arrogance. There is no doubt that by the iddle of the eleventh century the impetus and zeal imparted to the nglish church by Dunstan, Ethelwold, and Oswald a century before ad virtually spent itself, except in parts of the West Country. On the ther side of the Channel, however, for more than fifty years before the onquest, the Normans had been in the throes of a reform movement hich had completely transformed the religious life of their Duchy. similar movement was active farther north, in what was then called ower Lorraine, and is now called Belgium. Even before the Conquest dward the Confessor had recognized the merits of this reformed ontinental clergy by importing men from Normandy and Lower orraine to fill high offices in the English church. After the Conquest Villiam the Conqueror found the majority of the native-born English ergy not merely unimpressive, but in many cases far too deeply ivolved with the displaced Saxon aristocracy for them to be entirely ustworthy. So it is hardly surprising that as soon as he was firmly stablished on the throne he started to do systematically what Edward ad attempted spasmodically—*i.e.*, to fill all important ecclesiastical acancies in England with reliable and well-qualified Continental hurchmen. Drastic action such as the deposition of Archbishop tigand of Canterbury was exceptional. The transformation was ffected slowly and patiently as the vacancies occurred. By the end of Villiam's reign, however, there were only four native-born English hurchmen left in high places: Bishop Wulfstan, of Worcester, and iree abbots.

The connexions between this transformation of the English clergy nd the introduction of Norman architecture into the country are close nd obvious. The lofty conception of the Church as an institution, hich inspired the reformers of the eleventh century, required for its isible image increasingly majestic church buildings. As we have seen om the donations which Abbot Leofric made to Peterborough, Saxon hurches were not lacking in material splendours, but we can only infer om the consistent attitude of the Norman clergy that the buildings emselves fell far short of the magnificence of their contents. It was most certainly the 'provincial' character of Saxon architecture, not ie specific manifestations of Saxon taste, which the Normans despised. i fact, there were already symptoms in the time of Edward the onfessor (see page 32) that some English patrons were aware of the iscrepancy between the standards of architecture current in England

and on the Continent; and their efforts to have copies made in Englar of interesting Continental designs suggest that even if there had bee no Norman Conquest an attempt would have been made in the secon half of the eleventh century to rebuild at least some English cathedra and abbeys in conformity with the more ambitious standards in vogu across the Channel. Without the Conquest, however, it is doubtf whether the transition to the Continental idea of what a great churc should look like would have been effected so quickly, so thoroughly, with so few concessions to insular waywardness. From the point of vie of the development of English architecture in the Middle Ages, th supremely important thing about the Conquest is that it brought to a end a long period when England had been to all intents and purpos a backwater. By establishing contacts with some of the main curren of Continental architecture at a critical period it secured the conditio for what amounted to another fresh start.

While it is true that in almost every case the appointment of a Norma bishop or abbot was followed sooner or later by the rebuilding of h church, the circumstances varied from place to place. The first tw Norman archbishops, Lanfranc and Thomas of Bayeux, reached the respective cathedrals at Canterbury and York in 1070 to find them ruins. When Paul of Caen came to St Albans in 1077 material fo rebuilding was already being collected by his Saxon predecessors fro the Roman ruins at Verulamium. It was a fire in 1087 that gave Bisho Maurice the opportunity to rebuild St Paul's, in London, and anoth fire, in 1116, was responsible for the reconstruction of Peterboroug The number of Saxon buildings which were deliberately pulled dow to make way for larger Norman structures was perhaps not very grea although some of the most imposing monuments of the new sty resulted from such actions—for instance, Winchester, Bury St Edmund in Suffolk, and Durham. Even the Saxon Bishop Wulfstan of Wo cester felt constrained to follow the fashion set by his Norman colleague although he at least wept over the passing of Oswald's church. The of course, there were many new foundations such as the Conqueror own abbey at Battle, in Sussex; and refoundations such as Glouceste and a whole series of new cathedrals had to be built because severa Saxon village bishoprics were transferred to towns after 1072. This wa how Lincoln, Chichester, Norwich, and Old Sarum acquired thei cathedrals, and Bath Abbey was rebuilt with the intention of replacin Wells. A similar explanation accounts for the abbey of Tewkesbury.

It is clear from all this that the Norman building campaign wa spread over a long period, and the individual works were undertake spasmodically. Except for Canterbury and the abbey at Battle, ther ems to have been a time-lag of several years after the Conquest before e movement got under way. Lincoln was begun about 1073; but it is not until the late 1070's and the 1080's that there came the full ate of what might be called the first generation of English Norman ildings: churches like St Albans, Winchester, Ely, and Worcester. ıen in the 1090's we encounter the earliest of another series which m a second generation. Durham Cathedral and the abbey at wkesbury are the outstanding works of this period. There was a rtain amount of overlapping between these two groups; but it is very portant to distinguish them from one another, and also to realize at both were patronized by the new Norman clergy. It must be phasized that this clergy, while passionately interested in having eat and splendid churches, was not exclusively attached to one rticular style of great church. As we shall see, it is only among urches of the first generation that we find evidence of really close inities with buildings in Normandy, and even among these there are tain differences which suggest that other Continental influences were work in England as well as those which were specifically Norman. ıe connexions with Normandy, which are implied in the name we to distinguish English architecture during the century which lowed the Conquest, tend to conceal the fact that Norman archi- ture in England was always Norman architecture with a difference, d that as time went on the differences became greater and greater. hen we come to buildings of the second generation it is much less sleading to use a term like 'Anglo-Norman,' in so far as this carries th it the implication that Norman architecture in England began to quire distinctly insular characteristics from about 1090 onward; hough even this is perhaps not entirely straightforward, because it ght convey too strongly the impression that there was a revival of glo-Saxon influences at that time. It would certainly be wrong to ke any very sweeping claims of that sort. All that we can say is that ne of these second-generation Norman buildings make use of specific glo-Saxon ideas. What is more important, they tend to make their ects in ways which seem to anticipate the remarkably consistent out- k of our later medieval architects. Their 'Englishness' is something t is more apparent if we look forward than if we look back. But ain it is dangerous to be too dogmatic, precisely because we do not ow what the best Saxon buildings were like just before the Conquest. e inordinate love of decoration which is so characteristic of later glo-Norman buildings, and which contrasts so strongly with the sterity of the first-generation works, may very well have been a nptom of the resurgence of Anglo-Saxon taste. But however we interpret these facts, the important thing to have in mind when attempt to understand Norman architecture in England is that it w not a static style, complete and perfect when it arrived, but somethi which showed a remarkable capacity for developing new forms. If o compares the choir of St Albans (*c.* 1080) with Oxford Cathed (*c.* 1160) the extent of this metamorphosis seems almost sensational. Y both are called Norman. It should be abundantly clear from this co parison that if the term has any meaning at all it cannot be confin merely to what these two buildings have in common. St Albans a Oxford represent extremes of primitive simplicity and ultimate sophis cation, and if there is any case for using the same word to describe the it must be shown that they belong to a common tradition with a lo series of legitimate intermediaries and exhibit a recognizable proc of change.

In a book of this kind discussion of all the buildings which contribut their distinctive nuances to the evolution of Norman architectu would be out of place. It will be more to the point to examine in det a few of the salient works which form landmarks between St Albans a Oxford. But first, because it is impossible to explain many of the featu of Norman churches in England without alluding to Normandy, it necessary to start with an example of the kind of great church bei built in Normandy just before the Conquest.

The abbey-church of St-Étienne, at Caen, was founded by Willia the Conqueror himself between 1064 and 1066, and was finished 1077. Of the original building, only the lower part of the west fro the nave, and transepts are still standing, and even the vaulted roof the nave was an addition of the early part of the twelfth century. In original state only the side aisles were vaulted; the nave was cover with a wooden roof. This seems to have been the usual arrangement Norman churches until well into the twelfth century, although know of some cases where the walls of the nave were joined overhe by a series of transverse, or 'diaphragm,' arches.

When all these things have been taken into account the arc tectural interest of what is left of the eleventh-century work centres the walls of the nave. When we compare these walls with even the m ambitious of our surviving Saxon examples we are at once struck by t very much greater degree of articulation in the Norman work. Nothi could be further from the bare surfaces of a church like Deerhurst. Caen we are confronted not so much by a surface as by an organiz system of arches raised in tiers one above the other. The three sectic of the elevation are almost equal in height. The main arcade, whi opens into the side aisles, and the arcade above, which opens into t llleries, each consist of large single arches. The clerestory openings ·m a triple-arch unit, or at least they did so before the vaults were :roduced. Between each vertical section of the wall is a semicircular ıll-shaft, and these, in conjunction with the well-defined horizontal visions, break up the wall into a network of rectangular compart- :nts—an effect which must have been considerably more pronounced ıen the clerestory was wholly visible. Although so much of these ılls has been cut away to form the arches, it is not difficult to realize at their basic dimensions would define an extremely sturdy block of ısonry. It is perhaps in the clerestory that the thickness of them is ɔst easily grasped. At that level the wall is visible in two planes. On : inside the surface is broken up by the triple-arch unit; while the ıter plane is represented by the clerestory windows. Between the two a continuous passage cut through the residual masonry. The lower :tions of the wall were obviously designed to carry this broad clere- ·ry, but there the bulk is all concentrated in the piers. It follows as a ıtter of course from this thick-wall construction that pier design was und to assume considerable importance. The same is true of the :hes between the piers. Basically, we may think of the core of the pier being formed by the residue of wall left when the arches have been t away, and the simplest kind of pier would therefore be square or :tangular in section. Such piers can actually be found in the most imitive Romanesque churches, but in the course of the eleventh ntury the practice of embellishing the core with subsidiary forms came fairly general. Definite rules governed these accretions, and ey are beautifully illustrated at Caen. The dominant idea was that ery arch, or visible part of every arch, should be supported by its own pporting member. This usually took the form of a half-column, mplete with base and capital. The nave at Caen shows us how this inciple was applied to a thick wall. The great arches of the main :cade and the gallery all have contiguous subsidiary arches to offset eir width. These are carried on half-columns, and so are the exposed rts of the main arch. The effect of all these half-columns, together th the wall-shaft on the side facing into the nave, is to produce a aracteristic congestion of forms around the exposed parts of the piers. ıis congestion reaches its climax in the capitals of the half-columns ıich are carved in crude imitation of classical acanthus capitals. The :hes themselves are left comparatively plain, although the exposed .rt of the main arch has a simple roll-moulding.

It is necessary to describe this Norman thick-wall technique in some tail because it was by far the most important contribution which the ɔrmans made to architecture in England. More than any other factor, it separates post-Conquest from pre-Conquest buildings—least among those known to us. So completely was it adopted in Engla that it persisted in use long after it had been abandoned on the Co tinent, and we can still find traces of it in purely Gothic buildings of t thirteenth and even fourteenth centuries. The form in which it found in England is not always identical with that of St-Étienne, Caen. A very common variation is the arrangement known as t alternating-system, where, instead of the piers forming a unifo series, two different kinds of pier alternate with one another. This ty of elevation had already been introduced into England before t Conquest if, as we think, it was copied from the Norman abbey Jumièges, in the Confessor's church at Westminster.

Neither St-Étienne at Caen nor any other Norman cathedral abbey built before the Conquest preserves its original choir in anythi more than plan. This is a pity for several reasons, but in particul because one choir would have told us much more than any of t surviving naves as to the precise point which the Normans had reach —if they had reached any point at all—in the matter of vaulting wi spans. Two types of choir-plan are known: one in which the side ais are continuous right round the apse, forming what is called an ambul tory, and sometimes, though not always, having chapels opening fr it; and the other in which the side aisles terminate in chapels flanki the choir, and other chapels open from the eastern walls of the tra septs. The former of these dispositions seems to have been regarded the more ambitious; but the latter probably maintained its importan during the eleventh century because it could be more easily and saf adapted to receive a choir vault. It is known that in some cases t walls between the choir and the side aisles consisted of solid mason which would be perfect supports for a barrel-vault, and not easy explain otherwise. Be this as it may, it is certain that when vaults we introduced into Norman churches in England it was in choirs of t kind just described that they appeared first. It was natural that t choir, which was the focus of all the liturgical activity of these gre churches, and which housed the relics and altars which were th *raison d'être*, should be distinguished from the rest of the building having this more imposing form of roof. So far as we know, nearly eve Norman building of the first generation in England conformed in t plan of its east end to one or other of these types; but it is high significant that among works of the second generation both beco increasingly rare.

Outside the outlines of Norman churches were dominated by towe The most important of these was usually placed over the crossing, b ɹas accompanied in the more important buildings by a pair of towers the west end of the nave, rising out of the west front. This arrange-nt can still be seen at Caen, although in a modified form. Like other

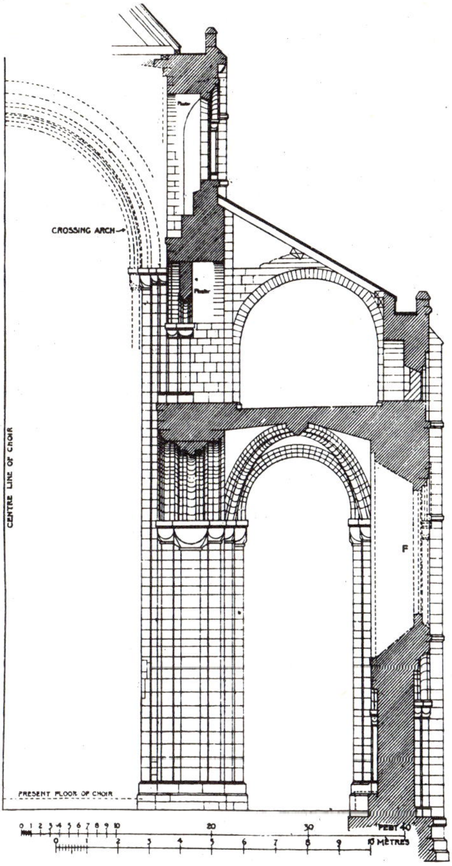

6. Half Cross-section of the Choir of Durham Cathedral

rman ideas, it was brought over to England, and although very few he original towers can still be seen, Norman ancestry can be detected the grouping of several Gothic cathedral towers. But again it is portant to realize that there were Norman towers in England which re not inspired by prototypes in Normandy.

When we turn to England—and once we have recognized things like Norman elevation, the thick wall, the two kinds of choir-plan, and the characteristic distribution of towers—what is apt to strike us m forcibly is a general increase in size. Naves in particular were m very much longer—even twice as long; although choirs also w extended. In fact, the dimensions of Norman cathedrals and abbeys England place them in the very largest class of medieval churches. T responsibility for this increase rests with the Norman clergy and th demand for great churches. Although by itself a change of scale d not constitute a change of style, in this particular case we can see h it entailed many of the detailed changes which mark the movemen Norman architecture in England away from the standards of Ca At Caen the average thickness of the nave walls was about 4 f 9 inches; at Canterbury and Lincoln it was the same; but at St Alb it was over 7 feet, and at Durham, Norwich, and Peterborough e more. It should be readily apparent that as the walls got thicker so articulation of the piers and arches became a more and more co plicated problem. Perhaps the best way to approach the question of historical development of Norman architecture in England is to st with a series of buildings such as Winchester, Ely, Norwich, a Peterborough, all of which are descended from the Caen type elevation, and see how the appearance of their walls was gradu transformed by the increased articulation of their piers and arches.

Although Winchester is perhaps the English building which sta closest to Caen, at least among those which survive, there are spe reasons for considering St Albans first. The St Albans walls h different proportions, and they give the impression of being much m primitive than those of Caen. This is no doubt due to their grea bulk, and to the absence in the recesses of the piers of the half-colur and capitals which were so conspicuous at Caen. And instead of se circular wall-shafts there are broad, flat buttresses. The removal of original fillings of the gallery openings also contributes to the effec simplicity. Comparison with Caen is not quite fair, because St Alb was built very largely of Roman brick, which is a material that can be made to take complicated forms. The austerity was therefore entirely a matter of choice. Be that as it may, the result is that the n walls of St Albans present us with the Norman thick wall in its m elementary form, with the barest minimum of articulation. It wo hardly be too drastic to describe them as crude masses of masonry w three rows of holes cut into them. This, so to speak, is the raw mate which was to be worked with ever increasing sophistication in the cou of the next hundred years.

Much closer in general effect to Caen is the architecture of transept arms of the cathedral of Winchester. These are all that is he great work begun in 1079 by Bishop Walkelin. The division into ee more or less equal storeys; the division into bays by means of l-shafts; the thick wall with its clerestory wall-passage; and the use

7. PART OF THE NORMAN NAVE OF ST ALBANS CATHEDRAL

secondary arches to articulate the piers—all this follows the prescrip-n of Caen and other Norman churches. Two features call for special mment, however. One is the division of the gallery opening by the roduction of a central shaft. This gives the middle section of the wall added degree of complexity which is appropriate to its position tween the main arcade and the clerestory. The other is the distinctive m of capital employed for all the small shafts and half-shafts. It is own as a cushion capital, and it is a form hardly known in Normandy. w it came to play such an important part in the decoration of glish churches is one of the besetting problems of this field of study, d one to which it will be necessary to return later. Winchester also eserves intact its Norman crypt.

The cathedral of Ely was begun by Walkelin's brother, Simeon, in e 1080's. Its original choir has disappeared, but there is a definite similarity between the transepts of the two buildings. At Ely, howev we encounter a version of the alternating-system, and when we come the nave which was designed and perhaps largely carried out in first third of the twelfth century we are confronted by a characteris development—namely, the use of two subordinate arches in the op ings of the main arcade and the gallery, so that now three arches visible in each opening; what is more, each now has its own r moulding. The alternating-system is not obtrusive, but it is interesti to see that where the cylindrical piers are used the principle of ev arch having its own support breaks down. Capitals are left projecti into space unsupported. On the other hand, the orthodox compou piers have correspondingly enriched profiles. But in spite of th anomalies, the nave walls at Ely represent perhaps the most satisfy stage in the transformation of the Caen type of elevation in Engla Conceived on a more monumental scale, and far more richly articula than any of their possible Norman prototypes, they have a weight a orderliness appropriate to their function as walls. At the same time th seem to achieve some of the decorative effects of abstract sculpture.

In later designs of the Ely type, of which Norwich (begun in 10 and Peterborough (begun in 1118) are the most outstanding, development of the plastic possibilities of the great interior walls taken even further. If anything, the walls are even thicker than at E and the enrichment is more profuse. At both Norwich and Peterborou we find arches covered with chevrons and billet-mouldings; and Peterborough there are areas of diaper pattern in the gallery arcad It is hardly surprising to find that the breakdowns in the logi handling of the supports now became numerous and blatant. Norwich the arcades and gallery arches have immense depth, but th are almost wholly unarticulated. Instead, we find them carried by many as three shafts side by side—an arrangement which recalls groups of shafts in the Anglo-Saxon church at Great Paxton, Huntir donshire. Again there are capitals which have no shafts to supp them. This is particularly disturbing in the side aisles at Peterborou which have ribbed vaults. The ribs seem to stop short, as thou suspended in space. These two features—increased decoration a increased dislocation of the Norman conception of structural logic— symptomatic of the change from the first to the second generation Norman buildings. Norwich and Peterborough are really 'overla buildings. If they derive from the first-generation type they were alrea responding to new tendencies which had their origins in the secor But before we turn to consider these new tendencies in their m radical forms this is perhaps the place to pause and mention one of t

8. The North Transept, Winchester Cathedral
Thomas Britton

greatest of the Norman buildings that have disappeared—an Abbey Bury St Edmunds—and to say what has to be said on the question early Norman crypts.

From what we know of it from written sources and its fragment remains, the nave of Bury belonged to the second quarter of the twel century, and was probably akin to the Ely–Norwich–Peterborou group. But perhaps the most interesting thing about Bury, if only knew more about it, would be its crypt, which, together with the chc was built much earlier—*i.e.*, in the time of Baldwin, who was Ab from 1065 to 1097. This crypt is still there, awaiting excavation, a until it has been excavated it is no doubt rash to venture any opini as to its significance. It is usual to explain the early Norman crypts England as variations on the precedent of the eleventh-century crypt the cathedral of Rouen; but the similarities are not very close. O important difference is that the English crypts make extensive a sometimes exclusive use of cushion capitals, a form which was har known in Normandy. The ultimate source of spacious crypts w Italy, but they were also common in the Rhineland in the elever century. Cushion capitals were also familiar there, and if crypts a cushion capitals came together the Rhineland would be the obvic centre from which they reached England. It is intriguing to learn th before he came to England Abbot Baldwin had been in charge of t Alsatian priory of Leberau, where he must have known some of t Rhenish crypts. Until Bury has been excavated it would be unwise pursue the hypothesis farther. The important thing is that Norman was not the only available source from which Norman architecture England could draw its ideas.

The building which more than any other marks the transition fr first- to second-generation Norman buildings in England is the cathed of Durham. The rebuilding of Aldhun's Saxon cathedral seems to ha been envisaged from the moment it was decided by the Lotharingi Bishop Walcher to introduce a community of monks in place of the Congregation of St Cuthbert, but the actual church was not beg until 1093, by Bishop William de Carilef. The choir was finished 1104, and the nave by 1133. The reputation which Durham enjoys being the most splendid of our Norman buildings is wholly justifi When we compare the walls of its nave with those of Winchester even Ely we are at once aware of a boldness and imaginative power the dispositions of the masonry which betoken a complete emancipati from the restraints inherited from Normandy. The proportions of t elevation have been drastically transformed. The main arcade n occupies a much larger part of the whole, and dominates the interi

9. The Nave, Durham Cathedral

The gallery has been reduced practically to the status of a triforiu while the clerestory seems almost to have disappeared among the ri of the vaults. At the same time the old unity of the wall has be seriously impaired. For one thing, the wall-shafts now project drama cally into the nave, and really disrupt the even flow of the horizont lines. Then again the walls seem to taper upward in the manner of tree-trunk or a lighthouse. All their bulk is concentrated in the arcad in the compound piers, and even more so in the cylinders who enormous girth is aggressively proclaimed by the eye-catching patter with which they are incised. By comparison the forms of the midd section seem almost slight, while the clerestory—partly because of t vaults—gives the impression of being more void than solid. T tapering is particularly evident in the choir, for which it is known ribbed vault was intended from the outset. So we may think of the walls, as it were, bracing themselves to bear the weight and thrust the vaults. Between the choir on the one hand and the nave and tra septs on the other there are slight but significant differences whi seem to imply that the decision to vault the rest of the church was afterthought. In the choir the wall-shafts which support the diagon ribs rest on the ledge left by the 'contraction' of the triforium; in oth words, the supports are themselves directly supported by the ma arcade. In the nave, however, the diagonal ribs are corbelled out of t triforium wall and have no supports of any kind. This change symptomatic of the growing indifference of the Durham masons things like the logical handling of supports. But either way the im pression of an intimate and organic relation between walls and vau is inescapable. Monumental though they are, the walls of Durham a no longer detached and self-contained monoliths like those of Ely. Th seem to grow together overhead, and a new and impressive shape thereby imposed upon the interior.

These famous vaults of Durham are clearly the clue to the unde standing of the whole design. So much has been written about the from what might be called the technical angle that it will do no har to approach them for once from the point of view of their contributi to the visual effect of the building. Nevertheless it would be wrong underestimate their importance as a feat of engineering. The task roofing a church in stone was one of the constant preoccupations European architects throughout the eleventh century. The simple form of stone roof, and the earliest to be used, is the kind known as barrel-vault. This is nothing more than a half-cylinder. It is easy to s how such vaults, with their evenly distributed weight, need more or le continuous supporting walls. This is the kind that may have been us ı those early Norman choirs which had solid walls between them and ıeir flanking aisles. It is perhaps worth mentioning that some of the arliest Norman churches in England had these solid choir walls—*e.g.*, Canterbury and St Albans; although of course nothing is known for ertain as to how they were roofed.

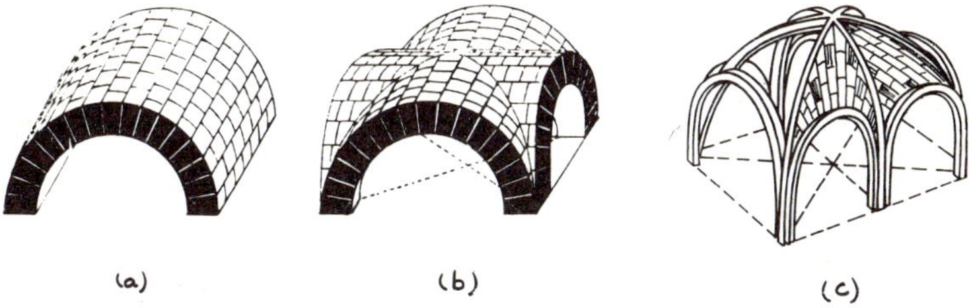

10. Types of Vaulting

(*a*) Barrel-vault; (*b*) Groined vault; (*c*) Ribbed vault

A more advanced form of vault is that which is called a groined ault. Essentially this consists of two barrel-vaults intersecting at right ngles. Where the two intersect, characteristic ridges appear in the ırface, becoming more and more pronounced towards the corners. This ›rm of vault had been systematically used in Continental churches for ıany centuries in side aisles and ambulatories, where the structural sks involved were slight, and a rough-and-ready finish did not matter. ut it was a long time before masons had the courage to use a vault of ıis kind for a major span. One of the things which may have deterred ıem is the fact that a groined vault is only really suitable for a more or ss square space. As soon as it is applied to a definite rectangle com-lications begin to appear. It can be done, but the construction of the ·ntring, and the cutting of blocks of stone to form the surface of the ıult, would call for a knowledge of geometry well beyond the capacity f most eleventh-century masons, at least in the north of Europe.

The ribbed vault was the solution which finally proved most satis-ctory. In appearance a ribbed vault is similar to a groined vault, with ıe addition of a rib along the edge formed by the intersection of the ɔmpartments. But whereas in a true groined vault the groins are in fect by-products of the intersecting half-cylinders, and in their simplest rm have an elliptical profile, in a ribbed vault the ribs are the starting-ɔint, and their profiles are always arcs of circles. The intervening ırfaces of the vault are no longer parts of a complicated set of geo-ıetrical relations, but present a series of separate and localized roblems that can be disposed of without undue difficulty. From the point of view of the people who invented the ribbed vault the geometrical simplifications were perhaps the aspects which recon mended it most strongly. But of course its possibilities extended f beyond considerations of this sort, and eventually the ribbed vau became one of the constituent elements of Gothic architecture.

In several respects Durham anticipates early Gothic buildings. N only is it vaulted throughout with ribbed vaults, but in the nave son of the transverse arches are pointed; while under the roof of the na triforium can be seen arches abutting on to the upper walls of the na which in function, if not in appearance, foreshadow the Gothic flyin buttress. In spite of all this, however, it would be a paradox to ca Durham a Gothic building. The massive strength of its walls is alor sufficient to dispose of any such idea. Although we habitually associa ribbed vaulting with Gothic buildings, it is not difficult to see how tl practice could have developed naturally within the Norman traditior and if the similarities mean anything it is not that Durham is Gothi but that Gothic has its roots in Norman Romanesque. All this gives special reason to deplore the series of historical accidents which ha robbed us of the stages leading up to Durham, and so left that buildin in a position of splendid isolation. One fairly certain predecessor seen to have been the choir of the Norman cathedral of Lincoln, begu somewhere about 1073.

Although the vaults of Durham are its most celebrated feature, it rather disconcerting to find that their immediate influence on Englis architecture was well nigh negligible. This is all the more surprisin because the theme of ribbed vaulting was at once taken up seriously Normandy, and transmitted from there to the adjacent parts of Franc but in England, apart from an isolated case, such as the vaulting of tl nave of Lincoln in the 1140's, it was not until well into the second ha of the twelfth century that it became at all common. Perhaps there we vaults directly inspired by Durham which failed to stay up (like tl vaults of the choir of Durham itself), but even if this were so it is st tantamount to saying that English architects were easily discourage and that their main interests lay elsewhere.

This brings us to other aspects of Durham. By comparison with tl vaults, the success of the new decorative techniques which seem to ha made their appearance at Durham was immediate and widesprea Apart from the incised patterns on the great cylindrical piers of tl main arcade, three other new elements contribute to the enrichment the interior. First, there is the addition of a roll-moulding in the cent of the arcade arches. This imparts a characteristic V-profile to the arc and, although in itself a comparatively modest addition, it has tl ffect at Durham of combining with other innovations to destroy the rdered sequence of arches within arches, and to substitute for it that of freely designed arch moulding. In this respect the Durham arches and at the head of a long and extremely rich tradition in English edieval architecture, and mark a definite bifurcation between English nd Continental ideas on this subject. Moreover, this is one of the atures of Norman architecture for which definite Saxon antecedents an be found. Second, there is the use throughout the nave of the hevron ornament. Once it had been adopted at Durham, its use spread ery rapidly throughout the country, and it became perhaps the most biquitous of all the later Norman decorative motives for the embellish- ient of doorways, windows, vault-ribs, and chancel arches. The third f the new decorative ideas found at Durham is the interlaced arcade long the aisle walls. The effect of this is undoubtedly to bring the outer alls of the church into line with the main walls of the nave, and to omplete the general impression inside the building of what has been alled an 'all-over linear pattern.' In this respect Durham anticipates ne of the fundamental trends of later English medieval architecture, ne which can be traced right down to the sixteenth century; although e linear quality of its later manifestations might make one hesitate to se the same word of a building like Durham, where so many of the rms assert their bulk rather than their surfaces.

The monastic movement in the North of England, which culminated the rebuilding of Durham, was initiated by a group of monks from e abbey of Winchcomb. It is not easy for us to follow the development f Norman architecture in the West of England, but the situation there ust have been more complicated than in any other part of the country. n the one hand, it was the only part of Saxon England in which the thusiasm kindled during the tenth-century Monastic Revival had not iminished; and it is possible—although it could not now be proved— at its architecture in the eleventh century was more enterprising than sewhere. Unfortunately, we know nothing whatever of the appearance f Winchcomb or any other Saxon monastery in the West, except eerhurst, which was too small and poor to be representative, although is interesting to find at Tewkesbury and Gloucester a type of apse hich seems to reflect the influence of the arrangement at Deerhurst. nother factor which is possibly relevant is the presence of a number of ontinental churchmen holding high ecclesiastical positions in the Vest during the eleventh century. The Diocese of Hereford seems to ave been particularly exposed to Continental influences from a variety f sources. The priory of Chepstow in Monmouth, which was founded on after 1071, and was a dependency of the Norman abbey of

Cormeilles, shows signs of having been vaulted throughout, probabl with groined vaults. At Hereford itself the Bishop's Chapel, nov destroyed, seems to have reflected methods of construction used i Burgundy; while in the cathedral itself, started *c.* 1110, the aisles of th choir terminated in towers—an arrangement that can be paralleled i German, or even Italian, churches of this and earlier periods. With s many different factors involved it is a pity that we know so little of th circumstances in which this West Country school of architecture cam into being, but by 1090, when both Tewkesbury and Gloucester ha been started, the school was evidently capable of producing design that were in some ways even more precocious than that of Durham.

If at Durham the orthodox Norman thick wall was freely adapted fo the task of supporting a stone vault, in the naves of Tewkesbury an Gloucester it was virtually replaced by a continuous series of monu mental drum-piers which must have occupied in their original contex nearly two-thirds of the total elevation. Nothing known to us in earlie Norman or Saxon architecture prepares us for this drastic deviation. I antecedents are to be found it is as far away as Tournus, in Burgundy or Como, in Italy, that we have to go to find drum-piers equall impressive. The possibilities inherent in such connexions are fascinating Above the drum-piers at Tewkesbury we find a series of very squa openings which give access to a passage in the thickness of the wall— which is none other than the old clerestory wall-passage detached fror the clerestory, and turned into an independent feature of the elevation followed above by a clerestory which is now no more than a series c small windows. The nave of Gloucester follows almost exactly the sam pattern.

What we find at Tewkesbury and Gloucester is, in effect, a three storey elevation which implies a completely new conception of a wal The visual importance of the vertical members which is strong enoug at Durham, is now overwhelming. And when we proceed from th naves of these buildings to their respective choirs which were earlier and attempt to reconstruct their original state, we find the same ide used in a less dramatic, but perhaps even more suggestive, way. Bot choirs were remodelled in the fourteenth century, but the survivin Norman masonry at both places is sufficient, if we put them together, a it were, to allow us to understand how their structural systems worked By contrast with the very high aisles flanking the naves of Tewkesbur and Gloucester, the choir aisles and ambulatories are reduced to th status of low tunnels. At Gloucester enough survives of the upper part of the Norman choir for us to see that these low choir aisles were sur

11. The North Transept, Tewkesbury Abbey

ιounted by a true Norman gallery. The one at Gloucester has half-
rches leaning against the choir walls in the manner of those of the
ave of Durham, and whether or not the original choir was vaulted, it
eems clear that these buttresses were built with the intention of
ıpporting vaults. In effect, the aisle and gallery together in the choir

correspond to the aisle alone in the nave. It follows from this that the upper parts of the choir were treated in the same way as the uppe parts of the nave the choir must have had a four-storey elevatio In the transept at Tewkesbury we can see that this was in fact th case.

It is well known that the four-storey elevation played an importa part in the development of Gothic architecture in Northern Franc but, so far as we know, there are no surviving examples in that part the world earlier than the choirs of Tewkesbury and Gloucester. It ma of course be the case that the idea was invented in the English We Country, but in view of the fact of its wider use, and much great development, in the Low Countries and Northern France, one tempted to postulate earlier instances there which have disappeare Here the Lotharingian clergy of the West Country come again to min Another feature of the choir of Tewkesbury seems to strengthen th point of view. Enough remains of the original piers for us to be able t infer that from the interior of the choir they would seem to rise witho a break from the floor to the top of the gallery. In other words, the would have the same general appearance as the drum-piers of the nav only with arches joining them in the middle to form the floor of th gallery.

Although both Tewkesbury and Gloucester no longer show th arrangement, they were undoubtedly the buildings to which the cred should go for the innovation, at least so far as the West Country concerned. The idea was evidently popular, for it was used agai several times in the course of the twelfth century—for instance, in wh is now Oxford Cathedral. Even later it appeared in a Gothic form i the abbey of Glastonbury. What beautiful and delicate architectur effects were made possible by means of this idea we can see perha best at the east end of the nave of Romsey Abbey. The term 'Gia Order' has been used to describe this device for making one arch spa two sections of an elevation, and it rightly suggests that the ultima origins of the idea are to be found in classical architecture. Th immediate source, however, was Germany. There is a Roman buildin at Trier where the arrangement can still be seen, and in the elevent century this building seems to have inspired the architects of th Rhenish cathedrals of Speyer and Mainz. The transept façades Romsey have this feature more or less in its German form, but hardl anticipate the boldness and beautiful effects found in the Romsey nav bay. The whole idea clearly underwent some development either i England or *en route* to England—*i.e.*, in Lower Lotharingia.

Tewkesbury and Gloucester form the starting-point for the mo

12. THE NAVE, GLOUCESTER CATHEDRAL
Thomas Britton

apricious and imaginative variations on the original Norman theme. ·ut the most characteristic expressions of Anglo-Norman taste throughut the twelfth century are to be found in the field of decoration. We .ave met this tendency already in the nave of Durham; but the chief ›urce from which it spread was probably Canterbury.

At Canterbury the first thirty years of the twelfth century saw th building of a new and very much enlarged choir in place of the shor eastern limb of Lanfranc's cathedral. According to William of Malmes bury, who saw it, there was nothing like it in all England "either fc the brilliance of its glass windows, the beauty of its marble pavemen or the many coloured pictures which led wondering eyes to the ver summit of the ceiling." This choir was not vaulted in stone like Durham for it was destroyed by a fire in the roof in 1174, which left only th outer walls of the aisles and the crypt. Both were preserved when th Gothic choir was built after 1174, and in the crypt especially we can ge some idea of the splendours which dazzled William of Malmesbur from the paintings in St Gabriel's Chapel and from the wonderfu series of carved capitals.

A distinctive feature of this new choir at Canterbury was the fac that it opened into a second, or eastern, transept. This was almos certainly derived from the plan of the great Burgundian abbey c Cluny, whose third church was begun in 1088, and the idea may hav reached Canterbury through the mediation of the Cluniac Priory c St Pancras, at Lewes, which is known to have also had this secon transept. Cluniac churches were famous, and even notorious, for th extravagance of their decoration, and the few fragments which surviv of the Lewes priory suggest that it conformed to the general practice c the Order in this respect.

Even more magnificent must have been the favourite foundation c King Henry I, at Reading, in Berkshire, which was colonized b Cluniac monks without being attached to the Order. The abbey a Reading was begun in 1121, and although again we know what it wa like only from a few fragments, it seems certain that it played a ver important part in spreading the use of decorative sculpture as a forr of architectural embellishment.

Yet another work of this period which has completely disappearec but which probably vied in splendour with Canterbury and Reading was the eastern extension of Old Sarum; and finally, although i belongs to the second half of the twelfth century, the new choir of Yor Minster ought perhaps to be added to this list. It was begun in 1154 evidently with the intention of making the appearance of the minste match the pretensions of its archbishop to be the equal of Canterbury

Although fragments are no substitute for the overwhelming effects c the total ensembles, we can still get some idea of the richness of th sculptural decoration of the twelfth century from doorways like thos at Ely and Malmesbury; and where the great works have disappeare there are sometimes humble parish churches in the vicinity whic reserve less grandiose, but not less interesting, records of their carvers' :t. Kilpeck, in Herefordshire, is perhaps the outstanding example.

Toward the end of the twelfth century the number of large-scale orks in the Anglo-Norman style gradually declined. The church at the .ospital of St Cross, Winchester, begun soon after 1151 but often terrupted, has a lavish display of the chevron ornament which is ombined with a number of new structural ideas from across the hannel. Elsewhere, however, buildings on a smaller scale gave the nglo-Norman decorators untrammelled scope, and it is at Durham, the 1170's, that we find what are perhaps their most extreme chievements in the galilee of the cathedral, and in the doorway of the ishop's Hall in the castle. Work of this delicacy has a *fin de siècle* uality which prepares us for the imminent arrival of a new style.

In all this drift toward the rich, the subtle, and the complicated, iere was one oddly discordant note. It was during this period that one the most distinctive features of later English church architecture .ade its appearance. This was the straight, or flat, east end, which was referred to both the earlier Norman round types. Undoubtedly this d to a simplification of plans; but there was a good deal of experiment efore the final clarification was reached. Thus at Hereford Cathedral ie central apse rose less than half-way up the eastern wall, the upper art of which was flat. At Southwell Cathedral, in Nottinghamshire, ie old three-apse plan was modified by the squaring of the central one; id at Chertsey Abbey (started 1110), in Surrey, the old semicircular nbulatory became rectangular, the radiating chapels acquiring a ctangular form and being placed side by side. This latter configura- on was further developed at Romsey Abbey, Hampshire, and received hat was to become its standard form at Old Sarum between 1125 and 130. The square ended chancel had already been adopted for other :asons by the Cistercian Order of monks, and when they arrived in ngland (see chapter 3) they did much to ensure its continued use. The :sults of this simplification were most apparent from the outside. lthough the external walls of English churches received their share of namental enrichment—for instance, the choir of Canterbury Cathe- ral—their actual silhouettes seldom seem to have been considered pable of yielding aesthetic effects. With the transformation of the st end the central tower could no longer serve as the climax of a refully graduated hierarchy of ascending forms, and it became creasingly an object which rose in splendid isolation above the long orizontal roofs of nave and choir. The two-tower façade was certainly iown in England; at Canterbury, Lincoln, Durham, and Southwell, r instance, it was combined with a massive central tower in the

Continental Norman manner. But the inordinate extension of the nave in English churches required something more impressive than tw small towers to give an adequate accent to their west end. Thus a Lincoln we find the two towers embedded in a massive block, and a Bury St Edmunds there was an elaborate complex involving corne

13. The First Bay of the Nave, Romsey Abbey

turrets which turned the façade into a great screen—perhaps the fir of what was to become a long series. At Ely the western emphasis wa even greater. Here the western transept with corner turrets and projecting porch verged upon a great monolithic tower. The idea of single central tower at the west end may be regarded as an Angl Saxon survival; and it is possible that a similar great western tower wa intended at first for the abbey of Tewkesbury. The other Angl Norman solutions also had their origins outside the Continent Norman tradition, and a search for them would lead us to the Lo Countries, Germany, and even to St Mark's, Venice. Few of the towe which remain—*e.g.*, those at St Albans, Norwich, and Tewkesbury- are now to be seen in the settings for which they were originally designe ll three have become the only external features of importance in their spective buildings.

At the beginning of the twelfth century no one in England would ıve considered building a great church in any other style than the nglo-Norman. After the middle of the century, however, this was no nger so. Yet the style lingered on for nearly fifty years, and exercised strong, if indirect, influence on English Gothic architecture of the ıirteenth century. The situation between 1150 and 1200 was, in fact, :tremely complicated. The essence of the matter was the rapid growth the new reformed monastic orders during the middle years of the :ntury—chief among them the Cistercians. With their arrival, :clesiastical patronage bifurcated. The Cistercians were not satisfied ith the Anglo-Norman style, and they insisted on a kind of architecture ıat was in keeping with their own astringent tastes. Henceforth the nglo-Norman style tended to become more and more the architecture what we might think of as the High Church party of the day. Its :rsistence was really due to the conservative outlook of its patrons. ıt the situation was confused still more by a third factor. This was the owing influence of French Gothic on both the Cistercian and the nglo-Norman styles. On the whole, this Gothic aspect is perhaps .e most important, so perhaps the best way of dealing with the hole problem is to make it serve as an introduction to the question of othic architecture in England.

CHAPTER 3

Gothic Church Architecture before Westminster

IN the year 1114 or thereabouts a group of monks from the Frenc abbey of Tiron was settled at St Dogmells, in the far west of Wale Some ten years later another foundation, this time from Savigny-l Vieux, was established at Tulket, in Lancashire. Later it moved Furness, a name which is perhaps better known. The first of th Cistercians followed in 1128. The earliest of their houses in England wa at Waverley, in Surrey. Tintern, Monmouthshire, was founded in 113 and Rievaulx, in Yorkshire, the following year. After Rievaulx th movement assumed the dimensions of a torrent. Between 1128 an 1150 there were thirty-five Cistercian (and twelve Savignac) founda tions. With these ought to be included the numerous priories of Augu tinian canons which sprang up everywhere during the same perio All these movements were animated by a common desire to puri regular religious life from what was regarded as the contagion worldliness; and renunciation and privation played a prominent pa in their respective programmes. Eventually the Cistercians became b far the most important of these reformed orders. Not only were they th most numerous, but also the best organized. Under their patronage wa conducted a very considerable proportion of all the building operatio in the country during the middle years of the twelfth century, and t some extent the orders which shared their sympathies in religio followed their example in architecture. Inevitably their attitude o matters of architectural style was bound to have tremendous reper cussions.

In the past a great deal of attention has been given to Cistercia architecture on account of the rôle which it is supposed to have playe in the evolution of English Gothic. Because it is so emphatically th antithesis of everything Anglo-Norman, it has been felt that in som way it must belong with what eventually took the place of Anglo Norman—*i.e.*, Gothic. Perhaps this was partly due to the pointe

:hes which were used systematically in Cistercian churches. But inted arches alone do not make a Gothic church; and in general it :ms to have been the case that so long as Cistercian architecture in igland remained truly Cistercian it was not Gothic; and when it came Gothic it ceased to be distinctively Cistercian. The only ception is at the critical point where we find at least one building that is both Cistercian and Gothic; and it cannot be denied that the stercian Order functioned to some extent as a catalyst in the great ocess of change from Anglo-Norman to Gothic, especially in the orth. But the situation was extremely involved, and requires very reful analysis.

The Cistercian movement began in Burgundy, and the only interest iich its early leaders had in architecture was to ensure that the onastic buildings, and chief among them the abbey-church, were itable to the way of life which was to be lived within them. The one ing on which they insisted was the exclusion of all superfluous nament, which they regarded as distracting, and therefore as an omination. Apart from this, they wanted buildings that were con-nient to use, and simple to the point of severity. Accordingly they opted the starkest form of contemporary Burgundian Romanesque, d when the need arose they devised a standard church-plan. The in they took with them everywhere, and it became for many years an mistakable and indispensable feature of every Cistercian church. But ey were less insistent about the style. In countries like Germany and orthern Italy, where the local versions of Romanesque were severe ough to meet with their approval, they were quite willing to com-omise. In England, however, the situation was different. Here the ablished style was, from their point of view, hopelessly contaminated, d their attitude toward it was therefore much more critical. That is iy we find so many purely Burgundian features in the earliest English stercian churches: relatively unarticulated piers, pointed arches, and rrel-vaults over the chapels and aisles set at right angles to the main lls. Yet even so there was no question of importing the Burgundian le whole. We have only to compare the substantial remains of the ve of Fountains Abbey, Yorkshire (some time after 1135), with ntenay (*c.* 1140), in France, which is the best preserved of the truly rgundian Cistercian churches, to realize the extent of the variations iich were tolerated in England. At Fontenay there is no clerestory, d the nave has a pointed barrel-vault; at Fountains, on the other nd, there is a clerestory, and the nave had a flat wooden roof. rhaps these ought to be regarded as concessions to the English nate rather than to English taste. But it is difficult to explain the other deviation at Fountains—namely, the central tower. This is qu remarkable, for towers were specifically prohibited by Cisterci regulations, and we know that an architect was sent from Clairvaux Fountains to ensure that the buildings of the new foundation shou conform to Cistercian practice. But although Master Geoffroi Ainai came from France, most of his masons were Yorkshiremen, a certain reminiscences of their previous experience were bound intrude. Central towers were common among Anglo-Norman buildin And in spite of the tower, Fountains must have presented an appearar of formidable austerity; there was never any question of contraveni the spirit of the Order.

The concessions at Fountains are none the less significant. If slightly earlier nave at Rievaulx Abbey had survived it would ha been a little more severe and a little more Burgundian than Fountai On the other hand, at Kirkstall Abbey, near Leeds (*c.* 1152), wh was the next great Cistercian church in the North after Fountains, relaxations and the infiltration of Anglo-Norman forms went a sta farther. The simple square or cylindrical piers at Rievaulx and Fou tains were abandoned in favour of a compound pier whose shape v generated from an eight-pointed star. The incipient mouldings on arcades of Fountains were developed into a definite echelon profi and there are several instances of the discreet use of Anglo-Norm ornament to be seen at Kirkstall. Even more important was the use Anglo-Norman ribbed vaults instead of the Burgundian barrels for choir and side aisles.

If Kirkstall shows Cistercian architecture in the process of be domesticated the development of the style was soon to be deflected another direction altogether. The abbey of Roche, at Maltby, Yo shire, was founded in 1147, but the church is certainly later th Kirkstall, and its design ought to be assigned to about 1160. T features distinguish Roche from all its Cistercian predecessors. One the appearance of a third storey in the elevation between the ma arcade and the clerestory. The other is the fact that the whole chu was vaulted. In both these respects Roche drew its inspiration fr France, not England. The vaults in particular, with their support wall-shafts running right down the walls, were conceived wholly in French manner, and they make Roche the first English church wh has any serious claim to be called Gothic.

To use this famous word for the first time in connexion with Roc is apt to suggest that it was an epoch-making building. Yet it is an thing but revolutionary. To appreciate just how conservative the Got of Roche is, we should compare it with a really advanced Frer ilding such as the cathedral of Laon, which was begun almost actly at the same time. At Laon the walls no longer seem massive or id. They have been hoisted up, as it were, on long rows of slender umns; and wherever possible they have been perforated by rows of enings. Each aperture is framed by a pointed arch with a simple l-moulding, supported by colonnettes or detached shafts; and the

14. The South Transept, Roche Abbey

erall impression is not so much that of a wall as a seemingly endless tem of arches, shafts, and spaces. This effect is intensified by the ndles of wall-shafts which carry the ribbed vaults. At first sight it is rather bewildering; but the more one looks at Laon, the more dent does it become that everything has been thought out with the ne kind of thoroughgoing logic as that which characterized the liest Norman architecture. The visible system of forms symbolizes structural system of the actual building. In fact, French Gothic, garded from this point of view, can trace its ancestry back to Norman hitecture no less convincingly than Anglo-Norman itself. The point divergence began at the point where logic and decoration came into collision. As we have seen, the English readily sacrificed the logi clarity of their buildings as soon as they set out to explore new deco tive possibilities. The one principle of Norman architecture which th never seriously questioned was that represented by the thick wall. Th changed its proportions, turned it into cylindrical piers, cut away la parts of it; but always in the last analysis they were left with a resid that could only be described as thick. The French, on the other ha assimilated the Norman logic with avidity. But at the same time th made a fundamental distinction between the logic as such and t thick-wall system within which it had been developed. The latter th rejected; and in its place they gradually evolved a new and revo tionary structural system, in which the diffused supporting strength the thick wall was replaced by a much more rational and economi system of supports applied at the points of real stress. This allowed t non-essential parts of the wall to be handled with unprecedent freedom. The relations between solid forms and voids became mu more complicated, and windows began to assume a new importan There was certainly much more to Gothic than the invention of a n kind of structural engineering; but this was undoubtedly the essence the new style during its formative period, and the extent to which was understood and reproduced elsewhere is a sure index of the pe tration of specifically French Gothic influences.

By this criterion the Gothic of Roche is extremely tentative. T solidity of the walls has certainly not diminished. Indeed, we can see Roche the reappearance in a Cistercian context of the Anglo-Norm wall-passage; while the new intermediate section of the elevati indicated by pairs of blind recesses hollowed out of the thickness of wall, merely accentuates the massive effect. Apart from the wall-sha the vaults, and the third storey, very little has changed. When it co to the point we call Roche Gothic only because, in a superficial w it reminds us of real Gothic works.

Nevertheless Roche is a remarkable building. It will not do explain its Gothic features simply on the grounds that it belonged to Cistercian Order. It is true that by 1160 the Cistercians had started come to terms with the new style in France; but in England there w no uniform trend in this direction. It was only in the North that th took the lead in adopting Gothic. The explanation is perhaps to found in the close commercial bonds that were developing between sheep-farming Cistercians of Northern England and the cloth-ma facturing towns of Northern France which bought their wool. It was these towns—Douai, Arras, Valenciennes, etc.—that the new arc tectural style developed most rapidly during the 1150's and 116 oche probably took its inspiration from some Cistercian house in the cinity.

The next great Cistercian abbey in the North of England, Byland, Yorkshire, survives only in fragments. Yet there is enough for us to be ole to reconstruct its elevation, and to infer that it must have been work even more decisive than Roche in the formation of the first stinctly English school of Gothic architecture. In one important spect Byland was less French than Roche. It was not vaulted. On e other hand, there seem to have been a great many more arches and afts used in the design, and to the casual observer the effect must have en far more reminiscent of buildings like Laon. Yet a closer comarison would have disclosed a fundamental difference. To anyone ho could understand it, Laon was an intricate system; but to the ninitiated it might seem that Gothic was nothing more than the use shafts and arches in large numbers—a way of making the walls teresting to look at. When Englishmen made the acquaintance of othic this was in fact precisely how they saw it. True to their insular as they chose to regard it, not as an alternative system of construction, ut as an alternative system of decoration. In a sense they completely issed the point of what the French were doing; but because of this ey created a totally different kind of Gothic of their own. It was at yland Abbey that this insular twist first became apparent. If Roche as the first Gothic building in England, Byland was the first English othic building. It was dedicated in 1177, and it must have been under onstruction before Canterbury choir was started in 1175. The new ollegiate church at Ripon was probably slightly later than Canterbury. oger of Pont l'Evêque, whose chief concern as Archbishop of York as to keep abreast of Canterbury in all things, had already provided is minster at York with a choir commensurate with the Anglo-orman splendours of Canterbury. Now the new Gothic choir at anterbury goaded his pride once more, and he resolved to rebuild ipon, one of his subsidiary minsters, in the new style. But if the imulus came from Canterbury his masons came from Byland. Ripon important because enough survives for us to form an impression of e Byland style; and also because it marks the point where this cipient Gothic of the North was emancipated from the exclusive atronage of the Cistercians. The Gothic of Ripon is purely an affair of oplying arch mouldings and shafts to the openings in thick walls. This clear enough in the transepts and choir which still survive. But it must ave been even more obvious in the twelfth-century nave which, for asons not wholly clear, was built without side aisles. Enough of the riginal dispositions were left when side aisles were added in the

15. RESTORATION OF THE ORIGINAL ELEVATION OF THE NAVE, RIPON CATHEDRAL

fifteenth century for us to be able to imagine how it must have looke On each side there were two wall-passages one above the other. The opened on to the nave through rows of arches which were grouped in patterns. Two patterns appear in each row, and they were repeat alternately along the nave.

Nothing could illustrate more clearly the almost exclusive pr occupation of these Northern masons with the articulation of wall and it is a great pity that the nave of Ripon has gone the way of many other large buildings in this style. Time has in fact dealt ve severely with them. The only mature example which survives in an thing like its original condition is the abbey-church at Hexham. The the choir and transepts have escaped destruction, but only at the pri of heavy restoration. Otherwise we have the romantic, often splendi but melancholy ruins of Whitby Abbey, in Yorkshire, Tynemou Priory, in Northumberland, and the Gothic choir of Rievaulx. Althoug they are picturesque, ruins are no substitute for complete building save perhaps in so far as they serve as skeletons on which to condu classes in architectural anatomy. At Whitby and Rievaulx, for instanc the ruined state of the structures allows us to see heavy masses masonry which originally must have been concealed behind a pure rnamental screen of shafts and mouldings. Here, if anywhere, it is oundantly evident that early Northern Gothic was only skin-deep; at the shafts and mouldings were no more than a veneer masking the epth of the wall perhaps more effectively than the old Anglo-Norman atterns, but not differing from them at all in purpose. Later, as in the noir of Rievaulx or the presbytery at Tynemouth (both early thirteenth entury), stone vaults were introduced; but in the earlier stages of the yle vaults were certainly not considered an essential feature of a othic building. To a Frenchman all this would have seemed little etter than heresy; yet in the North of England it meant merely that e local masons were slow to cut the traces linking them with their nglo-Norman past. For that reason alone it is perhaps more illuminat-g to approach English Gothic from the North than from any other rection.

Early Gothic in the South was more or less dominated by the new noir of Canterbury. Already at St Cross and elsewhere there had been asmodic signs of French influences penetrating across the Channel,

16. THE NORTH TRANSEPT, HEXHAM ABBEY

but at Canterbury the authorities went a stage farther and summon(a Frenchman, William of Sens, from what was then undoubtedly tl region of the most advanced Gothic buildings—the vicinity of Arr and Valenciennes. Had their patrons wished them to do so, Engli masons might very well have learnt to build a purely French Goth church at Canterbury. But the monks insisted that whatever could l salvaged from the old Anglo-Norman choir should be incorporat(into the new building. In effect this meant retaining most of the ear twelfth-century plan, which, from William's point of view, was not very suitable starting-point for an up-to-date Gothic design. At tl same time adequate provision had to be made for the rising cult St Thomas à Becket. In this respect the disaster of 1174 could hard have occurred at a more propitious moment. To accommodate Becke shrine it was decided to extend the church still farther toward the eas This made the plan even more rambling and irregular, and still le amenable to William's style. It is not surprising, therefore, to find th in the event his design for the new choir of Canterbury was a good de less revolutionary than it might have been if he had been given a fr(hand.

Even so, Canterbury is more French than any other English buildir before Westminster Abbey. Here we find walls raised on rows columns in the French manner; and in the first part of the choir at lea there are circular and octagonal columns alternating with one anothe and corresponding to the double-bay system of the sexpartite ribbe vaults overhead. And there are wall-shafts systematically relating tl ribs of the vaults to the columns of the main arcades. The walls abo these columns are not thick walls in the technical Anglo-Norman sen at all. Although the traditional wall-passage appears at clerestory leve this is not a true indication of the thickness of the wall, for the clerestor is built out over special arches which rest, not on the main column but on the haunches of the transverse arches across the side aisles. N doubt this represents a compromise between Gothic and Angl(Norman practice. But the point from which the compromise starts very much farther in the Gothic direction than was the case in th North.

Canterbury was conceived first and foremost as a splendid approac to Becket's shrine. As the work proceeded eastward, so the level of th floor rose, and the richness of the decoration steadily increased, unt the climax was reached in the Trinity Chapel where the shrine wa to be housed. After the second transept we find some of the ston columns of the main arcades festooned with supporting shafts of dar marble. Then the columns are doubled, as in some French churche

17. THE CHOIR, CANTERBURY CATHEDRAL

ıd finally when we come to the Trinity Chapel the columns themlves are made of richly coloured and highly polished marble. These .rround the apse, and together with the marble-shafted upper storeys, e tiled floor, and the stained-glass windows, they must have formed setting of unprecedented brilliance for the shrine.

In all this Canterbury probably owed as much to the memory of its nglo-Norman predecessor as to the contemporary Gothic buildings known to William of Sens; and, as one might have expected, it was th decorative display rather than the original structural features whic made the deeper impression on English masons and their patrons. Eve when something new appeared like the marble shafts, which seem t have come from Valenciennes, the extent to which they were used a Canterbury was far more lavish than in Continental Gothic, and already anticipates the extraordinary vogue which Purbeck marbl enjoyed in England during the thirteenth century.

More indirectly, however, the importance of Canterbury was nc that it represented this or that kind of Gothic, but that it was Gothi and not Anglo-Norman. It marks the point at which the higher Englis clergy abandoned their conservative attachment to the older style an set out to bring themselves up to date. Perhaps it was not entirely coincidence that this should happen almost immediately after th Cistercians had come to terms with Gothic on their own account. A any rate, from this time onward it is no longer possible to think of th differences in English church architecture as manifestations of high and low-church policies. Canterbury being a metropolitan church, i example was sufficient to establish Gothic of whatever kind once an for all as the fashionable style for great churches; and when every on went over to Gothic the only significant differences left were thos between regional schools.

The immediate influence of Canterbury is evident in the columns o the retrochoir at Chichester Cathedral, which was remodelled afte 1187; and one may suspect that the Gothic elements which appear s curiously mixed with pure Anglo-Norman survivals in the round nav of the City Temple church (dedicated 1185), in London, came from th same source. But to see what English masons could do with Canterbur themes when they were freed from all restraints, one must turn t Lincoln. First, however, the West Country school of early Gothi remains to be discussed.

The origins of Gothic in the West Country are more obscure than i the North or the South-east. The rôle of the Cistercians, so far as we a now in a position to judge, seems to have been less crucial than in th North. The earlier parts of Abbey Dore (1170's), in Herefordshir represent a later stage than Roche. Already in the nave of Malmesbur (*c.* 1165) some Anglo-Norman masons had gone over to pointed arch for their main arcades. The same thing happened in the two bays a the west end of the nave of Worcester Cathedral, which seem to hav replaced a part of Wulfstan's church that was damaged by the fall of western tower. They belong to the 1170's, and perhaps more than an other design of this period, they merit the description 'transitional ere wall-shafts and ribbed vaults appeared side by side with Anglo-orman ornament and in conjunction with Anglo-Norman thick alls. The handling of the piers is particularly interesting, for the wall-afts and the shafts in the angles of the set-backs together produce a amond shape with a rippling profile that foreshadows in a rudi-entary way the purely Gothic piers at Wells.

In 1184 the abbey-church at Glastonbury was destroyed by fire. At ace all the abbey's considerable resources of relics and legend were ared to the task of raising money; and with help from the King, the lebrated Chapel of St Mary, or *vetusta ecclesia* as it was called, was built in well nigh record time. This chapel itself had been something a relic, and in its new form it was lavishly decorated. Much of the nament was Anglo-Norman, and in many ways it can be regarded as e last important Anglo-Norman work to be started in England. But is a complicated building, and there are several concessions to the w taste. The capitals have early Gothic leaf-forms, and it was com-eted with a ribbed vault. In the abbey-church itself, which was arted only shortly after the chapel, the Gothic idiom was much more ominent. The only considerable fragments that remain belonged to e transept walls; but they are sufficient for us to see that the elevation as a transcription of the Romsey–Oxford type of Anglo-Norman, with considerable admixture of Worcester influence, especially in the erestory. We find at Glastonbury clusters of shafts with a very distinc-ve form. They are arranged in threes, and their capitals are in effect unches of curly leaves. With or without the capitals, this motive pears in many West Country and Midland churches of the period, d suggests that there was a definite school with common pattern-oks.

The church with the closest links to Glastonbury in this respect is the thedral of Wells. The two buildings must have been nearly con-mporary. Work on Wells was certainly in progress during the 1180's, d the latest views seem to imply that Wells was slightly earlier than lastonbury, although of the two it makes the more definite break with e past. Here in fact West Country Gothic assumes a precocious aturity. Although it is later than Canterbury, it shows singularly tle Canterbury influence; and although there is perhaps a vague debtedness to the Cistercians, it is far more advanced than con-mporary work in the North. The design underwent a slight but gnificant change as it passed from choir to transept and from transept nave. This is most readily apprehended in the treatment of the iforium and the vertical divisions between the bays. In the choir and ansepts the triforium section of each bay consists of a double-arch unit.

The wall-shafts which separate the bays are not taken down to tl ground as at Worcester and Glastonbury; or to the capitals of the pie of the main arcade as at Canterbury. They reach only to corbel where the main arcade and triforium meet. These vertical divisions i the choir are by no means conspicuous; but even so in the nave the are attenuated still further. Here a third arch is introduced into th triforium, and this has the effect of 'squeezing out' the wall-shafts an merging the discrete sections of the triforium into a band of contiguou arches.

This tendency at Wells to stress the horizontal divisions of tl building at the expense of the vertical was to become very characterist of English Gothic in the thirteenth century; and it is one of the thin which distinguishes English Gothic of this period from all Continent versions of the style. Whatever else English masons may have bee trying to do, there was no question of their buildings soaring heave ward. This was even more apparent from the outside. The silhouett of early English Gothic churches were uniformly long and low, wit occasional squat towers. The taller towers and spires which now ador them all belong to a later age. When they were built the only extern features which really disturbed their outlines were the high-pitche gables of their numerous façades. With a sure instinct, the Englis realized that their particular kind of Gothic was most effective when was allowed to form long, receding vistas. In the nave of Wells tl effect of recession is particularly vivid, and this is due as much to tl conception of the walls as a series of self-contained horizontal strat as to its actual length. Below the triforium the piers and arches of tl main arcade make an even more emphatic and clearly defined zone patterning. Their profiles and mouldings and, above all, their folia capitals, to which the not very appropriate designation 'stiff-leafed' usually applied, leave us in no doubt at all that this was the aspect Gothic design which exercised the deepest fascination for Englis masons. Even when we realize that the piers are simple crosses masonry with groups of triple shafts placed against each face and each angle they remain visually bewildering. It goes without sayir that such richness and profusion of form was only possible because tl whole wall was conceived on Anglo-Norman proportions. There is tl traditional wall-passage at clerestory level, and the external buttressir of the main vaults is still concealed under the aisle roof. The vaults an clerestory, which constitute the third horizontal section of the nav have sometimes been criticized on the grounds that there the patternir is weaker—*i.e.*, less dense than in the lower parts. The fact may l admitted, but it is not necessarily a defect. To see Wells in this way

18. The Nave, Wells Cathedral

to see it in the light of Lincoln. But it is at least arguable that the W designers thinned out their patterning deliberately with the intenti of suggesting that the lighter parts of the building were at the top.

The work at Wells culminated in the great west front. This seems have been started about 1220, by which time two other import cathedral façades in the Gothic style had been designed in Englanc those of Lincoln and Peterborough. At Lincoln a flat, screen-faça had been built around the old Norman west front, and its ances clearly goes back to Bury St Edmunds. The Peterborough design v far more original and impressive, comprising three enormous port which occupy the whole façade. This is the only instance in Engla where we find deep portals like those of the French High Got cathedrals, but it was very much a case of beating the French at th own game, and it does not seem to have provoked the sort of admirati which leads to imitation. Although the Wells façade was intended accommodate a vast array of figure sculpture devoted to eschatologi themes, such as the French deployed in their cathedral portals, design followed the example of Lincoln rather than Peterborough, least in the fundamental respect of being a screen. This projects beyo the church to north and south to embrace the roots of the fourteen century towers. The actual portals are insignificant, the main pub entrance to the cathedral being through a splendidly decorated por on the north side of the nave. This was not the only difference betwe Wells and French Gothic cathedrals. The French figures were alw crowded together in rows; at Wells they are dispersed over the wh façade, and even spread round the corners of the towers to their easte sides. Moreover, while the French statues tended to come right aw from the walls to which they were attached, so that they could be se in the round, at Wells they were set back into niches in the buttress where they could be seen only from the front, and then not easily. fact, everything about this façade is as wilfully insular as the arc tecture behind it.

And so to Lincoln. From Canterbury and from Wells streams Gothic ideas converged on Lincoln, and mingled there with others t were wholly new, to produce what is by common consent the mast piece of the style. An earthquake in 1185, which broke the back of Anglo-Norman church, provided the opportunity for a compl rebuilding; and the resources of patronage were equal to the m extravagant demands that could be made upon them. So apart from re-use of the old Norman west front, hardly anything at Linc Cathedral can be blamed on the exigencies of economy or compromi We can sense that it was built as a *tour de force*, and it is no accident t

19. The Nave, Lincoln Cathedral

all the churches of its period it is the one that seems to embody most
mpletely the English ideal of what a great Gothic cathedral should
ok like.

Work began in 1192. The original apse, a singular arrangement with almost triangular sides, has gone, and the earliest surviving parts a the eastern transepts and the choir called St Hugh's Choir after t bishop who built it, to distinguish it from the later eastward extensi which is known as the Angel Choir. The idea of a church with t transepts suggests at once a link between Lincoln and Canterbury, a many of the details of St Hugh's Choir owe their inspiration, if not th exact form, to the Gothic work at Canterbury. There are also structu similarities. But it is characteristic of Lincoln that the enrichme should be taken to a far greater pitch of sophistication. Purbe marble now appears everywhere. The piers of the main arcade in t choir, which are variations on the Canterbury theme of shaft-suppor piers, each have their own peculiar design. And the arcades along t aisle walls replace the simple arches or intersecting arches which suffic in Anglo-Norman times by two rows, each with its distinctive ar form, and one superimposed on the other in what can only be describ as a kind of architectural counterpoint. It is in keeping with this tre that the capitals should follow the stiff-leafed type of Wells rather th the more formal convention at Canterbury.

But the most important contribution of Lincoln to English Got was in the field of vaulting. The vaults in St Hugh's Choir are fam for their bizarre asymmetry, and they are not at all easy to understa Both transepts have orthodox sexpartite vaults, and it has been su gested that the choir vaults were intended to produce something like t visual effect of a sexpartite vault without having to find room for intermediate transverse rib. One can see well enough what the intenti behind this curious formation was, by comparing the clerestories of t eastern transepts and St Hugh's Choir. In the transepts where the are ordinary sexpartite vaults there is room for only two lancets, a these are heavily obscured by the converging ribs. In the choir t intermediate transverse rib has, as it were, been shifted to one sic and this makes room for a third lancet. Moreover, the other two adr a great deal more light. Another advantage of such a vault is that could be placed over a crossing as well as an ordinary bay. At Cant bury there was an anomaly between the choir and the crossing whi arose from the necessities of sexpartite vaulting, and which was avoid at Lincoln. This explanation may contain part of the truth, but it is r entirely convincing because the Lincoln vaults do not really resembl sexpartite vaults at all, except at a great distance when they are heav foreshortened. They differ from sexpartite vaults in two ways. One the presence of what is called a ridge-rib, which runs right along t crest of the vaults, and joins all the keystones together to provi another and very effective longitudinal accent. This idea had alrea ɜn used on a small scale at Ripon. The other was the provision of ɔ keystones instead of one for the ribs in each bay. This was not :irely unprecedented, for some such arrangement can be seen in the ve of Durham. It is true that at Durham the vaulting-compartments

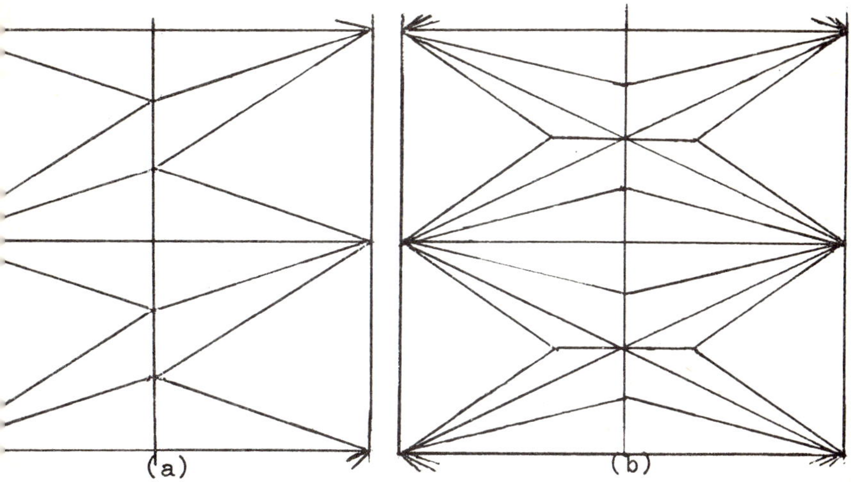

20. LINCOLN CATHEDRAL

(*a*) The vault system in St Hugh's Choir
(*b*) The vault system in the nave. (Not to scale)

re related to a double-bay system, and treated like two bays in one. t at least in respect of the two centres the parallel between Lincoln d Durham is exact, and at this point it becomes pertinent to wonder ıat form the ribbed vaults took in twelfth-century Lincoln.

Together these differences are crucial. The essence of a sexpartite ult is that it spreads like a canopy over its bay or double bay. The s, converging on a single and isolated centre, bind the space below o a unified and clearly defined spatial compartment. This effect is tirely due to the converging ribs, and as soon as they cease to con- rge it is lost. This is precisely what happens at Lincoln. There the ttern made by the vaults is clearly based on the notion of divergence :her than convergence. The ribs spread out in groups from points ɔng the walls toward the ridge-rib. The importance of this change n hardly be overestimated. It implies a totally new conception of the ıction of vaulting, one that is visual and decorative rather than uctural. Lincoln marks the point where the English discovered that ɜy could do with ribbed vaults what they had already done with ıer Gothic elements—namely, to transform them into devices for pattern-making. To this end they were prepared to dispense with hitherto unquestioned assumption that vaults should be related to bay-system. The diverging ribs of St Hugh's Choir, in fact, cover pa of adjacent bays.

What makes it almost certain that the designers of St Hugh's Ch were thinking along these lines is the fact that in the nave, only a f years later, a much more mature and ambitious system of divergi ribs was carried out with complete assurance. There are two differen between the vaults of the choir and those of the nave: one is that latter are perfectly symmetrical; and the other is that they conta more ribs. These facts have a common explanation. Within each b of the nave there are now three centres instead of two. This means th the number of ribs in each diverging group has increased from four five (in fact, there are seven, but two of these do not reach the rid rib). It needs only a little thought to realize that for any vault to both continuous and symmetrical, there must be an odd number centres; and it is a standing wonder that this never occurred to designers of St Hugh's Choir. But it must be remembered that th were feeling their way toward something entirely new, and we probably not clear as to what they really wished to achieve when th began. The idea of two centres may have been given to them as a fix starting-point, and they only emancipated themselves from t restriction when they reached the nave.

The result of all this was a vault pattern which is as interesting look at as the rest of the building below; and for the first time we c say that all the exposed surfaces have been accorded equal empha In a sense this is an extension of the Wells principle; but it also invol to some extent a repudiation of Wells, and with it the first signs o revision of English thinking on the subject of the thick wall. This po can easily be spoilt by being overstated. The walls at Lincoln are s thick enough to carry wall-passages at clerestory level, and the mou ings of the arcade arches are as florid as ever. But there is a defin shift of emphasis. The main arcade at Lincoln is not so massive as Wells, and it is far less obtrusive. This is because the span of the arch has been increased. The Lincoln arcades are wider than any others England, except those of the nave of York, which are much later. A result of this we can look right through them to the aisle walls beyor and these are allowed to participate directly in the overall effe Quite apart from making the interior lighter and more spacious, means that we tend to see it in terms of its peripheral surfaces. Pi and columns which are surrounded by space are inevitably appr hended as solid volumes. This was frankly admitted and deliberat ploited in Norman times; and although the early Gothic masons sed their piers with rippling profiles, these scarcely concealed their ılk. At Wells we feel that they were making a virtue of necessity. But Lincoln the trend is reversed, and although it is too early as yet to eak of linear, as opposed to plastic, patterns, there is undeniably mething about Lincoln which foreshadows the later development of ıglish Gothic.

Yet there is no question of external—*i.e.*, French—influences. We alize this if we compare Lincoln nave with the elevation of the inner oir aisle at Le Mans, which is almost exactly contemporary (*c.* 1218), d has almost exactly the same basic design, but which seems almost overty-stricken when it is set against the profusion of English decora-e forms. The change at Lincoln is wholly a change within the context English taste and English presuppositions, and it is perhaps typical English waywardness that though Lincoln was frequently copied in is or that particular, the further implications of its design were not plored until much later in the thirteenth century.

In spite of its importance, the nave of Lincoln was neither the end or the climax of the first Gothic building period there. It is in the apter-house that we find the most perfect expression of the aesthetic int of view which developed as the work progressed. In plan this is a ntralized figure with ten sides. Centrally planned chapter-houses ere adopted in the West Country during the twelfth century as an ternative to the more usual rectangular form. The earliest seems to ve been at Worcester, which still survives. Two more are known at e Cistercian abbeys of Margam, Glamorganshire, and Abbey Dore; d another was planned at Wells, although it was not built until much ter. Perhaps it was from Wells that the idea reached Lincoln. The ntralized plan was well suited to the special needs of the Lincoln yle. The walls are all shafts, arcades, and lancet-windows; and the of offers an unprecedented display of purely decorative rib-vaulting. he whole building was really designed around a central column hich branches out into a lovely cone of no less than twenty ribs. hese correspond to smaller groups of ribs which start from the corners the building. The cone of ribs was the final achievement of the ries of vaulting experiments at Lincoln, and its success was im-ediate and lasting. The idea haunted the imaginations of English asons almost down to the end of the Middle Ages.

Most of the buildings which followed Lincoln inevitably seem some-ing of an anti-climax by comparison. In the new choir at Worcester egun in 1224) the triforium has an enlarged but diluted version of the ntrapuntal arcades of St Hugh's Choir. There is also a ridge-rib, and the pier design perhaps owes something to Lincoln. But the Worcest piers have a bulk that seems more akin to Wells than Lincoln. The ar mouldings are the most extravagant in the whole repertoire of Engli

21. THE CHAPTER-HOUSE, LINCOLN CATHEDRAL

Gothic. On the other hand, the vaults, in spite of the ridge-rib, a treated with a restraint that again makes us think of Wells. The sar mixture of influences can be seen in the early parts of Lichfield Cath dral, which were more or less contemporary with Worcester.

It is significant that in the only two cases where systematic attemp were made to go one better than Lincoln, one—the new choir of E (*c.* 1238)—is little more than a copy of the Lincoln nave; while t other the transcpt at York (*c.* 1230)—overreached itself, and f victim to the necessities of compromise. It is clear that before t rebuilding of Westminster Abbey Lincoln represented a limit beyor which no one could see any way of advancing farther. The oth Northern minster, Beverley, in Yorkshire, which was rebuilt at abo the same time as the York transept, was more modest. Several of t Lincoln decorative techniques were used, notably the contrapunt arcades, which, as at Worcester, were transferred to the triforium. B ie Northern masons remained curiously shy of vaulting in the Lincoln anner. At Beverley they were content with simple quadripartite aults; and at York there were no vaults at all. At one time vaults em to have been projected, but either the designers baulked at the chnical problems involved, or they simply did not leave themselves ifficient room. As a result of this infirmity of purpose the York transept only succeeded in becoming a rather more splendid version of iose at Byland and Hexham.

Two other buildings in the North call for special mention. These are ie eastern transepts at Fountains Abbey and Durham Cathedral, both which are known as Transepts of the Nine Altars. The type may be iought of as a special version of the double-transept plan in which iere is no extension beyond the eastern transept. The origin of this odification is obscure. Fountains is the earlier of the two, and there ie primary consideration seems to have been liturgical. But at Durham iere were severely practical reasons. The nature of the site precluded ny considerable building to the east of the Norman apse; and when ishop Poore decided to repair and extend the choir of his cathedral ist before his death in 1237 (work did not begin until 1242) the choice this particular form was virtually forced upon him and his successors. i spite of the fame of these two buildings it must be admitted that the sle-less transept hardly offers much scope for architectural invention, nd in almost every other country apart from England it would have een abandoned as an intractable problem. At Durham the full pertory of marble shafts and wall-arcading was brought to bear, and ie building is saved by the sheer weight of ornament with which it is icrusted. At Fountains it is more difficult to judge, for there we see ie Nine Altars roofless, and denuded of its marble shafts. One suspects iat time and decay have endowed it with a more potent magic than ie men who built it. The incredibly slender cores of the free-standing iers which formerly rose sheer from floor to roof, and which now stand it against the sky, contrive to evoke the vision of an ethereal Gothic hich never existed in England save in Romantic imaginations.

Bishop Poore, who was responsible for the decision to build the Nine ltars at Durham, was already an experienced patron of cathedral othic before his preferment to Durham. In 1220, as Bishop of Salisury, he had decided to abandon his episcopal church inside the amped fortress of Old Sarum in favour of an entirely new site by the ver Avon a few miles away. Opportunities of this kind, which gave esigners almost unrestricted freedom, were becoming very rare in ngland, and one might have expected that the occasion would have een graced by a magisterial affirmation of the current style. The result was rather less than this, but it remains interesting as the o serious effort that was made before the rebuilding of Westminst Abbey, to escape from the tyranny of Lincoln. One would hesitate say that Salisbury offers a genuine alternative to Lincoln; but tl

22. SALISBURY CATHEDRAL FROM THE NORTH-EAST

similarities and debts to Lincoln are less obvious than in any oth important church of the early thirteenth century.

In plan Salisbury Cathedral conforms to the double-transept typ with a single-storeyed Lady Chapel projecting eastward from t ambulatory between two subsidiary chapels. All these features tend make the outline of the building complicated, and there are ma façades and gables, especially at the east end, which gave the exteri the little interest it had before the tower and spire were added in t fourteenth century. But all the changes of direction are made throu right angles, and in each panel of wall the articulation comprises group or series of groups of lancet-windows. Together these introdu an element of order, simplicity, and even monotony into the desig Inside the lancets are equally prominent, not because they are larger

23. THE LADY CHAPEL, SALISBURY CATHEDRAL

ɩore numerous than in other churches, but simply because everything se has been handled with unusual restraint so that there is nothing to ɔmpete with them. The main piers are far less elaborate than at incoln. The aisles are high, and simple quadripartite vaults reappear.

Wall-arcading under the aisle windows is conspicuous by its absenc It is almost as though Lincoln did not exist. The only part of tl building where we find a rich display of marble-shafting is in tl triforium. Elsewhere, although there is marble to be seen, it is used wi extraordinary discrimination.

It is clear that the Salisbury masons were trying to do somethir quite different from their colleagues at Lincoln. The question i What? The stress on the windows suggests that they were much mo interested in lighting-effects than in surface-patterning of the Lincol kind. To-day light comes flooding in through the lancets, and Salisbu is perhaps the brightest church of its period. But it must be remember that originally these windows would be filled with stained glass, and i the first half of the thirteenth century stained glass tended to be dar toned and brilliant in the intensity of its colour. Salisbury would ha been particularly well suited for the presentation of a display of suc glass; and the chromatic effects still evident in the alternating hor zontal bands of dark and light material in the nave seem to imply th colour was the primary consideration, as it had been at Canterbur The Lady Chapel probably reveals the kind of architecture which tl masons of Salisbury had in mind more truly than any other part of tl building. Although it was designed with two rows of supports for tl vault, which turn it into a sort of miniature hall-church, these suppor are so attenuated that we hardly notice they are there at all. They a no more than free-standing marble shafts, and they leave an almo uninterrupted view of the surrounding lancets. The damage an drastic restorations that Salisbury has suffered in the course of i history have robbed it of almost all its original character, and it is no a deceptively difficult building to appreciate. Even so, the shift emphasis to the windows is symptomatic of one of the most importa developments in English Gothic that started at Westminster Abbe and it is well known that Westminster was indebted to Salisbury mo than to any of its other English predecessors.

At Salisbury the idea of a church designed wholly or mainly as frame for its windows was no more than hinted at. Even if the intentic had been there the means were not yet to hand. Simple lancets a hardly capable of sustaining our interest by themselves, and we ca sense a growing dissatisfaction with their limitations in the attemp that became steadily more impressive, as the thirteenth century u folded, to combine them into larger patterns occupying whole façade Perhaps the most imposing of these are the groups of five at Lichfiel and York, which treat the whole wall of their respective transepts as unit, and make no concessions to the divisions of the elevation. Wi

24. NORTH TRANSEPT ELEVATION, YORK MINSTER, WITH THE FIVE SISTERS WINDOW

these groups of lancets the great traceried windows of the next gener tion do not seem far away. By 1240 England was ripe for the introdu tion of tracery; and even without Westminster it would have mad its appearance more or less when it did. The west window of Binha Priory, in Norfolk, for instance, may even pre-date Westminster by few years. Westminster, however, was undoubtedly the building whic put tracery 'on the map' in England. And in many other ways as we it cut right across the native Gothic tradition. It marks the beginnin of another of those momentous periods when Englishmen turned asid from their insular preoccupations, and took a long look at what wa happening in the main stream of Continental architecture. As on oth occasions, they were immensely stimulated by what they saw. Th whole question of how they wanted their churches to look was re-opene and when the upheaval eventually subsided an entirely different Goth style was established. It is not true to say that the late Gothic style i England was created at Westminster; but the early Gothic perio certainly came to an end there.

CHAPTER 4

From Westminster to Gloucester

HE first move in the rebuilding of Westminster Abbey was made in 220, when Henry III laid the foundation-stone of a new Lady Chapel. ıst what was projected in 1220 remains obscure; but it seems to have ıvolved the transformation of the east end of the Norman abbey, hich was round, by squaring off the presbytery, and adding chapels ı the eastern side. The problem seems to have been roughly similar to ıat at Chichester in 1187, and the solution was also essentially the me. How far they got with this enterprise is not known, although the ady Chapel was being roofed in 1234, and some work 'on the church' as in progress at the same time. But it was certainly never finished, r in 1245 the King took over the whole financial burden, and romptly began to rebuild the abbey anew to his own liking.

This royal intervention at Westminster marks the emergence of the ing and Court as the most important source of architectural patronage the country; and although there were lapses and intervals when ttle was done, this remained the case down to the time of Henry VIII. ı two ways the patronage of the Court differed from that of the earlier shops and abbots. On the whole, these had been content to use local lent; and although occasionally, as at Canterbury, they were pre-ıred to call in foreigners, they were undoubtedly responsible for the sular and regional character of early English Gothic. The King, on ıe other hand, could and did procure the services of the best masons om all over the country. We find names like Richard Canterbury, oger Luton, John of Gloucester, and John of Beverley on his pay-roll. oreover, his territorial, ecclesiastical, and dynastic connexions with urope put him in a peculiar position of advantage when it came to ıowing about the contemporary state of art on the Continent. Other ımes, such as Richard of Paris, John Norman, Henry of Reyns, Peter Rome, and Peter of Spain, show how far afield he was prepared to ok for his artists. It is clear that royal patronage created the conditions in which a national style of Gothic could be formed; and at the san time ensured that it should be, if not exactly cosmopolitan, at least Gothic strongly flavoured with Continental ideas.

The man placed in charge of the work at its inception was Henry Reyns. A great controversy has raged around the nationality of th man. Protagonists of the Englishness or the Frenchness of Westminst have claimed him with equal vehemence for their respective causes. is true that if we try hard enough Reyns can be found in England; b for the Middle Ages the Reyns par excellence was Reims, in Franc There are certainly echoes of Reims Cathedral at Westminster. Th was only to be expected, for Reims was the coronation church of th French kings, and Westminster was its equivalent in England. B Reims was not the only source of the French influences at Westminste Amiens is often mentioned; and another no less important was th abbey of St-Denis, near Paris, which was another counterpart Westminster in so far as it enjoyed the special and intimate protectic of the French kings. Finally, there was the Sainte-Chapelle, which w being built for the palace of St-Louis in Paris at the very moment th Westminster was started. On the whole it seems necessary to postula the presence at Westminster of someone who had a long, close, ar up-to-date knowledge of French architecture; and we can admit th Master Henry was a Frenchman without prejudice to the Engli contribution to the building.

King Henry's interest in Westminster did not spring from a desire emulate any or all of the French buildings which it resembles in par but from his personal devotion to St Edward the Confessor. In a ve literal sense his plan for the abbey centres on the Confessor's shrin The very point where the head of the saint was to be placed is the ape of a right-angled triangle of which the hypotenuse is the baseline the transept; and from this point the whole system of radiating chape is generated. Master Henry made very skilful use of the restricted spac at his disposal. He adopted the latest French scheme for a five-side apse which is in effect five sides of an octagon. This allowed him to g half a chapel on either side behind—*i.e.*, to the west of his startin point. (There is a slight modification apparently due to the necessi of incorporating the already completed Lady Chapel into the desig This took the place of the axial chapel, and it entailed reducing th sides of the octagon by a small amount. This has left the two outermo sides of the apse canted inward.) Another desideratum was a broa and spacious transept with two aisles. The transept of the Norma abbey had only an eastern aisle. The new western aisle had of necessi to be placed on the western side of the baseline, and this results in th

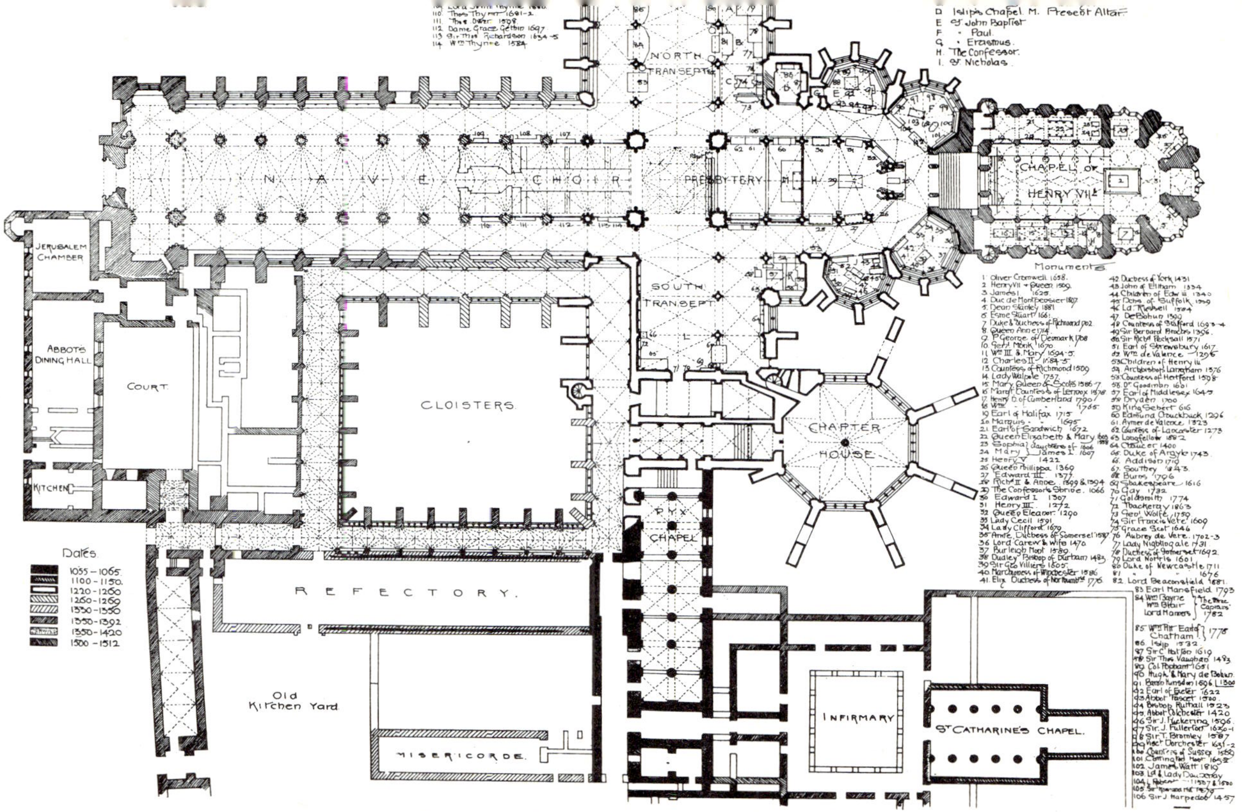

25. Ground Plan of Westminster Abbey

curious compromise on the south side where the western aisle is, as were, superimposed on the eastern arm of the cloister.

On this plan was raised the closest approximation that was ever ma in England to a French High Gothic chevet. Although Westminster c hardly compare in absolute height with cathedrals like Amiens Beauvais, it remained higher than any other English medieval churc and it tends to look higher than it is because it is relatively narrow. a whole the elevation has the characteristic French dispositions: comparatively narrow triforium with a high arcade and a high clere tory on either side. There is no question of a wall-passage, and t stability of the upper storey is ensured by means of flying-buttress All the windows in the chevet are filled with tracery.

The traceried window may be thought of as a much more versat alternative to the idea of increasing window space by grouping lanc together. Instead, the lancet itself is enlarged, its shape altered, a thin strips of stone inserted to form a pattern. The essential point is th the stonework is never thick enough to suggest that it is part of the wa In order that the pattern made by the tracery should register, it w necessary that it should stand out against the surrounding glass; a it was about this time that the deep-toned glass of the early thirteen century began to give way to the much lighter-toned 'grisaille.' Tl was used in the chapter-house windows at Westminster. In the choir Westminster the patterns of the tracery derived mainly from Reim although in the triforium there are triangular windows that came frc Amiens or Notre-Dame, Paris; the chapter-house windows also repe a design from Amiens. At the time, *c.* 1245, these were already out date in France. The transepts at Westminster, however, have tv enormous rose-windows in which the tracery followed the latest Pa fashion. Windows of this kind had been invented only a few years befc at the abbey of St-Denis, near Paris; and those at Westminster we among the first imitations. Even more up to date were the angels on t transept walls, just below the rose-windows. These are Westminste clearest obligation to the Sainte-Chapelle.

When all these debts to France have been acknowledged what is l to form the English contribution? The answer is more than might ha been expected. The main columns of polished marble are clearly in t Salisbury-Canterbury tradition, and lead us to suppose that colo played an important part in the decoration of the abbey. Around t transept walls there is a zone of carving in relief which was inspir from Worcester. And in the roof a ridge-rib makes a solitary concessi to Lincoln. But over and above these specific features there is a gene richness of form and texture which in its way is as English as anythi

Lincoln. The triforium, for instance, is far richer than its prototype Amiens. Another case in point is the diaper pattern which is liberally plied to the upper surfaces of the choir and transepts, and which alls to mind the Anglo-Norman use of such patterns. The same is

26. ROSE-WINDOW, NORTH TRANSEPT, WESTMINSTER ABBEY

ne outside. The main façade of the abbey was on the north transept, ing the Palace of Westminster. Its inspiration seems to have been e west front of Amiens without the towers; but even when allowances ve been made for the several restorations it must have been a very e transcription. In the process all the French features except the se-window were drastically altered, and none more so than the rtals. These were reduced in size, and tracery patterns took the place figure sculpture. The result was a compromise of the worst kind, and is not surprising that as an essay in façade composition it was quietly gotten.

The hostility of the English to deep sculptured portals was matched ly by their allergy to flying-buttresses. There are flying-buttresses at estminster, but it is only on the cloister side of the nave that we find bank upon bank of them, as in France. Around the chevet in particu they are almost completely obscured by the upper storeys of t radiating chapels—a feature without parallel in France, but whi occurred occasionally in Anglo-Norman churches—*e.g.*, Gloucest It is a measure of the reluctance of the English to use flying-buttres that they were prepared to use iron tie-rods inside as an alternat means of ensuring stability. In the abbey itself these were only co plementary to the buttresses; but in the chapter-house the wh structure was apparently held together by them at first. In the e however, it had to be admitted that the expedient was a failure, a within a century the hated buttresses made a belated appearance.

In other ways as well, the chapter-house was the building at We minster where the English tradition re-asserted itself most vigorous Being centrally planned, it had no counterpart in France, and we a consequently in a much better position than in the abbey itself to s which of the new ideas made the deepest impression on English tas Without question it was the traceried windows. Although the chapt house windows must have been contemporary with those of the abb choir, they are more than twice as large, and occupy practically all t surface on each side of the building. It is natural to compare We minster chapter-house with that at Lincoln. These great windows a the obvious innovation, but there is another difference, hardly l important. In deference to the shape of the windows the radius of t vault-ribs at Westminster has been reduced, and this means that t cone of ribs in the centre has been pushed up into the roof, where i far less conspicuous than at Lincoln. Both vaults and windows Westminster are nineteenth-century reconstructions, but Salisbu where the chapter-house was a direct copy of the one at Westminst confirms the impression in every detail. By comparison with the twen ribs that made the cone at Lincoln, there are only sixteen at We minster and Salisbury. But whereas there are ten sides at Lincoln, the are only eight at Westminster and Salisbury. This means in effect th the sides have been enlarged, and the cone reduced; or, in other wor ribs have been sacrificed to windows.

Put like this, the comparison between the Lincoln and the We minster chapter-houses might suggest that there was present from t start an antithesis between two different aesthetic programmes, o represented by the rib-patterns at Lincoln, and the other by the windo patterns of Westminster. With the advantage of hindsight, we m perhaps feel inclined to be dogmatic about this; but a great deal experience and experiment was required before the people direct concerned—*i.e.*, the designers—reached this conclusion for themselv

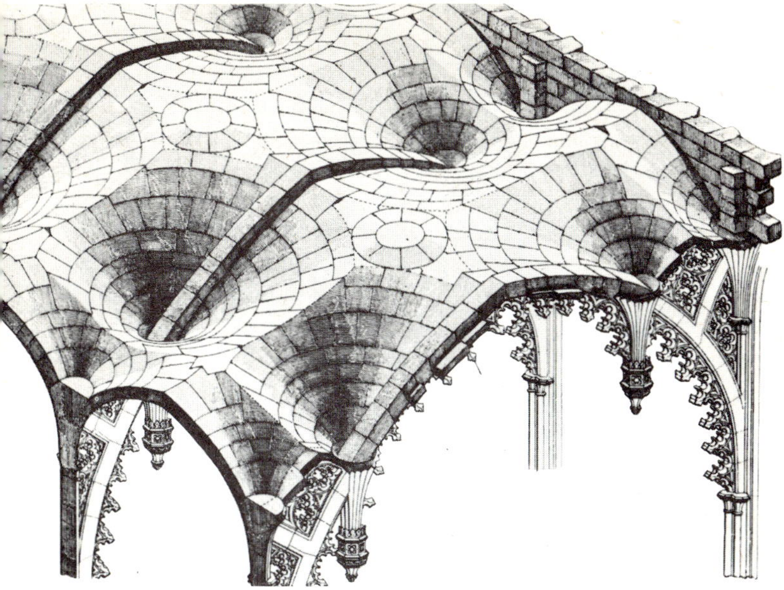

27. Vault System, Henry VII's Chapel, Westminster Abbey

28. The Chapter-house, Salisbury Cathedral

It is true that in the two chapter-houses which followed Westmins and Salisbury, those of Southwell and York (both *c.* 1280), the infere was drawn that central columns and cones of ribs were inconsist with traceried windows; and the former were duly dispensed with. it was in the nature of the case that this problem should be more ac in centrally planned buildings than in ordinary churches. And e in chapter-houses at least one attempt was made to demonstrate compatibility of the two ideas. This was at Wells.

The most general reaction to the development of traceried windc was to try and have the best of both worlds; and for at least a generat after Westminster masons went happily about the business of achiev richer and richer effects by making both kinds of pattern more and m complicated. We can see the first signs of this at Westminster itself, the main vaults of the nave where the full Lincoln pattern was adopt The three most important designs of the late 1250's—namely, Angel Choir at Lincoln, the nave of Lichfield, and the choir of old Paul's—all followed suit. In the Angel Choir, which takes its na from the rows of angels over the triforium—a clear indication Westminster influence—the result was particularly felicitous. Exc for a slight modification of the vaults to accommodate an enlarg clerestory, the nave-design at Lincoln was readily adapted to rece the new windows. Yet even at Lincoln the designers were aware of inherent conflict between tracery on the one hand and the implicati of thick-wall construction on the other. They repeated the clerest tracery on the inner side of the wall-passage, and thereby preserved three-dimensional homogeneity of the wall itself, without losing essential flatness of the tracery pattern. It was a solution that followed elsewhere, especially in the North.

The most important of the Lincoln windows, however, was at east end. Already at Binham in the 1240's the Westminster chap house pattern had been used for a façade window. Now at Lincoln find two of these patterns placed side by side, with another circu pattern, or 'oculus,' above and between them, to form the first re elaborate tracery composition that occupied the full height and wi of a cathedral façade. A little later at old St Paul's there was an equ impressive and no less influential east window combining the W minster rose with a series of lancets. Once the type had been createc wonderful succession of similar designs followed. Almost at once great window was accepted as the dominant feature of church façac In west fronts it replaced the old idea of a screen of niches, and so m possible a new version of the Norman two-towered façade. The w front of Exeter (begun *c.* 1327), which contrives to have both a scr

29. The Angel Choir and East Window, Lincoln Cathedral

d a great window, might almost be regarded symbolically as the nt where one idea gives way to the other. But it was in the North, ere the deeply rooted tradition of cliff-like east ends provided ready pe for ambitious schemes, that the most impressive of these great windows were made. Intact, restored, or in ruins, we find them Yorkshire at Ripon, Guisborough, Howden, Selby, York, and Cumberland at Carlisle. For a hundred years the designing of trac patterns was one of the chief forms of creative activity in England. T geometrical principles on which they were based became steadily m and more involved, and by the second quarter of the fourteenth cent the rigid formality of the earliest examples had given way to a luxuri and almost lyrical freedom. At York, Selby, and Beverley, for instan we find heart-shapes, and raindrops, and tongues of flame wh anticipate by more than half a century the French Flamboyant trac which was based on these motives.

The lead given by the great windows was closely followed by smaller windows of the aisles and clerestories. In becoming denser a

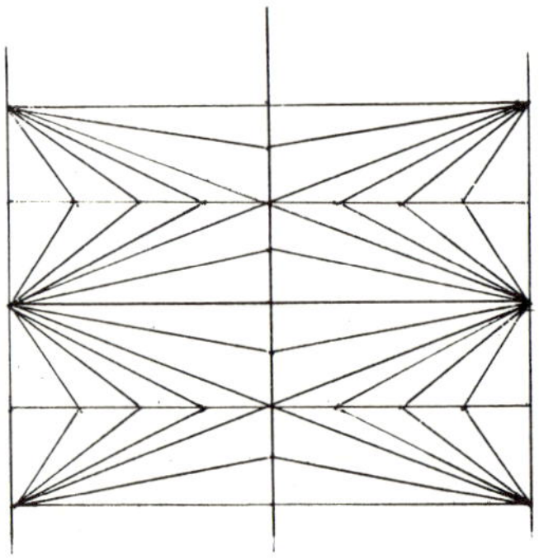

30. THE VAULT SYSTEM IN THE NAVE OF EXETER CATHEDRAL
(Not to Scale)

more elaborate window-tracery followed the same law of developm which we have already seen operating in the cases of pier profiles, a mouldings, and vaulting-ribs. The building which marks the criti stage in the assimilation of tracery to these older forms of decorat was Exeter.

Exeter Cathedral was started before 1280, and although it took m than eighty years to complete, its design was fixed in the early stag and hardly altered except for details. It is clear that the designers out with the Lincoln idea of an all-over surface-pattern in mind; they also set themselves the task of intensifying it to a very much hig degree. This is most apparent in the handling of the vault-ribs. T maximum of seven in each diverging set of ribs at Lincoln has beco eleven at Exeter. The vaults are now so thick with ribs that ther hardly any exposed surface between them. Moreover, every part of

31. THE NAVE, EXETER CATHEDRAL
John Britton

ult is covered, not just the centre. By comparison with Lincoln, this ıs going to extremes; and if the main arcades had been as light and ·en as those of Lincoln the building would have seemed top-heavy. To mpensate for this exuberant vault-pattern it was therefore necessary stress the main arcades as well; and so it is that we find at Exeter ərs and arch mouldings as bulky and obtrusive as any at Wells or orcester. The vaults and arcades are in fact so prominent that to all :ents and purposes Exeter looks like a two-storeyed building. It is not rprising to learn that the original design made no provision for a ddle section. The unobtrusive triforium that we now see was introıced in the course of construction. Despite its presence, Exeter still oks like a long vista through a forest.

In earlier Gothic churches the middle section had often been the ıce for a display of coloured marble shafts. But by the end of the rteenth century the vogue for this particular kind of ornament was ssing, and the triforium became henceforth increasingly redundant. it did so interest shifted to the arcades below and the clerestory above.

The thickening and coarsening of the rounded forms in the piers a mouldings at Exeter are evident enough. But any gain in the clerest fails to register because the clerestory is lost to view among the vau ribs. The windows are set back behind a wall-passage, and the trac has not been repeated on the inside as in the Angel Choir. As a res their contribution to the general effect of the interior is disappointi The aisle windows are equally discreet. Yet when they are examin in detail it is clear that the windows are every bit as elaborate as t masonry, and there is no doubt that they were intended as a co plement to the stonework in achieving an ideal of total decoration.

But they failed to do so. Exeter remains a brilliant piece of masor in which there happen to be windows. There is no organic un between them; there is not even an element of deliberate contr between stone and glass. Impressive as it undoubtedly is, Exeter was the *tour de force* that it was meant to be, and perhaps it was the d appointment that forced English masons to realize that tracery was just another decorative device to be used at will in conjunction with existing repertory. When it comes to the point shafts, mouldings, a vault-ribs are all very similar to one another. Either they are vertic or they follow smooth curves. And they are all plastic forms. In sh they cohere into a system. Tracery patterns, on the other hand, hav different rhythm. The strips of stone are lighter; their changes direction more rapid; their intersections more violent. The conditi under which they are seen are totally different. Above all they are f patterns, and will not readily combine with plastic forms. The m they will do is to provide under favourable conditions an element contrast. But in a building like Exeter, where the plastic forms w emphasized to an unprecedented degree, they had no chance.

Whether or not there was a general inquest along these lines, Exe was followed by a remarkable series of buildings, all of which can regarded as being to a greater or less extent reactions. The half-cent from 1285 to 1335 witnessed the most brilliant display of sheer inventi ness in the whole history of English medieval architecture. Sometin the works of this period are grouped together under the label 'Decora Style.' But quite apart from the fact that this is a singularly inept te by which to distinguish one set of English medieval buildings from rest, it is doubtful whether the notion of stylistic unity which it imp will stand up to analysis. The name Decorated was first used distinguish windows with elaborate patterns of tracery from the sim lancets which preceded them and the Perpendicular panelled windo by which they were followed. It is easy enough to extend the mean of the word to include the new kind of vaulting which was inven

1290, to which the name 'lierne' is given; but whether we can go rther and speak of Decorated buildings, as well as Decorated tracery nd vaults, is another matter. By comparison with the impressive milarities between early Gothic buildings on the one hand, and erpendicular buildings on the other, it is the variety—one might lmost say the experimental character of the so-called Decorated esigns—that is the salient fact about them. It is true that they often now an interest in complicated spatial shapes and spatial relations, nd recently this has been used as a stylistic criterion. But one hesitates o assume that spatial considerations were fundamental. More often han not they seem to have been means to other ends. Perhaps one gets better insight into the great buildings of this period if they are egarded as so many essays in the quest for a new style. One of these venues of research led directly to Perpendicular, and the kind of olution which Perpendicular offered sheds a good deal of light upon he general problem with which the discarded alternatives were concerned as well.

By a curious inversion of the normal order of progress, the two esigns which were to be of greatest significance for the future—the nave f York Minster and St Stephen's Chapel in the Palace of Westminster —were the first to follow Exeter. St Stephen's is best left until we come o discuss the origins of Perpendicular. The nave of York, however, eserves to be accredited with more importance than is usually attached o it. The chapter-house at York had already provided an introduction o the problems of tracery. The decision to abolish the central column annot have been taken lightly, for it involved a structural difficulty of ome magnitude—namely, how to vault the building. Without the olumn the span became something like 60 feet. This was far beyond he normal limits of English experience, and in the end the York nasons handed the task over to their colleagues, the carpenters, who roduced a wooden imitation of a stone vault. This was not the first ccasion when the carpenters had come to the aid of the stonemasons. t had happened at Lichfield as far back as 1240, and at Henry III's hapel in Windsor Castle soon after. But the success of the sham vaults t York marks the emergence of timber architecture into the front rank f importance, where it was to remain for the rest of the Middle Ages. f anything were needed to prove the point that in England visual ffect was the primary consideration in the construction of vaults this s it. We are often told that vaulting in stone was invented precisely in rder to avoid the risk of fire to which wooden roofs were liable. Now he wheel has moved full circle. Eventually the whole of the nave and he transepts of York were given sham vaults as well. Although the nave

32. THE NAVE, YORK MINSTER

vault was not put up until the middle of the fourteenth century, it wa probably designed along with the rest about 1290. It is very differen from Exeter vault. Instead of a dense system of ribs there is mparatively sparse pattern of an entirely new kind. Between the main s, of which there are only three to begin with, a subsidiary system of nnecting ribs has been introduced. These small ribs, which start and d on other larger ribs, are known as liernes. At York the idea may ve developed naturally from the unified pattern on the roof of the apter-house. But there are several other instances from the last cade of the thirteenth century, the choir of Pershore Abbey (1288) ving perhaps the earliest dated example. The importance of this ıd of vaulting is that it results in a kind of pattern that is distinctly alogous to the kind of pattern produced by window-tracery. The ain ribs correspond to the mullions of the windows and the liernes to detailed designs at the top. It is not too fanciful to see in this novation the germ of the idea of applying a tracery pattern to a roof.

In other respects also York is a complete antithesis of Exeter. The ndows are far more prominent. The arcades are high and wide, like ose of Lincoln. The upper walls are thin and flat. There is no wall-ssage, and the clerestory windows are brought into the plane of the ier surfaces of the nave walls. Even more remarkable is the handling the middle section of the elevation. York was built as a two-storeyed sign. The window-tracery of the clerestory comes right down to the ing-course above the main arcade. The upper parts are glazed; the ver parts, which correspond to the aisle roofs, are not. That is the ly concession to the old notion of a structural triforium. When npared with the cathedral designs that preceded it York nave was cidedly revolutionary. This is perhaps concealed by its great height d width, which put it in a class apart among English cathedrals, and o by the fact that there were few later buildings of the kind to follow lead. Nevertheless it is the starting-point for late Gothic cathedral-sign in England, as comparisons with the naves of Canterbury and nchester will show.

The second series of works at Wells, which began in 1285 and con-ued for half a century, presents us with a much more complex reaction Exeter. The first of them, the chapter-house, was almost certainly lt by men from Exeter. It has without doubt the finest cone of ribs be seen in England. There are no less than thirty-two of them; and h the corresponding ribs that spring from the corners of the building effect is overwhelming. It is just the sort of chapter-house vault that should have expected from Exeter masons. The windows are initely subordinate partners in this composition, and the overall ect represents a return to the Lincoln, as opposed to the Westminster, e of chapter-house.

The success of this cone of ribs so endeared the motive to the designers

33. THE CHAPTER-HOUSE, WELLS CATHEDRAL
John Britton

of Wells that they retained the idea when they began to remodel t east end of the cathedral. This work falls into three well-defined stag an extension of the choir; a new Lady Chapel; and a retroch between them. The starting-point for this complicated design was type of east end which had started at Chichester *c.* 1187, and which h worked its way across Southern England during the thirteenth centu to reach Wells via Winchester, Salisbury, and Exeter. But at Wells customary gridlike arrangements were drastically altered. The La Chapel became an irregular elliptical polygon, while the piers of retrochoir were disposed in the form of a hexagon with very little reg for the main axis-lines of the building. This extraordinary plan o makes sense in terms of the visual effects which it made possible. I often claimed that the subtlety of Wells arises from the relation betwe the Lady Chapel and the retrochoir. This is true up to a point, but clever handling of these spaces was a means to an end, not an end itself. The relation between them has been described as 'interpenet tion'; but this is surely a mistake. The Lady Chapel pushes into

34. The Retrochoir, Wells Cathedral

:rochoir, but there is no reciprocation, and neither lose their identity. r real interpenetration it is necessary to look back to Salisbury. At ells the Lady Chapel is to all intents and purposes a self-contained ilding. This is evident from its shape, and still more from its vault, iich is a unified star-pattern based on liernes. We can think of it as eccentric modification of the York chapter-house idea. The retro- oir flows around this building, but the contrast between them is very arked. They do not rise to the same height; their vaulting is quite fferent; and even the piers which they have in common present fferent faces in different directions. It is not easy to describe the Wells trochoir as a clearly defined spatial entity. Although the supports m themselves into an elongated hexagon on the ground, the vaults ove them bear no relation to this figure. It is almost certainly a istake to attempt to think of it in terms of spatial geometry. Our certainty as to its precise limits seems to have been deliberately ntrived. Instead of a spatial configuration, it is objects in space that are meant to see. Whichever way we look there are branching cones ribs, and beyond them other cones of ribs, with only the aisle windows and those of the Lady Chapel seemingly far away to suggest where comes to an end. Although there are some lierne ribs, the retrochc does not have a true lierne vault. Fundamentally, it is an extension the chapter-house idea, but instead of a single cone we now have whole series of them; and their triangular dispositions allow them to l seen effectively from almost any point of view. There are so many ri in play that it proved quite impossible for them all to be matche symmetrically; and so we find two conveniently placed lion-heade keystones, each of which contrives to swallow a couple of ribs when the have performed their allotted function. In any other context this woul have been outrageous, but here it hardly seems to matter at all, whe everything else is arbitrary, irrational, and exquisitely mysterious.

As a solution for a particular problem the Wells retrochoir was triumph of imagination; but its very perfection made it the sort thing that could not easily be done again. If it had been generalize into a type of church architecture the result would have been a hal church. But the demands of regularity would have reduced it all to tl level of the commonplace. The men who built the extension to tl choir of Wells proceeded as though the retrochoir did not exist. Ril cones are given up altogether, and the vault has become a pattern squares and hexagons embedded in the solid material of the structur The texture of this pattern matches that of the window-tracery ve well. The unity of clerestory and triforium, however, is disrupted by tl wall-passage which was continued from the earlier work, and this only partially offset by the extension of the triforium downward, so th the niches of which it is composed rest directly on the haunches of tl arcade arches. With its strong vertical lines, the choir of Wells seems share the mood of Perpendicular without actually using any specifical Perpendicular forms. Later, when work shifted to the towers, th Perpendicular quality became more explicit.

It is curious that while this second building campaign at Wells w in progress a kind of hall-church was commenced only a few mil away at Bristol. This was for the choir of St Augustine's Abbey (no the cathedral). Work was already in progress by 1306. It might ha been expected that the Bristol designers would have followed the san lines of thought as the men who made the Wells retrochoir. In fac however, they avoided making any direct allusion to Wells, and to ar of the other great building projects of the time in England. The resu is undoubtedly the most unusual and original of our great mediev churches.

Much attention has been given to the fact that Bristol has the for of a hall-church—that is, a church with aisles and nave of the san

35. Section and Plan of the East End of Bristol Cathedral

ght. But as soon as we compare it with conventional hall-churches in rmany or Western France it becomes abundantly clear that the stol masons were either being wilfully obtuse, or else they had some-ng else in mind apart from the simple desire to build a hall-church. e aisles and nave at Bristol do not merge to form a unified interior, ich is what one expects; and the aisles have a deceptive ambiguity ich from some points of view almost destroys the hall-church effect. e only feature of a Continental hall-church about which there can no dispute at Bristol is the absence of a clerestory. From this it ows that all the windows, except the great east window, are con-trated in the aisles; and instead of being dispersed in two rows, they now unified, and occupy more or less the full height of the wall. a counterpart to this bringing together of the windows the arches of the main arcades and those of the vaults can now form themselves ir a single system. What has happened in effect is that ribs and ar mouldings on the one hand, and window-tracery on the other, ha been rigorously segregated. In other words, the indiscriminate mixi of decorative elements which was so obvious at Exeter has been repu ated. This seems to have been the fundamental idea which inspired t Bristol masons. The thoroughness with which they applied it in det emerges if we study the windows a little more closely. The only wind which was not banished from the choir proper was the great e window. But here the question of segregation did not arise. The Bris designers seem to have agreed with their colleagues elsewhere tl there was nothing wrong with windows in terminal façades. Inde this was the only place for them. To prove the point, they went to t trouble of placing each of the aisle windows at the end of a miniat replica of the structural system of the choir. The design of the dividual aisle bays at Bristol is extremely subtle. Each has its o arcade of one arch on either side—*i.e.*, east and west—and its o vaulting-system, aligned by a ridge-rib running north–south at rig angles to the choir. The terminal façades of these bays are occupied simplified versions of the great east window of the choir. From t point of view the windows are set back from the choir in what app to be lateral recesses from the central space—detached from, but wholly unrelated to, the arcade openings. But these aisle bays thoroughly equivocal. The designers never lost sight of the orthod conception of a side aisle as a subordinate vista parallel to the m axis of a church. The cleverness with which they contrived to have t best of both worlds, and at the same time ensure the stability of t whole building, gives Bristol a claim to be considered the most sophis cated piece of architecture in the whole of Europe at the time. At t points where the thrust of the main vaults is received by the arca stone girders span the aisles, and allow the outer walls to resist strain. Below these girders are skeleton arches which support the gird in the middle, but otherwise carry no masonry. To anyone looki along the aisles, the receding vista of these arches gives a stro impression that the aisles are lower than the nave after all; and if t matter had been allowed to rest there the effect would have be similar to that produced by the Burgundian vaults over the side ais of early Cistercian abbeys like Fountains. But one final note of fant was introduced. Part of the masonry between the vaults of each co partment of the aisles was cut away to leave what appears from distance to be the base of a little cone of ribs resting on the centre each girder, and hinting at unexpected recesses of space above a yond. This strange but captivating caprice is perhaps the most ayward thing about this wayward building. The germ of the idea may ve been suggested by the free handling of cones of ribs in the Wells trochoir, but apart from one special adaptation of the motive at

36. The South Aisle of the Choir, Bristol Cathedral

loucester, there is nothing remotely like it anywhere else. It was one f those brilliant feats of imagination which could transform even a ommonplace building into a work of art. But as in the case of the Vells retrochoir, the talents displayed at Bristol were of a kind which ould not lead easily to the formulation of a new style.

The same is true of the octagon at Ely. This took the place of the old orman central tower which fell down in 1322. Several bays of the oir were damaged, and so also were those of the nave and transepts djoining the crossing. Instead of restoring these it was decided to build iagonal walls across the corners, and turn the crossing into an octagon. he sides of this octagon are not all the same length, but the design can e regarded as a vastly enlarged version of the Wells chapter-house ith the central cone of ribs taken out, and a lantern placed over the hole that was left. The result is splendidly spacious, and the lante offers an almost melodramatic solution to the problem of how combine lighting with vaulting. The vivid shaft of light that pass vertically through the gloom of the vaults creates an effect unlike an thing else in architecture, unless it be the dome of the Pantheo Building the lantern of stone proved a task beyond the capacity of t Ely masons, and once again it was handed over to the carpenters. Th time the King's master-carpenter, William Hurley, was summon from London to devise a solution in wood. The Ely lantern more th confirms earlier impressions of the virtuosity of timber construction, ar in this case there is the added interest that its style introduces us to t current taste of London and the Court.

By this time, *c.* 1330, the King's craftsmen were beginning to acqui a nation-wide reputation. At Lichfield a few years before, Willia Ramsey, the master-mason of all the King's works south of the Tren had been called upon to perform a similar task. The most outstandi instance of this tendency to fall back upon the King's experts was course the choir of Gloucester.

These royal craftsmen owed their authority very largely to the fan of one building—St Stephen's Chapel, in the Palace of Westminste This was started in 1292, and it marks the re-emergence of the Crow as the leading source of architectural patronage. Work on the abbey Westminster came to a halt before the death of Henry III in 1270; ar during the early part of his reign Edward I was chiefly concerned wi castle-building in Wales. In their way these splendid castles are them selves evidence for the continued penetration of Continental influenc into England. The master-mason in charge of their construction was certain James of St George, who seems to have come from Savo Welsh fortified towns such as Conway or Caernarvon are certain planned like the Savoyard town of Yverdon; while the isolated castl reflect theories of defensive warfare which had been formulated fro the experience of the Crusading kingdoms, and had spread acro Europe in the course of the thirteenth century. St Stephen's w Edward's first work of pure, as opposed to applied, architecture. It w started shortly after the King's return from a long sojourn in Franc and, like the abbey, it has to be thought of as a compound of Englis and French elements of which one particular French idea turned o to be all-important.

In form the chapel was modelled on the Sainte-Chapelle in Pari But it was fifty years later than the Sainte-Chapelle, and in the mea time masons of the French Court school had developed a new fashic in architectural decoration. In France the problems posed by windo acery never occurred in the acute form that we find in England. This as because from the outset Gothic architecture there had consistently oided the thick wall. Walls were treated as far as possible as plane rfaces; and consequently when tracery was invented in France it read with a sort of natural inevitability from the actual window-enings to the adjacent masonry. It soon became apparent that markably homogeneous effects could be achieved by this means, and uring the second half of the thirteenth century the whole aspect of othic churches both inside and out was transformed as the possibilities tracery were exploited. By 1300 the ubiquitous shafts of early Gothic d largely disappeared, and tracery had taken their place as the incipal decorative element in church-design. From the visual point view this change was perhaps the chief difference between early d late Gothic, not only in France, but in most parts of Europe as ll.

So far as we know, it was at St Stephen's that tracery was first used this way in England. It seems to have appeared in the form of panels ound the heads of the great windows, and short curtains of tracery re carried down over the lower windows. On the strength of these atures St Stephen's has been claimed as the first Perpendicular build-g in England. It is a great pity that it was destroyed in 1834 because e records of its appearance, though copious, are not sufficiently mplete to allow us to test this opinion. An equal misfortune was the s in the Great Fire of 1666 of the chapter-house of old St Paul's, hich was built *c.* 1330, and which had close stylistic affinities with Stephens. Here we know what the exterior looked like from a venteenth-century engraving, but there is no record of the interior. his is a serious gap in our knowledge, especially in connexion with the ecise form of its vault. As a result of these losses we depend entirely Gloucester for our first adequate impression of what could be done th this new type of decoration.

Building operations at Gloucester seem to have been more or less ntinuous from *c.* 1318 to the end of the century. They involved the pair of the south aisle of the nave, and the refashioning of all the urch east of the nave as well as the cloister. None of this work can be lled rebuilding in the Norman or early Gothic sense—it was con-rned only with the transformation of the appearance of existing asonry. But a decisive change of style took place *c.* 1330, at the point here the south aisle of the nave was finished and the south transept as taken in hand. The earlier work was essentially conservative and odest in character; but everything after 1330 was revolutionary, and ecuted on a grandiose and sumptuous scale. The event which precipitated this change was the burial at Gloucester of King Edward who had been murdered in 1327 at Berkeley Castle near by. In 13: after the execution of Mortimer, Edward III belatedly set abc restoring his father's reputation. It used to be said that the Perpendicul style was created at Gloucester out of the proceeds of the cult Edward II. But this cult was almost certainly fictitious, and we now s the Gloucester style of 1330 onward as that of London and the Cou brought to the West Country under the auspices of the King's fil piety.

The heart of this new work was the choir. The Norman apse was c off, and the clerestory removed. But the aisles and galleries remaine and formed a massive frame inside which a delicate scaffolding tracery was erected, running unbroken from the new and heighten clerestory to levels sufficiently near the ground to make the choir see entirely shut off from the surrounding aisles and galleries. Unlike t luxuriant patterns of decorated tracery, those at Gloucester are simp and spare. The motive on which the design was based is a rectangul panel with an arched and cusped head. The only virtue of these pan is that they can be repeated endlessly, and applied to any kind surface, or indeed to no surface at all. Some are occupied by gla others are backed by solid masonry; and still others pass over t openings of the old Norman walls. The biggest aperture of all is at t east end. This is completely filled with glazed panels to form the fi of the great English Perpendicular windows. In fact, the window slightly wider than the choir—the walls of which have been splay out to contain it. It is also slightly bevelled. The usual impression o window as a hole in a wall has been completely eliminated here. Inste the choir seems to terminate directly against a glass screen; and t whole structure takes on the character of a fragile glasshouse with pa of the windows blocked in or otherwise obscured.

It is clear that Gloucester choir is no ordinary choir. It is in fact enlarged chapel—a sort of Sainte-Chapelle, intended to receive t remains of the murdered king who in due course, it was hoped, wou become a royal saint. These hopes were not fulfilled; but elsewhere fourteenth-century Europe other buildings of the kind are to be foun Earlier and less elaborate than Gloucester is the choir of the prior church at St-Thibault, in France, where the ducal house of Burgun honoured the relics of a local saint. The glorious choir of Aachen, beg in 1355, was in effect another of these royal sanctuaries, built to ho the shrine of Charlemagne. The case of St-Thibault is particula interesting because there we find in rudimentary form the curtain tracery running from top to bottom of the building; partly glaz

37. The Choir, Gloucester Cathedral

partly void, and partly backed by solid masonry. If this represents wha French provincial masons were thinking *c.* 1300 the French ancestr of English Perpendicular becomes clear in principle. Nearly all the lat Gothic styles of Northern Europe, and some of the Southern as well have their origins in the art of tracery-design which the masons of th French court pioneered during the second half of the thirteenth century From this point of view, Perpendicular marks the completion of th process which started at Westminster Abbey, whereby English Gothi was brought into line with the main stream of Continental Gothic. Thi is not to say that it ceased to manifest insular characteristics. On th contrary, Perpendicular has been well described as 'the national styl of England.' Once more it is a case of Englishmen taking just what the wanted, and no more, from their Continental neighbours; and usin what they took in their own way to solve their own problems.

The name Perpendicular was invented with Gloucester in mind; bu its obvious appropriateness should not be allowed to obscure the fac that there is a great deal more to the style than the use of a lot o vertical lines. When we compare Gloucester choir with the othe experimental buildings of the previous fifty years the quality which i likely to impress us most forcibly is its clarity and straightforwardness There are no spatial complexities or irregularities; no asymmetry; n illusionistic cunning; no subtle play with half-light or indirect light Everything is what it seems to be, and everything tends to look the sam in all directions. Above all, there is a poverty of detail. This wa inevitable, granted the voluntary restriction of means which th architects imposed upon themselves. Clearly much was lost. What wa gained? If an answer has to be given in one word, it would be: Homo geneity. Buildings of the so-called Decorated period had at least this i common—namely, that confronted with the problem of how to com bine plastic and linear decorative forms—*i.e.*, shafts, vaults, and tracer —they did so by varying their mutual relations in highly imaginativ and sophisticated ways. They refused to sacrifice anything. Perpen dicular, on the other hand, confronted with the same problem, solve it by abolishing all the plastic forms. Only tracery was left. Eventuall even pier and arch mouldings were turned inside out, as it were, t become a series of lines between adjacent concavities. Gloucester itsel did not go quite so far as this, but even so an all-over pattern of a entirely new kind was achieved there. In its own way Glouceste re-affirms that persistent English preoccupation with pattern which ha already produced masterpieces at Durham and Lincoln. But now fo the first time we can speak of a truly linear pattern, and from this th homogeneity springs. For in this evenly distributed system of lines ther

: no accents—nothing in particular to distract our attention away m the whole. That is why it seldom takes long to look at a Perpen- ular church; but the total impression can sometimes be, as it is at ɔucester, overwhelming.

So far not a word has been said about the choir vaults at Gloucester. at is because they strike the only discordant note in the whole nposition. The vaults have what is undoubtedly the most involved ne pattern ever devised in England. There are no less than three rallel ridge-ribs, and several basic rib-systems—*e.g.*, quadripartite, partite, etc.—can be detected superimposed on one another, even ore the liernes are taken into account. Yet few people would acclaim : result as something visually satisfying. It is evident that the intense ıgestion was an attempt to match and complete the all-over patterns the walls and windows below. But whereas lierne vaults accord well h Decorated window-tracery, their irregular compartments merely k untidy when they surmount tier upon tier of rectangular panels. ere is another factor which interferes with the coherence between ılts and walls. The vault-pattern is still conceived in terms of ribs. is is an awkward residue, and there is no doubt that it was felt as h, even though it took a surprising length of time before a satisfactory ution was worked out.

It is not hard to see the crux of the problem. If walls and windows re covered with tracery-panels a completely homogeneous interior uired that the vaults should be treated in the same manner. But w to apply tracery to a vault? About the time Gloucester choir was ng built, not far away, at Tewkesbury, a similar reconstruction was progress, and there we can see vaults in which elements of tracery re introduced between the ribs to form rose-patterns—similar to the e which appears in one of the clerestory windows. The effect at wkesbury is extremely poetic—and it marks a step in the required ection. But Tewkesbury was not built in the Perpendicular style. For t something much more formal had to be found.

The ultimate solution makes its appearance in the cloisters at ɔucester. The name we give to it is 'fan-vaulting,' but this is perhaps nisnomer. The word 'fan' suggests something semicircular with kes of equal length. It is true that there are late fan-vaults with mbers that resemble spokes, but to think along these lines is to miss essential point of the original idea, which is that these vaults are irely composed of tracery-cells. Sometimes ribs are found with them, : they are always extraneous to the actual fan. Not only are fan- ılts made up of cells, but the cells are organized in the form of a -developing system. Each cell at the base of the fan bifurcates into

38. The Cloisters, Gloucester Cathedral

two; and each of these into two more; and so on. As they grow lar
they assume more and more the shape of typical Perpendicular pan
and at all stages there is an element of ordered inevitability which

erfect foil to the endless repetition of the wall and window-tracery. o Perpendicular interior in England can vie with the long vistas of loucester cloister, at least from the point of view of uniformity. Here, anywhere, the aesthetic ideal of the style finds its fulfilment.

Were fan-vaults invented at Gloucester? There is something about e complete assurance with which they are handled that suggests that least some experiments had been made before; but if so, nothing has rvived. In the 1360's, at Hereford, we know that the chapter-house ow destroyed) was vaulted with a circle of partial fans around a mplete fan, in the centre where the thirteenth-century cone of ribs ad been. It needs only a little thought to realize how perfectly the rinciple of the fan was adapted for this purpose, and we are apt to onder whether it did not originate in such a context. In essence the ells of a fan-vault are generated in the same way as the 'leaves' of irteenth-century French rose-windows—only in three, not two, imensions. This alone is sufficient to connect the idea with the London *ilieu* in which Perpendicular developed at the beginning of the four-eenth century; and in particular we would give much to know how t Paul's chapter-house was vaulted. The building was probably too nall to have a central column; but in other ways it might have applied links between the Gloucester and Hereford fans on the one and, and the French rose-windows of Westminster on the other. The ouble cloisters of old St Paul's also remain an unknown quantity. Whether or not fan-vaulting began as early as this, the fact that it was ot used in the choir at Gloucester has no bearing on the date of its vention. At the outset fans were essentially small-scale decorative rms with no structural utility at all. Accordingly, no one dared to use em for major spans until late in the fifteenth century. The successful ffort to overcome this limitation was, characteristically enough, the st great achievement of English medieval architecture.

CHAPTER 5

The End of the Middle Ages

THE architecture of the long period between 1350 and the Reformatic
is usually described as Perpendicular; but that should not be taken
meaning that all the buildings looked like Gloucester, or that it was
period of stagnation. The history of Perpendicular architecture is
very complex subject, and no really satisfactory study of it exists. S
either a great deal ought to be said about it here, or very little. Fro
the point of view which has been adopted so far in this book the latt
is perhaps the more prudent policy. Even so it is impossible to do justi
to the scope of Perpendicular by discussing it in terms of a sing
stylistic trend, as one can in large measure with the earlier periods.
is true that the masterpieces of the style are still to be found among tl
cathedrals, abbeys, or the royal chapels which emulated them in bo
scale and magnificence. But whereas in the twelfth, thirteenth, ar
early fourteenth centuries there was a constant succession of such work
in the subsequent two hundred years they were comparatively rare ar
spasmodic. On the other hand, the Perpendicular period was the gre
age for the building of parish churches in England; and although or
is tempted to dismiss parish-church architecture as a debased
simplified version of the grand manner practised elsewhere, there a
enough buildings of sufficient merit to justify the invention of a speci
category of Parish Church Perpendicular. Moreover, it was during th
period also that secular architecture, both in its public and priva
aspect, began to acquire a character of its own, and to display at tl
highest levels an aesthetic pretension which, if it did not rival those
its ecclesiastical counterparts, at least contained the promise of a
importance that was fulfilled after the Reformation. Except in matte
of detail this Secular Perpendicular, as it may be called, has little
common with either of the ecclesiastical varieties, and deserves to l
accorded a separate status within the family of styles that constitute ou
late medieval architecture.

In a book of this kind there is little room to discuss all these wider mifications of Perpendicular; but it must be remembered that as the ge-scale works became fewer and fewer, the threads of continuity tween them are to be found increasingly among the more modest orks of these other categories; and imperceptibly architecture lost a tle of its former preoccupation with the niceties of design, and assumed stead something of the highly organized appearance of the modern ilding industry. For most of the period the men who otherwise ould have been the patrons of English architecture were squandering eir not unlimited resources on a long series of wars: first, the Hundred ears War, in France, and then, at home among themselves, the Wars the Roses. While this did not put an end to building altogether, it s inevitably the expensive schemes that suffered most. The worst riod of all fell roughly between 1425 and 1475. Not until stable vernment was restored by Edward IV and Henry VII did circum- nces once more favour the most ambitious kind of Perpendicular; d at this level there is a distinct hiatus between two groups of build- gs: one belonging to the second half of the fourteenth century and beginning of the fifteenth; the other belonging to the end of the eenth century and the beginning of the sixteenth. It is significant that patronage of all these buildings was in the hands of the two institu- ns that were the traditional supports of medieval architecture— mely, the higher clergy and the Crown; whereas the men who paid the parish churches and the secular buildings were very largely to found in the ranks of the aristocracy and the prosperous middle sses. The development of this new source of patronage was to be of highest importance after the Reformation, when for a considerable riod both church and monarchy virtually dropped out of the picture.

It will be convenient to trace the fortunes of 'top level' Perpendicular t, before taking a brief glance at its other manifestations. Among the signers of large churches the immediate reaction to Gloucester was cumspect rather than enthusiastic. The special purpose for which the oir was built set it apart from the ordinary run of ecclesiastical chitecture. It remained a chapel 'writ large.' The decorative possi- ities of tracery-panelling were widely acknowledged, but nowhere e does it seem to have been handled with the same devastating effect. stead there followed a period of compromise in which the new motive s discreetly and innocuously used in the context of established forms. e result was a kind of hybrid between Perpendicular and certain tures of Decorated; and during this period the nave of York Minster s probably as influential as Gloucester in determining the designs great churches. This can be seen in the eastern limb of York itself, begun in 1361, where the elevation and the vaults follow the gene lines laid down in the nave, but where much of the detail sho Perpendicular influence. The eastern façade, where work started, covered with Perpendicular panels, and its principal feature is enormous Perpendicular window even larger than that at Gloucest All the window-tracery is affected by the new fashion, especially th in the dwarf transepts, which run from top to bottom of the wall. T detached mullions which form a sort of screen outside the clerestc windows of the Lady Chapel are an inversion of the idea which w used in the Lincoln Angel Choir, but it can be provided with a Fren ancestry like other Perpendicular motives.

Another example of compromise is the nave of St Mary Redcliffe, Bristol (third quarter of the fourteenth century). There the mullic of the clerestory windows are brought right down to the mouldings the main arcade, and to this extent the effect is closer to the Glouces conception of Perpendicular.

The climax of this phase was reached at the end of the fourteen century when the cathedrals of Canterbury and Winchester receiv their present naves. In both cases decayed Norman structures had to replaced or renewed. At Canterbury there was a total rebuilding, a the mason in charge, who was almost certainly Henry Yevele, had mc or less a free hand. More is known about this man than any oth medieval English mason, and his inventive capacity has perhaps be overrated. Canterbury nave is certainly a beautiful building by a standard, but it owes far more to its proportions than to the novelty its ingredients. The design owes a general debt to York Minster, a certain specific features to Westminster Abbey, where Yevele h recently completed the nave in accordance with the thirteenth-centu style of the choir and transepts. Yevele's distinctive contribution Canterbury was to heighten the main arcade at the expense of t clerestory. The result was a very subtle compromise between t traditional notion of a great church with soaring piers contributi strong vertical accents, and the spacious homogeneity of a hall-chur in which the aisle windows provide most of the light. The tracery of t aisle windows is the most obvious Perpendicular feature of Canterbu with the exception of Bell Harry tower.

At Winchester Yevele's contemporary, William Wynford, had rather more difficult task. There it was decided not to dismantle Norman nave entirely, but to retain as much of the old masonry could be incorporated into an up-to-date design. Although Wynfc solved his problem with great virtuosity, the result inevitably suffers comparison with the serene and noble nave of Canterbury. In particu

was impossible to reduce the piers to the slender dimensions of :vele's work; and the original thickness of the Norman walls is not tirely concealed by the skilful transition from one plane to the other clerestory level.

39. The Nave, Canterbury Cathedral

All these buildings, from York choir to Winchester nave, have lierne ults. As we have seen, there is nothing specifically Perpendicular about e origin of this type of vaulting, and no building in which it appears ictly deserves to be called wholly Perpendicular. Gloucester choir is fficient proof of its anomalous character. Why then did it go on being ed? As no one thought fit to record his views on the subject at the ne, we can only speculate; but in the absence of any evidence to the ntrary we may guess that the purely ornamental character of the gical alternative—*i.e.*, fan-vaulting—had something to do with it. It as one thing to put a fan-vault over a cloister walk, or even over a apter-house, and quite another to construct one over the main vessel a church perhaps 40 feet wide and 80 feet high. To do so required ill of a very high order; but even more it required nerve. For we must member that medieval masons had no means at their disposal for making rational estimates of the strains and thrusts generated in th buildings. They worked within the limits of well-tried rules of thun which summed up the traditional experience of their craft. Once th transgressed those limits they were lost in the unknown. Lierne vau had developed organically out of earlier and simpler forms of vaultin But fan-vaulting involved a very considerable break with tradition, a it was only very slowly that men screwed up their courage to put fan-vault over the main span of a church. A tentative move in t direction was perhaps made in the fourteenth-century nave vaults Hereford Cathedral (replaced at the end of the eighteenth centur where the ribs emerged from cells at the points where they reached t walls. The same sort of thing was done in the transept vaults at Tewk bury. But at Norwich Cathedral we still find a lierne vault being co structed over the nave in 1464 and even St George's Chapel at Winds which was designed for Edward IV, only had fans over its side aisl By this time, however, the decisive step had been taken successfully Sherborne Abbey.

The dating of Sherborne is not closely determined. A rebuilding w

40. Vaulting in the Choir of Tewkesbury Abbey

arted early in the fifteenth century; it was delayed and set back by a
e in 1437; and the recasing of the nave, with its vault, and the vault-
g of the north transept, were the work of the last quarter of the

41. THE NAVE, SHERBORNE ABBEY

teenth century. The fan-vault over the choir is certainly earlier than
at of the nave, and may very well belong to the first half of the
teenth century. If so, however, it is curiously isolated, unless some
nportant contemporary works have been lost. Apart from the conoid
fect which we find in the vaults of the choir at Winchester, and which
presents a transition from lierne to fan, we have to wait until the very
id of the fifteenth century and the beginning of the sixteenth for the
ate of large-scale fan-vaults in which Perpendicular architecture
scovered its second and last period of vitality.

The restoration of internal peace and strong government by Edward
V, and with it the resumption of royal patronage on a large scale,
itiated what has aptly been called the Indian Summer of English
edieval architecture. Three buildings in particular, each of them due
the munificence of the Crown, form a splendid climax to the whole

medieval tradition. They are St George's Chapel, Windsor; King College Chapel, Cambridge; and Henry VII's Chapel, Westminst Abbey.

St George's Chapel was started, and its design fixed, before tl impact of the Sherborne achievement was felt. Consequently the hig vaults were given a lierne pattern. This, together with the fact that has side aisles, make it far more reminiscent of the late fourteent century cathedral designs than Gloucester choir, in spite of the fact th it was meant to be a chapel. It is in fact one of the last great churc designs to be carried out in England before the Reformation. Tl traditional elements, however, do not conceal an internal effect that more radically Perpendicular than anything achieved since Gloucest choir. This is due partly to the ubiquitous panelling, and partly to tl proportions of the building which reproduce in elevation the square off aspect of the individual panels. This uniformity of appearance enhanced by the universal use of the flattened four-centred ar throughout the building.

St George's Chapel was completed by Henry VII. Another unde taking left unfinished by one of his royal predecessors provided tl occasion for another act of unwonted generosity. This was the chap of King's College, at Cambridge. The chapel had been conceived l its founder, Henry VI, not so much as an integral part of the colleg but as an immense affirmation of his personal piety. It was therefo modelled, not on previous college chapels, like that of New College Oxford, but on a cathedral choir. The nearest prototype is, in fac Gloucester, and of all the Perpendicular buildings in England whic were influenced by that precocious design, it is the only one whic deliberately takes up the problem of the homogeneous Perpendicul interior at the point where it was left at Gloucester, and finds for it wholly satisfying solution. Essentially the chapel was conceived Gloucester choir with all the extraneous masonry removed—that i with all the panels free to be filled with glass. What it would hav looked like if it had been completed by Henry VI we may surmise fro the Lady Chapel at Gloucester, which was started a few years late and which was itself a free-standing version of the choir on a small scale. But it was perhaps fortunate that the chapel at King's Colleg languished with the fortunes of its royal founder; for when Henry V provided the money for its completion fan-vaults were already practical proposition. They were started in 1508 by a group of me who had recently had experience of this kind of vaulting at Pete borough. They provided King's College with the finest array of fa ever achieved on a large scale, and the result is the most majestic of a

42. King's College Chapel, Cambridge

Perpendicular interiors, the only one in fact where vaults, windows, ar panelling have been allowed to find a perfect accord, and to define monumental vista. It is especially fitting that a building which depen so much on its windows should enjoy the rare privilege of preservir its original stained glass.

The classic dignity of King's College Chapel was something th could only be done once, and the third of these late Perpendicul masterpieces, Henry VII's Chapel, is utterly different from it in eve respect. Henry VII as a patron of architecture is a paradoxical figur Not particularly interested in building for its own sake, he neverthele has three works to his credit that not even Henry III can equal. Tl completion of the Yorkist Chapel at Windsor and the Lancastria Chapel at Cambridge may perhaps be regarded as gestures inspired b his policy of reconciliation. But in his own chapel at Westminster l was building for himself, and it is here alone that we encounter som thing of his own taste. No expense was spared. The old Lady Chapel the abbey was taken down, and a new plan laid out which is one of tl most intricate geometrical constructions in the whole of mediev architecture. For sheer density of ornament there is nothing like th building anywhere in England. Under it all we can perhaps detect basic debt to the design of St George's, Windsor; but whereas the everything is light, clear, and harmonious, at Westminster there is onl an impression of confused and congested forms which become steadi worse as we pass from the serried ranks of statues in the middle sectio to the vaults above. Nowhere else in England does sculpture play suc an important part in the interior of a great church; and nowhere a there vaults of such complexity. These almost defy description. Tw fundamental ideas are involved. One is the fan-vault, and the other the pendant. The history of the pendant motive in late medieval Englis architecture is long and fascinating. It originated in timber worl where there was a certain structural justification for it, although it wa often used as a purely decorative device. It seems to have been adopte by stonemasons at Oxford in the middle of the fifteenth century. I appears in the vault of the Divinity School there, and later in what now the cathedral, where someone had the idea of threading th pendants on transverse ribs. At Westminster the process was taken stage farther by making the pendants the centres of fan-cones. Th result is a series of fans which appear to be suspended in space fro transverse ribs. The Westminster fans are smaller than the elegan designs at King's College, and the density of the cells is very muc greater. Moreover, other fans are introduced between the pendan and the walls, and down the centre of the roof other pendants ar

43. Henry VII's Chapel, Westminster Abbey

pended, so that the overall effect resembles not so much a church as exotic cave with rows of fantastic stalactites. As an exultant gesture defiance at every orthodox conception of vaulting it is no doubt a · *de force*. But the extravagance verges on the vulgar, and we are left h the impression that the steady intensification of ornament has at reached saturation point.

Henry VII's Chapel was undoubtedly a special effort, and in its w like King's College Chapel, it leaves the impression that there was v little left for anyone else to do afterwards. This is confirmed in anot way by the last of the great medieval churches to be built in Engla Bath Abbey, which was under construction from 1499 until Reformation. The great Norman church had fallen into a state disrepair, and was far too big for the reduced circumstances of abbey; and rather than attempt a complete restoration, the Bisho Bath and Wells decided to build a new, smaller church on the sit the Norman nave. The bishop was familiar with the Court, and masons, the two Vertues, also came from royal service. The ab therefore deserves to be grouped with the other royal works of time; but the resources behind it were less substantial, and it is to seem a dull, lifeless building when compared with King's Colleg Westminster. The Vertues promised the bishop the most splendid v in the country; it is unlikely that what they had in mind was monotonous fan-vault which we see to-day, for the choir seems to h been designed to receive a very shallow vault, perhaps based on a f centred section, like that of St George's Chapel, Windsor. The were a not very happy afterthought, being so attenuated that the c become monotonous. The man who designed them either did not or did not wish to introduce the kind of counterpoint patterns wh make the vaults of King's College so much more satisfying.

It is always dangerous to speculate as to what might have happe if other things had turned out different. But it seems fairly certain when the Reformation put an end to the great tradition of chu building it was just about exhausted, and it is difficult to see from w source it could have been renewed because all the Continental vari of Gothic were more or less in the same condition. The plain fact is not many changes could be rung on the theme of fan-vaulting panelling. The aesthetic ideal of Perpendicular was far more rigid monotonous than that of early Gothic, and if circumstances had b more favourable to large-scale church-building the limitations of style would have been exposed long before the sixteenth century.

But if Perpendicular provided little scope for variations on the th of the great church-design it found compensation in exploring fields of design altogether. One of these was church towers. V vaulting and window-tracery becoming more and more stereoty aspiring masons found an outlet for their talents in transforming external appearance of the older cathedrals and abbeys. Already in first half of the fourteenth century Lincoln and Salisbury had set fashion—the latter crowned by its incomparable spire. During the ındred and fifty years Wells, Worcester, York, Beverley, Gloucester, ıd Canterbury, to mention only the most familiar, followed suit. The shion was by no means confined to the great churches. Boston church,

44. BEVERLEY MINSTER

Lincolnshire, Cirencester church, in Gloucestershire, the parish ıurches of Somerset, Merton and Magdalen Colleges, at Oxford, all stify to the zeal with which this particular form of architecture was llowed at other levels.

All these towers are essentially simple in form, depending on their oportions to make an effective silhouette rather than upon the tricacy of their details. In this they are totally different from the ntastic open-work constructions of their Continental counterparts, ıd as typically English as other aspects of Perpendicular.

The same is true of the Perpendicular parish churches. Many of em—for instance, at Hull and Coventry—are very large indeed. But in construction they tended to be as simple as possible. Hardly any them are vaulted. St Mary Redcliffe, at Bristol, is quite exception Instead of vaults, fine timber roofs were customary. These made possible to dispense with elaborate forms of buttressing, and masor was often little more than the provision of elegant arcades and fran for windows. The churches were extremely light and spacious, a often endowed with rich decoration, as in the sumptuous early sixteen century "Wool Church" at Lavenham, in Suffolk. But the glory of th churches, and the feature which makes it possible to set them apart a class of their own, is their timber roofs. Nothing comparable is to found in the city churches of the Continent, like those of Liège Nürnberg, which are nearly always vaulted in stone. The use of timb in cathedral architecture has been mentioned from time to time; b there, in spite of its many triumphs, timber was never more than seco best to masonry. In parish churches there was no break in the cc tinuity of the use of wood for roofing. In every church, whether vault or not, the actual roofing material was carried on a wooden frame; a where there was no intervening web of stone these timbers were giv a fine decorative finish.

As carpentry became more ambitious new methods of timber cc struction came into use to cover wider spans. The most spectacular these was the hammer-beam principle, which was used on the m lavish scale, not in churches, but in the great halls of palaces a colleges. The first and most impressive of all the surviving examples hammer-beam roofs is that in the hall of the Palace of Westminster. was devised by the King's carpenter, Hugh Hurland, in 1394, a spans no less than 68 feet. The roof is a superb mixture of constructio and decorative elements, the great baulks of timber being offset free-standing webs of wooden tracery panels.

Hammer-beam roofs continued to be made until well into t sixteenth century, and they tended to become steadily more elabora In the hall of the Middle Temple, in London, built in Elizabeth times, two rows of hammer-beams were used; and in Edward I Great Hall at Eltham Palace, *c.* 1479, pendants were suspended at t ends of the hammer-beams. The same device was used again Hampton Court. Pendants were also used on their own. On a mod scale they embellish the flat ceiling of Crosby Hall, in London; ar much more impressively, the roof of the nave of St David's Cathedr in Pembrokeshire. What happened when the motive was adopted stonemasons has already been mentioned in connexion with Hen VII's Chapel, at Westminster.

The royal halls bring us to the threshold of secular architecture.

r very little has been said on this subject, partly because what has rvived is disappointing by comparison with the large number of edieval churches, but also because it has to be discussed in a totally fferent way. The design of secular buildings varies far more than that great churches; and has to be thought of far more in terms of nction and general effect than in terms of decorative detail or con-uctional methods. To understand them it is necessary to know some-ing of the kind of life that was lived in them.

The most important thing to realize is the extent to which medieval : was lived in public—at least, by the kind of people who could ford to build themselves fine homes. The basic unit was not an dividual or his family, but a group or community. The most obvious amples of this were provided by the monasteries, where the con-ntual buildings were beautifully organized around their cloisters for e sake of the special kind of corporate life to which the monks were dicated. But even outside the cloister the great men of State were dom able to enjoy what we would recognize as private life. They ed the greater part of their lives before a constant audience of their pendents and retainers; and the history of secular architecture in the iddle Ages faithfully reflects this social pattern.

The worldly counterpart to the monastic cloister was the great hall. was the nucleus of every important medieval residence from Saxon nes to the fifteenth century. Around it were grouped the kitchen, rerooms, private chambers, and the chapel. The relations of these mponents to one another naturally varied. The first sizeable remains at we encounter are embedded in Norman castles. These castles, nich were spread in great numbers all over the country, were first and remost focal points of feudal power, and their dispositions were imarily military. At first they consisted of little more than a mound rmounted by a tower, and a fortified enclosure—hence the name at is usually given to this type of castle: motte and bailey. But castles re also places of permanent residence, and domestic apartments had be provided for the great men and their garrisons who lived in them. metimes these living quarters were built into the great stone keeps nich, in the course of the twelfth century, replaced the earlier wooden wers. In the White Tower, in London, or in the keep of Rochester istle, Kent, the hall and chapel, etc., can still be seen. But the keep is essentially an ultimate defensive position, and it was not a con-nient place in which to live when there was no emergency. Accord-gly a more general practice was to build the great hall out in the closure, at some distance from the keep. Thus the hall of Richmond istle, Yorkshire, stands in a far corner of its bailey. Later, when the modes of warfare changed and the keep lost its importance, it w sometimes transformed into what was in effect a residential block; a in the Pele towers of Northern England we have a survival of the ide the slight fortifications being designed to ward off marauding Scots.

As the king's government became more effective, and feudal war w gradually eliminated, so the need for the physical protection of stro walls became less pressing, and emphasis passed from the military the domestic aspects of castles. Already by the end of the twelfth centu castles were being built, like that at Oakham, Rutland, in which t great hall was by far the most important feature of the place. The le in this process was given by the bishops in the first place, and then the king. Bishop Pudsey's hall at Bishop Auckland, in County Durha and Henry III's hall for Winchester Castle, survive to illustrate t trend. Few of the royal castles or palaces preserve much of th medieval form; but in the case of bishops' palaces we are better place for at Wells there still stands the rambling and picturesque group buildings, erected at various times during the thirteenth century, whi must have been fairly typical of the class as a whole in spite of certa peculiarities. The domestic hall, the chapel, and the solar, to which second great hall has been added, are grouped with no appare system; indeed, they are in some cases barely contiguous. The co ception of the great house as a compact and unified building still lay the future.

From the purely military point of view the climax of English cast building was reached in the series which Edward I had made in Wa at the end of the thirteenth century. But these stand apart from t evolution of domestic architecture, except in so far as they anticipa certain features of the 'livery and maintenance' castles of the lat Middle Ages. After 1300 the feudal levy was no longer a serious milita factor. Its place was taken by professional mercenaries, or 'liverymen who, while being very much better soldiers, were liable to change sid at short notice. To counter the exigencies of this possibility, elabora precautions were sometimes taken to make it more or less impossib for a garrison to gain access to the private quarters of the lord of t castle. These can be seen perhaps most clearly at Bodiam Castle (138 in Sussex, where everything was done twice, once for the lord, and on for the men. Bodiam was one of the last castles in England to be bu for a strictly military purpose, and not every so-called castle of the lat Middle Ages went to quite such lengths. At Stokesay (*c.* 1291), Shropshire, all the fortification was concentrated in a strong tow built on to one end of the hall. We find the same idea on a very mu grander scale at Tattershall (after 1431), in Lincolnshire, where t ver itself became the main part of the residence, and its defensive pacity was reduced to a minimum.

The salient feature of house- and castle-design in the Perpendicular riod was undoubtedly the diminished importance of the idea of

45. ACTON BURNELL HALL

oviding a place of refuge and protection in time of war. Not that arfare disappeared as a social phenomenon in England. On the con- ary, the fifteenth century saw more violence than at any time since e middle of the twelfth century. But clearly it was not the sort of olence to be resisted with massive fortifications. The typical building the time was the fortified manor-house, such as we can see in the ins at South Wingfield (mid-fifteenth century), in Derbyshire, here again one large tower, this time built into an orderly plan based two courtyards, provided the only really strong position in the place. it already, long before South Wingfield, this relative indifference to rtification had produced some interesting experiments. At Acton irnell, in Shropshire, for instance, built at about the same time as okesay, Bishop Burnell of Wells, who added considerably to the palace there, built for himself what was in effect a country house. The trac tional residential elements were compressed into a neat rectangul plan, much as we find them in the twelfth-century keeps, but with concessions to the conventions of castle-building other than the use towers at the corners. These did little more than give the exterior symmetrical appearance. In the fourteenth century this rather pr cocious anticipation of the country house of the future proved less of inspiration than the ideals of chivalry, which required a background towers and battlements for its pageants, but which were often conte with a picturesque sham rather than the real thing. It would be pr mature to speak of bogus castles while the Middle Ages lasted; b there is a definite element of the spectacular in the entrance to Wardo Castle (1393), in Wiltshire; in John of Gaunt's hall (*c.* 1390), Ken worth; or in the distant view of Hurstmonceux Castle (1441), Susse which owes nothing to purely military considerations.

Another factor which helped to distinguish domestic from milita architecture in the later Middle Ages was the use of brick. This w introduced into the East of England during the fourteenth century, even earlier, from Germany and the Low Countries; and by Tud times it had spread over most of the country, and was used for t largest houses, such as Thornbury Castle (*c.* 1511), Gloucestershire, a Hampton Court. Brick architecture had its own decorative possibiliti which produced such fantasies as the chimneys of Thornbury.

Finally, there was the growing use of large glass windows. Wherev stone walls were the most important consideration domestic apartmer must have been extremely dark and gloomy; and conversely the we lit house was a sure sign that comfort and convenience had becor criteria to be reckoned with, even if they had not entirely replac security and defence. The Perpendicular house never dissolved in glass to the same extent as some Perpendicular parish churches; b the oriel windows which came into general use to light the high tab of domestic halls, the bay windows of the State apartments at Thor bury, and the large areas of wall given up to glass at Ockwells Manc Berkshire (*c.* 1450), or the abbot's lodging at Much Wenlock Abbe Shropshire, all indicate the point which this new fashion had reach by the eve of the Reformation.

So far as general planning was concerned, the decisive change seer to have taken place when the protective curtain wall of the earli castles was abandoned. This made it necessary for the domestic apa ments themselves to be grouped in a much more orderly way; and fro the nucleus of the hall, solar, and chapel we find them spreading arou courts, which often presented a continuous wall to the outside worl oken only by a great gatehouse. A tremendous impetus to this kind design was given by the development of the college system at the iversities of Oxford and Cambridge. The universities themselves isted long before anyone thought of endowing permanent institutions

46. OCKWELLS MANOR

iere scholars and masters could live together in carefully regulated mmunities, which is what the colleges were; and it was not really til William of Wykeham founded his New College at Oxford, in 79, that something like a definitive form was achieved. Wykeham is closely connected with the Courts of Edward III and Richard II, d his career as a patron of architecture was one of the most out-nding of the whole Middle Ages. Along with New College he inded a school at Winchester (Winchester College), and as bishop ere he was responsible for most of the transformation carried out by illiam Wynford on the cathedral. His acquaintance with the Court le began at Windsor Castle in the 1350's, and he it was who was ponsible for introducing the official Perpendicular style into the iversities, where it flourished for the rest of the Middle Ages. The sential ingredients for any college were a chapel, a hall, a library, and accommodation for the master, fellows, and scholars. The problem w thus similar to that of housing a family and its retainers, although t nature of the activities which were carried on there, and the great degree of communal life, gave the chapel and hall of a college mo importance than in an ordinary house. The grouping of the schola rooms around a court, or quadrangle, with the chapel and hall alo one side of it, was a very convenient solution, and the New Colle design exercised great influence over subsequent foundations at Oxfor

One might have expected that at Cambridge the place of New Colle would have been taken by King's College, which, in conjunction wi Eton, was deliberately planned by Henry VI to match Wykehan foundations at Oxford and Winchester. But at King's College t chapel consumed almost all the energies that could be mustered, and far as college-design was concerned it had less influence than its co temporary Queens' College, where the great gatehouse and the use brick anticipate the Tudor colleges of the sixteenth century.

Of the civic buildings which must have been a prominent feature prosperous towns in the later Middle Ages, not a great many ha survived. The Guildhall, at York, which was destroyed in the Seco World War, was a good example. Here and there a medieval i presents something of its original appearance, as at Norton St Phil and Glastonbury, in Somerset; while the Vicars' Choral Close, Wells, and the fifteenth-century houses of prosperous wool towns li Lavenham, preserve for us glimpses of a humbler order of domes architecture. We can hardly be satisfied with what remains. Yet the is enough for us to realize the vitality of Perpendicular architecture. fundamental achievement was not the solution of a single stylis problem, but its ability to cope successfully with a rapidly expandi range of problems, presented by a changing and developing societ In this sense it deserves to be called a national style; and it deserves t title more than its predecessors. Admirers of Perpendicular might al think that what came afterwards had no better claim.

Note

As far as possible, all the buildings described in Part II of this bo are reasonably accessible to the public. The reader is referred to t annual publication called *Historic Houses and Castles* (London, Ind Publishers), which gives over 450 houses, castles, and gardens open the public, together with details of buildings, times of opening, a routes.

Part II

CHAPTER I

Tudor and Jacobean Architecture

[EDIEVAL houses must have been very uncomfortable places to live . By our standards they had hardly any furniture, the chimneys were tle more than holes in the roof, and every one lived huddled together the great hall, choked by smoke, and frozen by the draughts from e front door. During the sixteenth century things changed consider-)ly, for, with the establishment of a strong Government under the udors, it became possible to build houses with an eye to comfort ther than defence; and, towards the end of the century, the new udor aristocracy, enriched by Church lands, had both the money and e desire to build 'prestige' houses in which to settle their ambitious milies. Another factor was the rise of the architect. According to the xford Dictionary, the words 'architect' and 'architecture' are first corded in English in John Shute's *The First and Chief Groundes of chitecture* (1563), which is also the first (and rarest) of English archi-ctural treatises.

In the sixteenth century both France and England became nation-ates in the modern sense, and both owed much of this, directly or directly, to the spread of ideas from Italy, the home of the New earning. Henry VIII was pleased with the picture of himself as a enaissance Prince and enlightened patron of all the arts, although he tually did very little apart from employing Holbein as his Court ainter; and his daughter Elizabeth was both too poor and too mean do more than encourage her nobles to ruin themselves in building. n fact, in spite of the legends which make every Tudor house built by alian workmen (and every portrait of Elizabeth painted by Zuccaro), ere was very little direct Italian influence on English architecture efore Inigo Jones. The French, with much closer contacts, were slow absorb Italian ideas, but by the time of Philibert de l'Orme (*c.* 1505–) they had developed a style that took full account of Italian ideas d Italian scholarship without being overwhelmed by them. In

England there was little or no Court patronage, and, after the bre: with Rome, no Church patronage either, so that there was no induc ment for any really good Italian artists to come here, with the sc exception of Torrigiano, who made Henry VII's tomb, in Westminst Abbey. Cellini's autobiography tells us how the barbarous Northerne appeared to a civilized Florentine artist: "Every day he [Torrigian had stories to tell concerning his brave deeds when he was living amo those brutes of Englishmen." Pietro Torrigiano's tomb was mac between 1512 and 1518, and it stands in Henry VII's Chapel, bu from 1503 to 1519; the tomb is the first pure Renaissance work to l seen in England, under a roof which is the last flowering of Gothi After the Reformation it was next to impossible to renew contact wi the new classicism of Italy, and England depended largely on tl hybrid versions current in France and Flanders. Indeed, it is likely th this impure Franco-Flemish style was actually preferred on account its very elaboration—"busie and fantasticall," as it would have seeme to the Elizabethans. Probably the finest example of this was Nonsuc Palace, in Surrey, one of the few large-scale undertakings of Henry VII begun in 1538 and destroyed in the seventeenth century. Drawings ar engravings, as well as a few surviving fragments—notably a gre fireplace—all seem to show that the exterior had the almost nigh marish elaboration of the Franco-Flemish style, although some of tl decoration was French and some Italianate.

The general type of a medieval house built round its great hall ca still be seen at Penshurst Place, in Kent, and in a few other house Parts of Penshurst date back to 1340, so that this type of plan w: already nearly two centuries old at the beginning of the sixteent century. A diagram based on Penshurst shows the two most importa aspects of this plan:

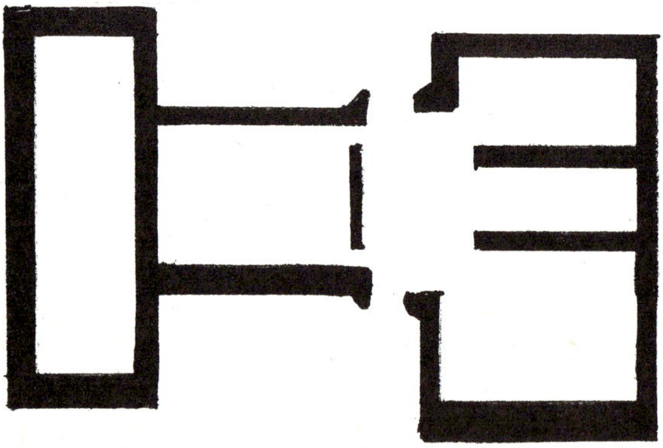

47. H-PLAN BASED ON PENSHURST PLACE

The reason why this plan is called the H-type is immediately vious, and this arrangement of the hall in the centre, with the ivate room or rooms of the owner on one side, and the service-block the other, was so sensible and practical that it lasted unchanged for nturies. The only important modification of it is the slightly smaller or half-H-plan, in which two of the projections are omitted, and the ntre of the E is the front door, thus: ⊓. The H-plan is based on the ea that the whole household ate together in the great hall, which was centre of the life of the house. At one end of the hall (here the left) ere was a dais for the master, and a way into the private rooms; at the posite end of the hall was a screen which separated the hall from the eens-passage, which in turn led directly to the kitchen, buttery, and ier service-rooms, while at either end of the screens-passage was a ain doorway. Clearly this type of plan is admirable, so long as the ilder does not mind having the front door off-centre, and is prepared make the wings of different shapes and sizes according to their nction—'expressing the plan,' as it is called. The struggle between convenience of the traditional form and the desire for a symmetrical in and façade determines much of the architectural history of the zabethan and Jacobean periods, and, as one might expect, the new eas come in gradually, and as decorative details rather than struc-al ideas. This can be seen in one of the greatest buildings of the age, ampton Court, and also in houses like Layer Marney Hall, in Essex, d Sutton Place, near Guildford.

Layer Marney has a great gatehouse, built for show rather than for fence, and is decorated with terracotta window-mouldings and stings on the sky-line which are purely Italian in feeling. Terracotta n hardly have been well known in this country when Layer Marney s built, about 1520, since it had probably been introduced by Torri-no himself only a few years earlier. The same kind of importation of corative details occurs at Sutton Place, which was begun about 1523. e plan was originally rather French, with a central court, and the ditional English gatehouse in the middle of the entrance side, but there two new features in the plan itself in addition to the Italianate terra-ta decoration. In the first place, the front door is set in the middle the hall block, and not at the end of the screens-passage, thus obtain-symmetry at the cost of convenience (and probably draughts); and, ondly, there is a Long Gallery. This was undoubtedly copied from mpton Court, for Sir Richard Weston, the builder of Sutton Place, d been to France, and was at the Field of the Cloth of Gold, so that was acquainted with the ways of the Court. The Long Gallery at mpton Court was built by Cardinal Wolsey, and it is a curious fact

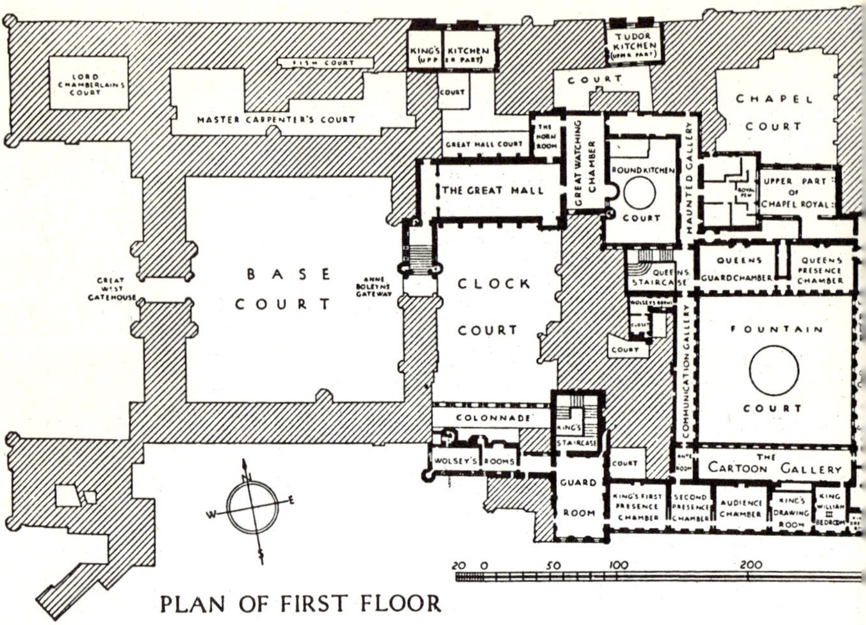

PLAN OF FIRST FLOOR

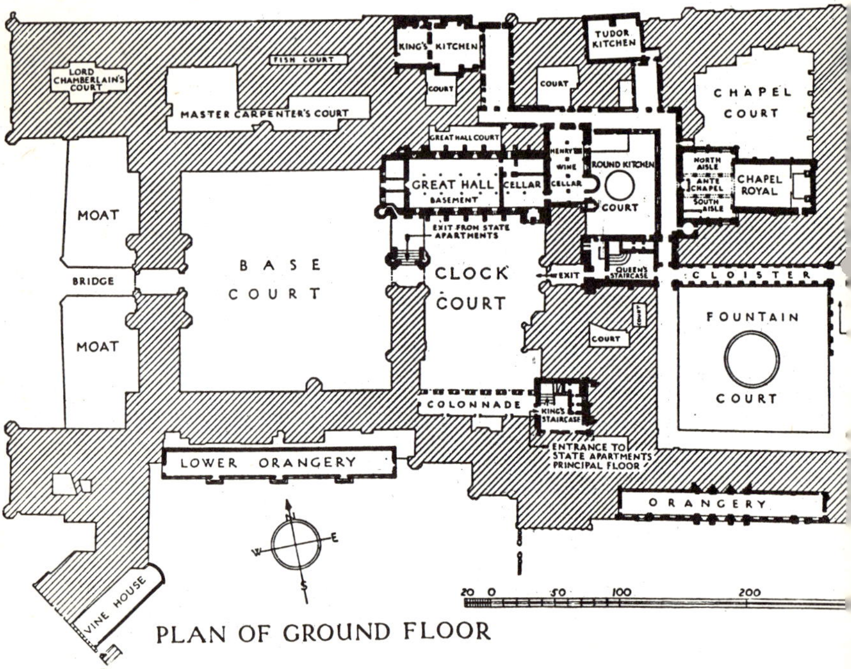

PLAN OF GROUND FLOOR

48. PLAN OF HAMPTON COURT PALACE
By Gracious Permission of H.M. The Queen

49. HAMPTON COURT PALACE

at no one has yet been able to explain its purpose. It is said that it as for the cardinal to take exercise in on wet days, but that hardly plains the speed with which it was copied in other great houses of the :teenth and seventeenth centuries.

The Palace of Hampton Court was begun in 1514 by Cardinal 'olsey on an enormous scale—his household numbered nearly five ındred—and he continued work on it until, in a desperate effort to ıve off disaster, he gave it to Henry VIII in 1529. After Wolsey's fall enry began to enlarge the house into a Royal Palace, and work ntinued until 1540. Later still, under William and Mary, Wren lded further ranges of buildings.

The original house was planned as a series of courts, exactly like a onastic or collegiate building, and the same design was used for the .rdinal's other great foundation, Christ Church, Oxford, begun in 25. As one passes from the Clock Court to the Base Court one goes rough Queen Anne Boleyn's Gateway, which still bears the arms of ardinal Wolsey in terracotta as well as part of a series of terracotta roundels of the Roman Emperors. These are of very high quality, a were probably the first such decorations in England; they are the wo of Giovanni da Maiano, and were paid for in 1521, but the buildi accounts show that the actual structure of the palace was the work Englishmen. Under Henry VIII the Great Hall built by Wolsey w greatly enlarged and enriched, and the wonderful hammer-beam rc was built between 1531 and 1536. The structure, which is of a ty invented in the fourteenth century at Westminster Hall, was probat the work of the King's Master-Carpenter, John Nedeham, but t superb carving is by Richard Rydge. These elaborate pendent lanter once more show the influence of Italian art, but again it is a questi of Italian details on an English body. The ceiling of Wolsey's Clos however, shows an attempt at an Italian coffered ceiling, but it is qui clear that the result is an English version, and not a copy of anythi recognizably Italian. The rest of the closet consists of traditional line fold panelling with Perpendicular tracery in the windows.

Henry VIII died in 1547, and the next two years were dominated the Lord Protector Somerset. Until his fall, in December 1549, Somer was responsible for a marked French influence in place of the wani Italianism, and his Somerset House, begun about 1547, and demolish in the eighteenth century, was one of the most influential buildings its day. Old Somerset House seems to have derived from the work contemporary French architects such as Philibert de l'Orme or Je Bullant, whose Château d'Écouen of *c.* 1545 was perhaps the actu model for the Protector's architect.

Longleat House, in Wiltshire, is one of the progeny of Old Somers House, and one of the finest examples of English architecture in t Age of Elizabeth I, but before we come to it a short digression on t Thorpes, the Smythsons, and John Shute is necessary. When Somers fell he was succeeded by the Duke of Northumberland, who sent Jol Shute to Italy in 1550 "to confer with the doings of the skilful maste in architecture, and also to view such ancient monuments thereof are yet extant." Shute was, so far as we know, the only English archite of the sixteenth century to have a first-hand knowledge of classical a modern architecture in Italy, but it was not until 1563 that he publish the results of his travels in *The First and Chief Groundes of Architecture*, short treatise based on the most influential of all Italian treatises of t earlier sixteenth century—Serlio's *Regole generali di architettura* . . translated into English in 1611. In 1562, the year before Shute's bo appeared, Vignola's treatise on the architectural Orders was publishe and this is perhaps the closest parallel with Shute. Whatever he m have learned and seen, however, Shute died in the year his book can

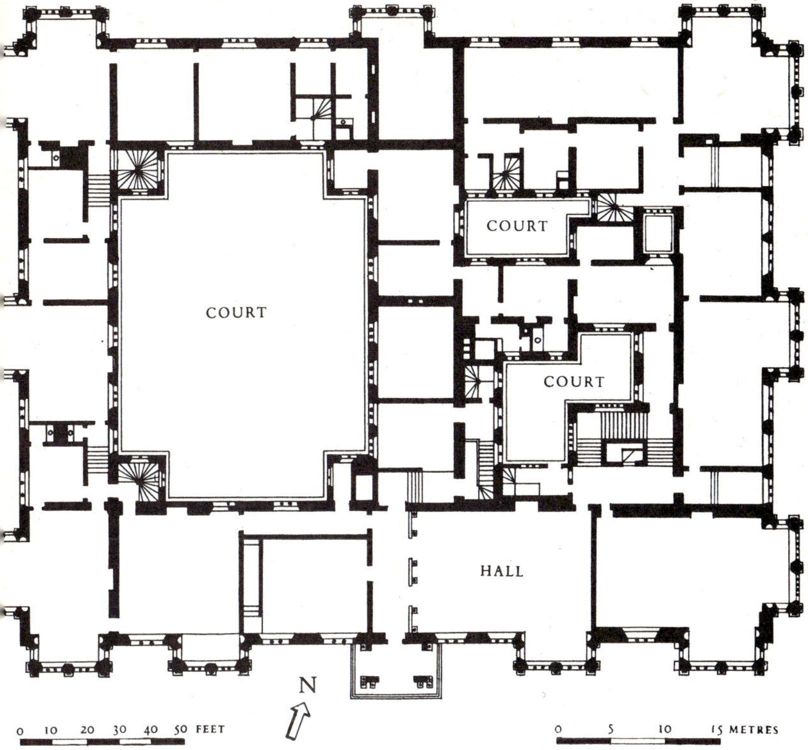

50. Plan of Longleat House

ut, and so we do not know what influence he may have had. On the hole, Flemish and German pattern-books, such as those of Ditterlin nd Vredeman de Vries, the latter published in 1563, probably had ıore influence in England than Shute's rather uncertain classicism, nd it was probably in imitation of such pattern-books that the two great ɔllections known as the Thorpe Drawings (London, Soane Museum) nd the Smythson Drawings (London, Royal Institute of British Archi- :cts) came into existence. Both collections may have been the work of ıore than one member of each family, and they can no longer be ɔnsidered as evidence that the men who made the drawings actually uilt the houses. The most important members of each family were ɔhn Thorpe (*c.* 1563–1655) and Robert Smythson (*c.* 1536–1614).

Longleat was one of the first of the great Elizabethan houses—the 'Prodigy Houses,' as Sir John Summerson calls them—and it is ertainly one of the great achievements of English architecture. Its uilder was Sir John Thynne, who had been in charge of the works at

Somerset House, and who had also visited France. He had considerab experience of building, and, as we have seen, Shute may have ha something to do with the original planning. The mason at Longle

51. LONGLEAT HOUSE

was Robert Smythson, and through him Longleat exercised a enormous influence on other houses, but it is impossible to say ho much the design of Longleat owes to him, and the position is furth complicated by the fact that there was a fire in 1567, and we do n know how much of the earlier house was incorporated into the ne model made in 1568. The latest view is that the present house dat from 1572, and that the top storey, formerly thought to have bee added after Thynne's death in 1580, was part of his original intentio Both in plan and in elevation the most striking thing about Longle is its symmetry and restraint, for the plan shows that the east, west, an south sides are designed with three projecting bays each, one in th centre, and one at each end, so arranged that the angles of the buildir appear strengthened, without using the more common device of angl towers such as we find in French work deriving from Serlio's plan fo the Château d'Ancy-le-Franc (1546). On the north, or entrance, fro there are five projections—two bay-window units on either side of th front door, which still leads into the screens-passage and the centre e house. This plan is based on internal courts rather than an adapta- ɔn of the H-type, but the much larger number of private rooms now ›nsidered necessary was bound to lead to several changes in design.

The first impression of the façade is of the amount of glass, the second its horizontal extent. The proportion of window to wall increased ıormously during the reign of Elizabeth I, perhaps partly on account ˙ greater security, but the fashion changed again under James I, and naller windows came back. These large windows recur in other ɔuses, such as Hardwick Hall, Derbyshire (another Smythson house), hich are related to Longleat, and so does the horizontality—indeed, ıis is a permanent feature of English architecture, and can be found in ıigo Jones at his most Italianate. In fact, the basic element of the Long- at façade is really a vertical one, consisting of two tall rectangular indows separated and flanked by three pilasters. Each of the bay indows is made up of three of these units one above the other, and this the most conclusive proof of Longleat's descent from Somerset House, here such units occurred in pairs at the sides. The essential horizon- lity is maintained by the entablatures of the pilasters and the string- ɔurse linking the bases which together produce the bands across the front ˙ the house; in addition to this the roof is flat, with only very restrained ecoration in the crestings over each of the bay windows. All through ıe decoration is surprisingly simple and classical in feeling, which is ore than can be said for Burghley House, Northamptonshire. This as begun as early as 1556, but the main front and the court are later. he plan is that of Longleat, with the addition of a gatehouse and ngle-towers. The court is dated 1585, and is much more French—we now that Lord Burghley sent to Paris for de l'Orme's books, and there a resemblance to de l'Orme's Château d'Anet—but the detail is lemish rather than French in character.

Not far from Burghley are the ruins of Kirby Hall, begun in 1570. It sed to be thought that the house was designed by John Thorpe ecause his drawings in the Soane Museum include a plan of Kirby ıscribed: "Kerby whereof I layd ye first stone Ao 1570," but Sir John ummerson has shown that he was only about seven at that date, so ıat he may have laid the first stone if his father was master-mason ıere, but hardly otherwise. The plan of Kirby is very French in that it ɔnsists of a court with an entrance front and loggia, two long wings of ›dgings for guests, and then the house proper, with the porch in the entre leading into the great hall on the right. On the left of the porch re two floors, but, to maintain the symmetry of the façade, the indows run right down like those of the great hall, which actually ses the full height of the house. On the walls of this front, and also

52. KIRBY HALL

down the side wings, there are Ionic pilasters of a Giant Order (*i.e* one that runs through two or more storeys). This is the first use of suc pilasters in England, and indeed the Giant Order was first used i Italy only a few years earlier. The porch, with its fantastic gable, dated 1572, except for the balcony window, which was inserted in 163

After 1580 two large and important houses were built, both of ther being linked with Longleat. They were Wollaton Hall, near Notting ham (now owned by the Corporation), and Hardwick Hall, which ha recently become national property.

Wollaton is almost certainly the work of Robert Smythson, since h is buried in Wollaton Church, and his tombstone calls him *Gent Architector and Survayor unto the most worthy house of Wollaton.* The owne was a coal magnate, Sir Francis Willoughby, and Professor Pevsner ha suggested that this may have something to do with the extreme elabora tion of the decoration, which, with its profusion of Netherlandis strapwork motives, might almost be Victorian. Wollaton is undoubtedl derived from Longleat, but the plan is quite different, and very curiou The general shape seems very close to the Serlio type, which may hav been the starting-point for Longleat itself, but Wollaton, like Burghley has the angle-towers; what is odd, however, is the fact that the centra court in Serlio's plan is here filled in by the great hall. This has th

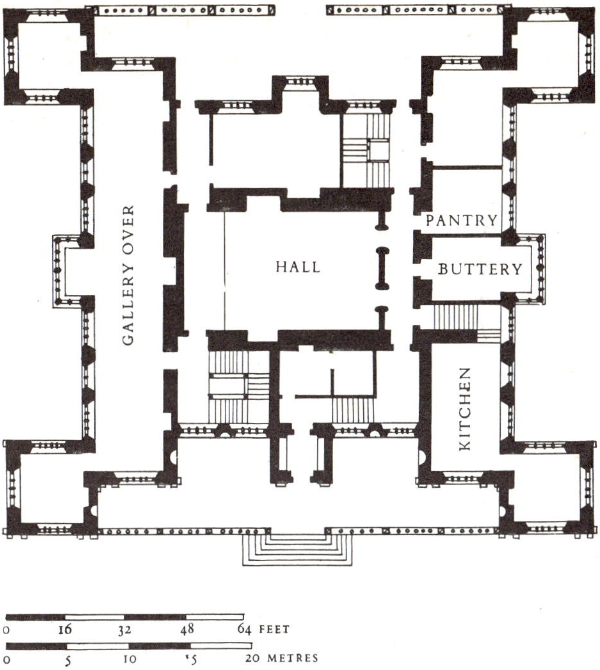

53. PLAN OF WOLLATON HALL

54. WOLLATON HALL

advantage that the front door no longer opens directly on to t screens-passage and thus the hall, so that there must be a welcor reduction in the draught; on the other hand, the hall is surrounded all sides by other rooms, and could not be lit except by carrying t walls up above the main block, and using a sort of clerestory. This turn made the hall block into the principal external feature, rising like a great tower, and this probably suggested the curiously mediev features of the angle-turrets, and the tracery in the windows of t 'great chamber' above the hall. Wollaton was built between 1580 a 1588. Two years later Elizabeth, Countess of Shrewsbury, known Bess of Hardwick, a much-married lady and an impassioned build began her great house at Hardwick. It was built at great speed, a was finished in 1596. The architect is unknown, but there are links wi both Longleat and Wollaton, so that Robert Smythson is a high likely candidate, especially as the plan shows yet another variati on the great-hall theme. The old H-plan is adapted for the gene shape, but at Hardwick the hall is made to run back at right angles the front door instead of forming the cross-bar of the H. By this mea the screens-passage is made into a vestibule at the same time as fulfils its original purpose of communication with the kitchens. Ext nally Hardwick is very like Longleat in its proportion of window wall—the local description is "Hardwick Hall, more glass than wal —and it also has something of Longleat's restraint in the detailir although the treatment of the towers recalls a plainer Wollaton. T interiors of Hardwick are important, since they contain some of t finest surviving Elizabethan decorative work in the gallery, a especially in the Great Presence Chamber, where the coloured plas frieze is a unique survivor of a barbaric but cheerful form of decoratic

Charlton House, Greenwich, built from 1607, was one of the f imitations of the Hardwick arrangement of the hall on the door ax Charlton also has an elaborate doorway which is the only record instance of an almost literal borrowing from one of the plates Wendel Ditterlin's architectural extravaganza. The date of Charlt takes us into the reign of James I (1603–25), and to a certain extent is possible to distinguish Jacobean from Elizabethan architecture, during James's reign many family houses were built, large in size, b not so exuberant as the Elizabethan ones, more sober in their deco tion, and usually built of brick, or brick with stone dressings, instead the stone favoured by the Elizabethans. The windows tend to be mu smaller, and they are usually long rectangles instead of the uprig shape in fashion earlier. Most of these houses were built by the seco or third generation of the new aristocracy, now comparatively settl

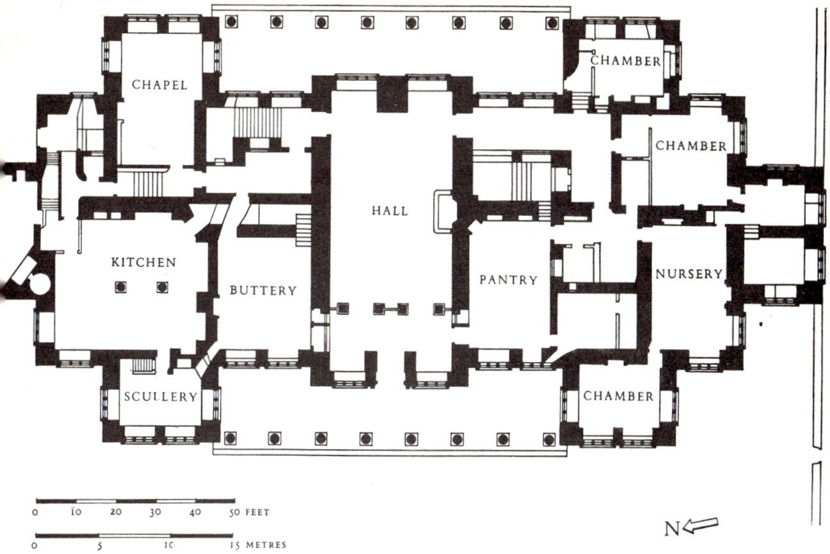

55. Plan of Hardwick Hall

56. Hardwick Hall

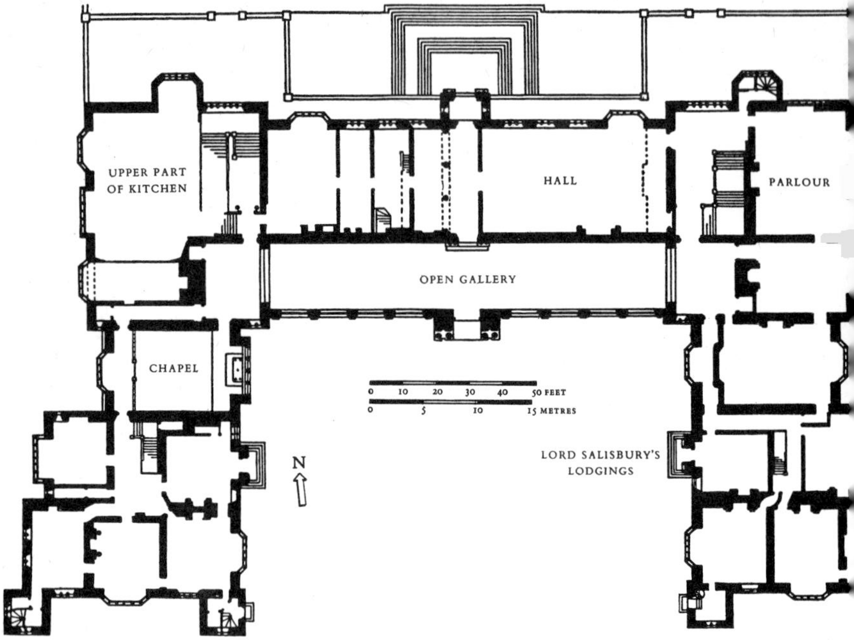

57. Plan of Hatfield House

58. Hatfield House

ıd they include such great houses as Knole, in Kent; Bramshill House, Hampshire; Audley End, in Essex; and, perhaps most typical, atfield House, Hertfordshire.

Hatfield was built by Robert Cecil, Earl of Salisbury, the second son Lord Burghley, Elizabeth's Minister. Like his father, Cecil was the ıding politician of the day and a great builder; Hatfield was far too rge for his needs, but it could house the entire Court on a Royal ogress if necessary. The house was built between 1607 and 1612, of ick and stone, and is much less extravagant than Burghley as well more comfortably planned. The plan shows that the great hall was tained, complete with a screens-passage, because this was the house a great personage, but at the same time the half-H plan is developed give a series of rooms in each of the wings, with the ends of the wings panded to three rooms thick. It was thus impossible to retain a mmetrical disposition, but this can hardly be seen when one is looking the house. The south front is much more classical in appearance, th a stone loggia and a central clock-tower, and it is now thought at this is one of the earliest works of Inigo Jones, since there is a yment to him in the Hatfield accounts of £10 in February 1610 "for awinge of some Architecture." The other people concerned in the sign were Simon Basil, the Royal Surveyor; Robert Lemyinge, who rtainly supervised most of the work; and Cecil himself. Much of the terior has been altered, but the splendid wooden staircase with its en well still exists, and was one of the first and finest of its kind.

Many other Jacobean houses of the same general type as Hatfield ll exist. To take only one smaller example, there is Aston Hall 618–35), now part of Birmingham City Museums. Swakeleys 1629–38), Middlesex, now a sports club, and Raynham Hall, orfolk, are also examples of the compact type of Jacobean house, many which still exist. All these are traditional buildings, almost completely touched by the new classical style of Inigo Jones, even though the nqueting House stood in Whitehall for all to see.

CHAPTER 2

Inigo Jones, Webb, Pratt, and May

INIGO JONES is the first British architect who is a clearly defina
artistic personality. This is because he appears as a completely n
phenomenon, the highly educated Renaissance ideal artist who w
able to work for the most exalted patrons without sacrificing
independence. The enormous gap between Jones and, say, Rob
Smythson is not so much one of artistic achievement as of intellect
attitude: Smythson was a tradesman who expected to be told what
do (though not how to do it), whereas Jones was an artist who expect
his patron to take an intelligent and informed interest in what was bei
done for him.

This emancipation came ultimately from Italy, where such a chan
in the status of the artist had taken place a century earlier, and it w
Jones's good fortune that he was able to study there, and that, on
return, he was to find a royal patron who both understood and symp
thized with this attitude. Charles I, for all his insistence on the Divi
Right of Kings, understood that great artists have an even closer relatio
ship with the Creator. We know that Inigo Jones was not the first Briti
architect to study in Italy—John Shute preceded him by half a centu
—but he was certainly the first who understood what he saw, and ga
himself wholeheartedly to the new ideals based on a fervent study
classical antiquity. Jones learned to speak Italian, and it is importa
to realize that the whole basis of his art was the knowledge of the gre
Italian theorists rather than his memories of actual buildings; abo
all his own style and his own theories were formed by a single boo
I Quattro Libri dell'Architettura, by Andrea Palladio, published in Veni
in 1570. Jones founded his style on Palladio, and a century later t
whole course of English architecture was modified by Campbell, Ke
and Lord Burlington when they chose to base themselves on Jones a
Palladio. The *Quattro Libri* was not, of course, the first Italian te
book to make a profound impression on English architects; as we ha

en, Serlio was one of the main factors in the Elizabethan and Jacobean
les, but it is true to say that Serlio's *Regole generali di architettura* . . .
s always used as a pattern-book, as a source for individual motives
decoration. Palladio's treatise was far more scholarly, and far more
mly based on the direct study of surviving classical monuments;
nes took over this more intellectual approach, and, in particular, he
lowed Palladio's system of harmonic proportions. According to this
stem the long and short sides of a room should bear a simple mathe-
atical relationship to each other, and also to the height; further, each
om should be proportioned to its neighbours, and thus to the block
the building as a whole. A simple example is a single-cube room—
y, 15 feet long, wide, and high—next to a double cube—in this case
feet long and 15 wide and high.

The other great factor in the creation of Jones's style is his ability as
draughtsman and as a painter. Most of his predecessors had been able
draw, with some difficulty, a 'plat' or an 'upright'—a plan and an
evation—but that was the limit of their ability as draughtsmen. Jones
s a trained artist; not, perhaps, a great one, but able to express his
eas on paper with ease, and a good part of his fame actually arose
om his skill as a designer of the elaborate costumes and scenery used
the royal masques. Scores of his drawings for these exist, and it is
ways necessary to judge his architecture in the light of his fame and
hievements as a masque-designer. He was probably the only man in
gland possessed of the technical skill needed for these elaborate
oductions, and this alone gave him a prestige at Court and among
erary men that made him seem altogether different from the masons
d carpenters who were the usual designers of houses.

Inigo Jones was born in London in 1573, and died in 1652. We know
ry little about his early years, but he was almost certainly in Venice
1601, for his copy of Palladio's *Quattro Libri* (now in the Library
Worcester College, Oxford) is so inscribed. Two years later he is
corded as a 'picture-maker' in the Earl of Rutland's service, but it is
ely that he had been to Denmark in the interval. There he worked for
hristian IV, but it is not known what he did. In 1605 he is documented
r the first time as a masque-designer in England, so it is likely that
had worked in Denmark as a designer of this kind, and had almost
rtainly studied in Italy, the only place where such elaborate forms
stage design could be learned. No painting certainly by Jones is
own to exist, and the work done in 1610–12 at Hatfield (if it is his)
so immature that it must be one of his earliest essays in architecture;
t in 1611 he had a job in the royal household, so that it is most likely
at his skill in devising elaborate pageants, and his knowledge of the

high-flown allegories and personifications usual in this type of ent tainment, were responsible for his advancement. He is known to ha continued to work as a masque-designer until 1640, and for ma years he collaborated with Ben Jonson until they had a violent quar over their relative importance. Both were prickly, and the quar produced some abuse which echoes down the centuries.

Meanwhile he had been back to Italy, about 1605, and he was France in 1609. In 1611 he was made Surveyor to Prince Henry, first certain architectural appointment, and in 1613 he was promis the reversion of Simon Basil's Royal Surveyorship. In that year he w once more in Italy, staying in a villa near Padua with Lord Arund the finest connoisseur and the greatest patron then in England. Fr Padua he went on to Rome, and it was at this time that he made sor notes in his Palladio, and filled a sketch-book, in which, on January 1615, he made his only general statement on the art of architecture. is ill-written, misspelled, and tortuous in expression as all his notes a but it contains a genuine aesthetic as well as a reasoned criticism Italian Mannerist art of the previous half-century, which were bo totally beyond the capacity of any other Englishman of the time. Th as much as his few buildings, is the measure of his importance. He say

> And to saie trew all thes composed ornaments the wch Proceed out of aboundance of dessigners and wear brought in by Michill Angell and followers in my oppignion do not well in sollid architecture [*i.e.*, as oppos to ephemeral work such as stage-sets]. . . . For as outwarly every wyse m carrieth a gravitie in Publicke Places, whear ther is nothing els looked f yet inwardly hath his immaginacy set on fire, and sumtimes licenciou flying out, as nature hir sealf doeth often tymes stravagantly, to delligl amase us sumtimes moufe us to laughter, sumtimes to contemplation a horror, so in architecture ye outward ornaments oft [ought] to be soll proporsionable according to the rulles, masculine and unaffected.

Later in the same year he succeeded Basil as Royal Surveyor, a pc he held until work was stopped by the Civil War, in 1642. All his maj work was done for the Crown. The Banqueting House in Whitehall w built to replace an older one destroyed by fire on December 12, 161 and the new one was completed in 1622. This and Jones's contempora work on the Queen's House at Greenwich must have seemed total alien to every member of the building trades as well as to most of t public (there is a contemporary reference to the Queen's House 'some curious devise' of Jones's), and indeed they are uncompromisi essays in the purest Palladianism. Two preliminary drawings for t Banqueting House exist, and either might well be mistaken for a desig

59. The Banqueting House, Whitehall
Aquatint by T. Malton, 1781

for a palace by Palladio, yet the building itself has an unmistakab character of its own. Jones began by deciding to make a double cu —it is 110×55×55 feet—with a single large room inside, but he th made the exterior like a Palladian palace in two storeys, where contemporary Italian architect would have made the exterior expr the interior by using a Giant Order. The two drawings show how began with a normal Palladian type, with a large pediment in t centre; but such a pediment is intended to mark the entrance fro and here the entrance is at the side. He therefore abandoned the pec ment, and kept his sky-line level, yet he still felt that a central empha was desirable, so he used four columns with projecting entablatur over them to stress the three centre bays, and pilasters to articulate t two side bays, doubling them at the ends to close the building. Su subtleties can hardly have been understood by any other craftsman the day, any more than the perfection of the detailing in the pedimer over the windows, straight on the *piano nobile*, and alternating segment and triangular on the ground-floor range, or the swags at capital lev (an unusual motive borrowed direct from Palladio), or the fine channelled rustication of the surface.

Inside, the Banqueting House is a beautifully proportioned sing room, with a gallery round it at the level of the first entablature outsic The panelled ceiling is as purely Italian as the rest of the building, b what makes this one of the noblest interiors in Europe is the gre painted ceiling by Rubens, put up in 1635. As a decorative whole t interior can be compared with the Carracci Gallery in the Palaz Farnese, in Rome; but one is unique in its time and the other a maste piece which is the culmination of generations of similar efforts.[1]

The design of the Banqueting House owes its origin to Palladi conception of a town palace, but Palladio himself was, and is, chie famous as a designer of villas for the Venetian noble families, and l designs of this kind formed the English country house of the lat seventeenth and eighteenth centuries. This was worked out in det by Lord Burlington and the Palladians, but the first example of Palladian villa on English soil is the Queen's House at Greenwich. T Queen's House was actually begun before the Banqueting House, 1616, but after two years' work was stopped until 1630, when it w begun again for the new Queen, Henrietta Maria. Her name and t date 1635 appear on the upper part of the north front, so the hou

[1] Until recently the whole floor-space of the Banqueting House was cluttered with exhibits of the United Services Museum, but now (1962) the Government is taking steps make it possible to see and enjoy one of the greatest achievements of two major artists.

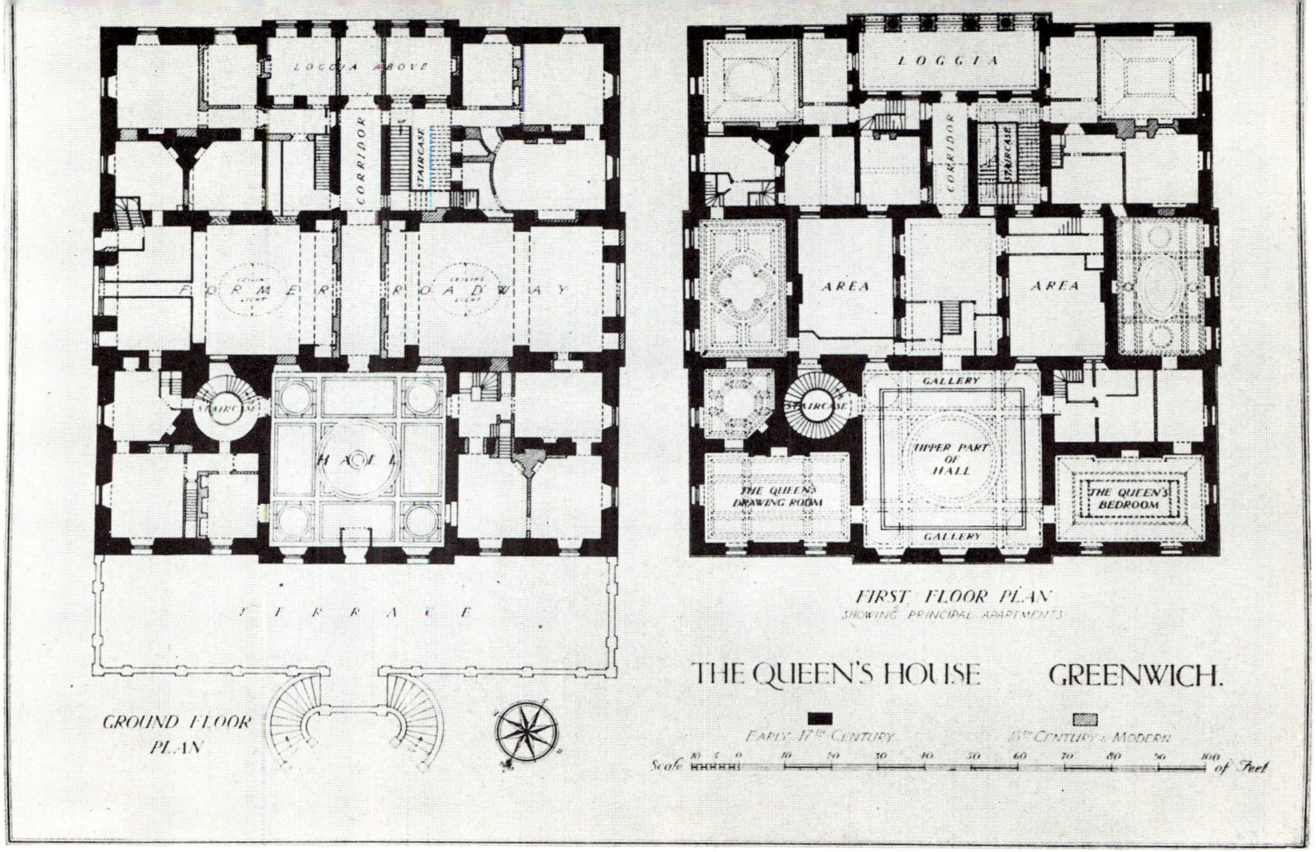

60. Plan of the Queen's House, Greenwich

61. THE QUEEN'S HOUSE, GREENWICH

must have been finished at about that time. The plan is distinctly od
for some whim of Queen Anne of Denmark made her choose in 16
to have her new house built across a public road, the main Deptfor
Woolwich highway. Later in the seventeenth century Jones's pup
John Webb, was called in to add bridges, and thus transformed t
house into the simple block we now see. Later still the colonnades we
added, and the road itself moved to where Romney Road now is. T
plan of the original house was thus an H, but a different H-plan fro
those we have seen since the cross-bar is a bridge at first-floor level onl
and the great hall is now the main feature of the entrance front, in t
north upright of the H. It is quite unlike any English great hall becau
it is now a single cube running up through the ground and first floor
like the Banqueting House, this hall is divided at half-height by
balcony which here serves to link all the rooms on the first floor. T
first floor is here the *piano nobile* of an Italian villa, and the ground floc
contrary to English usage, was treated as a rusticated basement to s
off the columns of the loggia on the south front. The loggia is, of cours
a purely Italian idea, and cannot have been used much in Greenwic
Originally the difference between the two floors was emphasized by t
fact that the windows on the ground floor were considerably smalle
but they were lengthened at the bottom in the eighteenth century. T

ape and size of the windows and the general outline of the building e the only two points which clearly distinguish it from an Italian la; the windows are, of course, far larger in scale than they would in an Italian villa where the intention is to keep the sun out, and e shape of the whole house is a long low rectangle of the traditional ıglish shape rather than the cubical block favoured by Palladio.

Most of the interior decoration has now disappeared, but it was obably originally very rich, and we can best get an idea of it from nes's work at Wilton. Among the other work done by Jones before e outbreak of the Civil War, the most important in the eyes of con- nporaries was the huge portico that he added to the front of the edieval St Paul's. This perished in the Great Fire, but we still possess ecimens of his ecclesiastical architecture in the Queen's Chapel, arlborough Gate, and—rebuilt in the eighteenth century—St Paul's, vent Garden. At Covent Garden, too, he did some town planning at echoed recent work in Paris, and left its mark on English archi- ture.

About 1628 the young John Webb (1611–72) became Jones's sistant, and later married his niece. Much of Webb's work consisted preparing drawings for the treatise on architecture that Jones prob- ly projected but never completed; Webb was also the draughtsman the palace at Whitehall which was planned by Charles I (though ere must, at that date, have been an unreal air about the whole thing). ıe original project of 1638 may have been feasible, but the drawings esented to Charles in captivity, about 1647, can hardly have been ore than wishful thinking. These he re-presented to Charles II, but thing came of that. The Whitehall Palace designs form a complicated d long chapter in the history of English monumental architecture, t as they were almost all grand projects rather than actual buildings, ey need not detain us.

During the Civil War, in 1645, Jones was taken prisoner by the rliamentarians at Basing House, Hampshire, but was later pardoned, d he and Webb worked at Wilton. The south front of the house was ilt by Isaac de Caux, but there was a fire in 1647, and Webb and nes made some repairs which probably included the towers at the ds—a motive to become important in the Jones Revival of the early hteenth century; more important, Jones designed the two splendid ate Rooms, the Single- and Double-cube Rooms. The Double-cube oom was designed to hold the great family portraits by Van Dyck in setting of the greatest richness, with superb carved swags and pedi- nted doorcases and a great coved ceiling. This is an important riation on the double-cube theme of the Banqueting House, for he felt here that the true double cube was too lofty, and the comprom was reached which enabled him to set his cornice at what he felt be the right height, with the cove leading up to the flat of the ceili at the height required by the double-cube proportion. The richness this decoration is perhaps more French than Italian, but it is the b evidence we have for the kind of decoration that must once ha existed in the Queen's House and elsewhere.

62. KING CHARLES'S BLOCK, GREENWICH HOSPITAL

After the death of his master in 1652 John Webb built Lamport H Northamptonshire, and hoped for better days. When the Restorati came he should have had the Surveyorship, but it went to the p Denham as a reward for services to Charles II in exile. The Whiteh Palace plans never materialized, but there was a project for a palace Greenwich, and some drawings were made by Webb. Once more project fell through, but one part of it was built, and was la incorporated in the huge scheme for Greenwich Hospital, now Royal Naval College. This one block—King Charles's Block—v built by Webb from 1665, and it is the most important work by him, a style which owes much to Jones, and more to the projects for palace in Whitehall, but which is nevertheless entirely personal, fo ɔws a trend towards the Italian Baroque, and a sympathy for its aims ıich we never find in Jones himself. In the Banqueting House there : two small orders to express a double-storey front, and all the units : correspondingly small; at Greenwich Webb built a great mass of ɜticated stonework, and then divided it into two storeys by a band of ılar stone below the sills of the first-floor windows, and another above ɜm. He then tied the whole front together by sets of four giant asters, one at each end, and the other set in the middle, and these ıphases are still further marked by the fact that the end bays have an ic storey over them, and the central entrance bay has attached .umns instead of pilasters and a pediment over. This awareness of the ity of large masses derives ultimately from seventeenth-century ılians like Bernini, whose work Webb can never have seen in the ginal; but his re-interpretation of such ideas makes him the essential k between Inigo Jones and Wren.

Before we come to the work of Wren himself only three houses need tain us—Chevening, in Kent;[1] Coleshill House, Berkshire; and :ham Lodge, near London. Chevening has been ascribed to Jones nself, and seems to date from 1630 or earlier. If these traditions are :rect (and it must be observed that an attribution of a country house Jones is almost always wrong), then Chevening was perhaps the first ɹntry house to break with the long, spreading type of plan, with vers at the angles, and other irregularities of outline. It is much more e a town house, since it is a simple block, rather high in proportion, d planned to be two rooms deep. The present house was refaced in : eighteenth century, and it is therefore impossible to be certain of : original disposition, but it seems to have been earlier than Coleshill. ıis was one of the most splendid of seventeenth-century houses, but vas totally destroyed by fire in 1952. It was the work of an amateur, Roger Pratt, who spent the Civil War years in France, the Low untries, and Italy, where he visited Rome with John Evelyn. On return he began Coleshill for a relative, about 1650, and although ıes was consulted, the house was certainly Pratt's work. The plan ɔws two major innovations. The old great hall has been transformed o a staircase hall, very Italian in feeling, with the splendid double ɜep of the stairs climbing round the walls to a landing at first-floor el. Behind the hall was the Great Parlour, but the two were separated a corridor which ran the full width of the house, dividing it into ɔ intercommunicating ranges. Pratt himself called this type of design double pile,' and it may have been invented by him, but, as it is ınd at Chevening, it is perhaps more likely that Inigo was the first

Chevening has recently been made over to the nation, but is not open to the public.

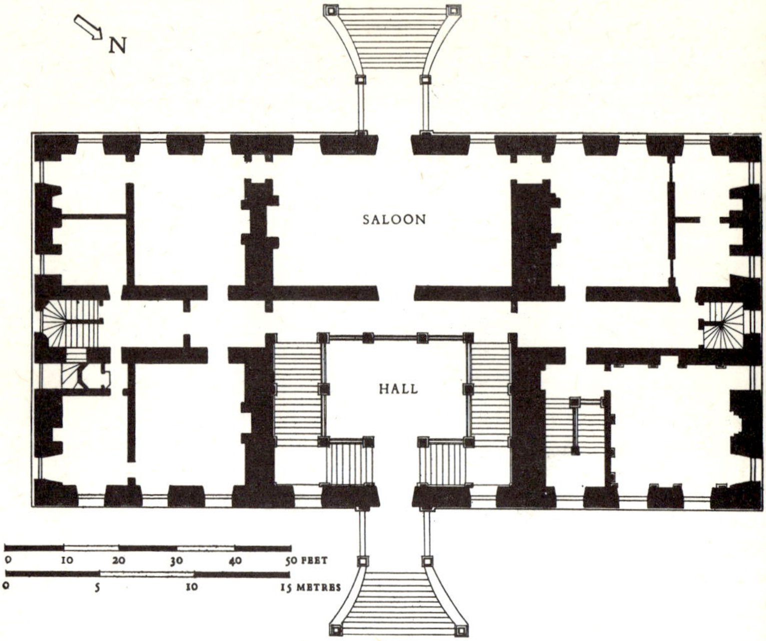

63. Plan of Coleshill House

64. Eltham Lodge

think of it. Yet when all is said there was a great deal of superb tailing and decoration at Coleshill that was not in Jones's style, and ıst have been Pratt's. He built little else, and spent most of his life a country gentleman, but he had a considerable influence, and he lped to popularize a type of house which used misleadingly to be lled the 'Wren type.'

The remaining house was built by Hugh May, in 1663–64, at Eltham Woolwich (it is now a Golf Club). Hugh May (1622–84) was rtainly in Holland during the Commonwealth, and was made Pay-aster of the Works at the Restoration, and it was for Charles II that did what was probably his most important work, now lost, at indsor Castle. His stay in Holland had given him first-hand know-lge of contemporary Dutch Palladianism, and Eltham Lodge reflects ry closely the style of such buildings as the Mauritshuis, in The ague, in its use of brick with stone pilasters, and the Giant Order th a pediment to emphasize the centre. Naturally enough, when the iled Court of Charles II returned from Holland a good many Dutch shions came with them, and the principal importance of May's tham lay in its influence on the smaller English house, and, still more ıportant, on the formation of the style of the greatest architect of the e, Christopher Wren. The Italian and the Dutch styles both con-buted to his development although he never visited either country; ıt the complex evolution of that wonderful mind owes much to Pratt ıd May as well as to greater men like Jones and Webb.

CHAPTER 3

Wren and his Successors

CHRISTOPHER WREN was one of the three or four greatest Englis men. This eminence is due as much to the amazing sweep of intellect as to any single aspect of his work, for the creator of the do of St Paul's is fit to rank as an artist with Shakespeare; while Wre own greatest contemporary, Sir Isaac Newton, reckoned him among t three best geometers of his day, and for the first thirty of his ninety ye he was exclusively a mathematician and astronomer—a 'Natu Philosopher,' to use the term current in his own time.

Wren was born in 1632, and died in 1723. He came to manho during the Civil War, and, like many others of his generation, turned away from politics towards the sciences. Newton was born 1642, and both he and Wren naturally became members of the Ro Society, founded in 1662, and still one of the great scientific societ of the world; both men became presidents of it, Wren in 1680–82, a Newton from 1703 to his death in 1727. In the second half of t seventeenth century men of this type were sickened by the Civil War, struggle in which there was evidently a good deal of right on both sid but in which the moderate and decent men were soon killed or thr aside by the fanatics. The whole world of scientific experiment— 'ingenuity'—offered a more rewarding occupation for a man of Wre talents, for Evelyn had called him 'that miracle of a youth' in 16 when he was still only twenty-one. Wren was the son of a clergyma and was brought up in a High Church atmosphere. His uncle, Matth Wren, Bishop of Ely, was bitterly opposed to the Puritans, and w imprisoned by them for eighteen years; he was released at the Restor tion, and his sufferings in the Royalist cause may have helped predispose Charles II in Wren's favour. It seems certain that t personal favour of the King was very helpful to Wren at the beginni of his architectural career, and in fact he soon became virtually Co architect, entirely superseding the official Royal Surveyor, Sir Jo enham. Nevertheless, before taking up his architectural career he had ready been successively Gresham Professor of Astronomy in London, ıd Savilian Professor at Oxford, retaining this post until his archictural practice in London took up so much of his time that he had to sign. His mathematical attainments probably caused him to be conlted on Old St Paul's for the first time in 1661, but very little is known this. With his first building, however, we are on surer ground. This as the Sheldonian Theatre, at Oxford, begun in 1664, and given to

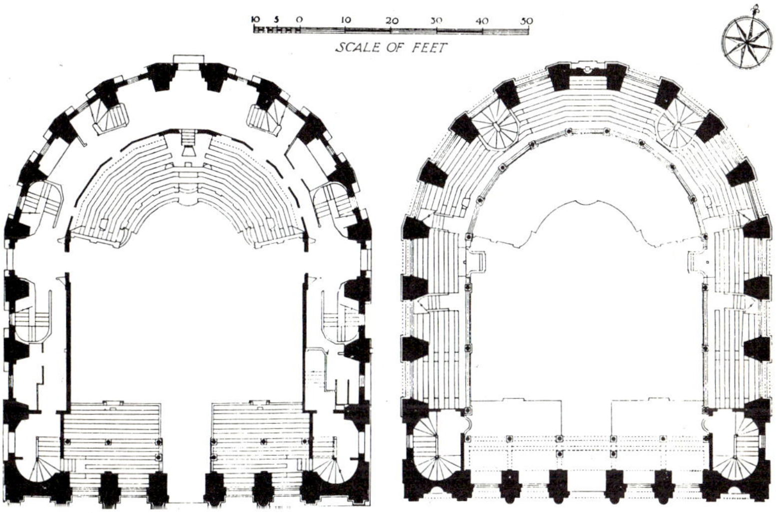

65. The Sheldonian Theatre

e University by Archbishop Sheldon as a suitable hall for the conrring of degrees and similar ceremonies. Since the purpose of the uilding was for solemn public acts, Wren chose a classical amphieatre as the basic form, and, like generations of Englishmen before m, he turned to Serlio for guidance. He adapted the D-shaped plan the Theatre of Marcellus, in Rome, shown in one of Serlio's plates, ıd then he added something of his own which is very typical. The heatre of Marcellus had no roof, but the sun was kept off by an awng of canvas. This was obviously impractical in the English climate, nd Wren had therefore to find some way of putting a ceiling over a)-foot span, and to do this he turned to a course of lectures given in 652 by Dr John Wallis, his colleague as Savilian Professor of Geoetry. Wallis had discussed the problems of a Geometrical Flat Floor;

Wren simply took his system of supports and turned them upside dow hanging a flat ceiling from a system of roof-trusses, and thus securir to the marvel of his contemporaries, a clear span of 70 feet tota unobstructed by any supports. To complete the classical allusion, t ceiling was painted to represent the sky with the cords and awning its prototype. In this, his earliest work, we have already the co bination of practical ingenuity and aesthetic feeling expressed in ter derived from classical civilization which is the hallmark of Wren as architect.

His next works were for the University of Cambridge, at Pembro and Emmanuel Colleges, but the turning-point in his career came wi great suddenness in the years 1665 and 1666, the years of the Gre Plague and the Fire of London, and also the years when Isaac Newt discovered the binomial theorem, and the differential and integr calculi. Wren went to France in the summer of 1665, and spent eig or nine months in Paris and the neighbourhood, returning in Februa or March of 1666. So far as we know, this was the only time he ever l England, and it was thus the only occasion he ever had to see a ful developed classical style other than that of Inigo Jones—for the rest his considerable knowledge of contemporary and earlier Europe work he had to depend on engravings. We know from a letter writt from Paris that he bought many of these in France, and he certain used many more on his return. The letter he wrote is undated, but w probably sent towards the end of his stay, and it contains some ir pressions which were to influence the course of English architecture:

> I have busied myself in surveying the most esteem'd Fabricks of Paris, a the Country round; the Louvre for a while was my daily Object, whe no less than a thousand Hands are constantly employ'd in the Worl some laying mighty Foundations, some in raising the Stories, Colum Entablements, etc., with vast Stones, by great and useful Engines; othe in Carving, Inlaying of Marbles, Plaistering, Painting, Gilding, e Which altogether make a School of Architecture, the best probably at t day in Europe. . . . Mons Abbé Charles introduc'd me to the Acquaintan of Bernini, who shew'd me his designs of the Louvre, and of the Kin Statue. . . . The Palace, or if you please, the Cabinet of Versailles call me twice to view it: the Mixtures of Brick, Stone, blue Tile and Go make it look like a rich Livery: not an Inch within but is crowded wi little Curiousities of Ornaments: the Women, as they make here t Language and Fashions, and meddle with Politicks and Philosophy, they sway also in Architecture; Works of Filgrand, and little Knacks are great Vogue; but Building certainly ought to have the Attribute eternal, and therefore the only Thing uncapable of new Fashions. . . . shall bring you almost all France in Paper, which I found by some

other ready design'd to my Hand, in which I have spent both Labour and ome Money. Bernini's Design of the Louvre I would have given my Skin or, but the old reserv'd Italian gave me but a few Minutes View; it was ive little Designs in Paper, for which he hath received as many thousand Pistoles; I had only time to copy it in my Fancy and Memory; I shall be able by Discourse, and a Crayon, to give you a tolerable Account of it. I have purchased a great deal of Taille-douce [engravings], that I might give our Countrymen Examples of Ornaments and Grotesks, in which he Italians themselves confess the French to excell.

Probably the most important event of this journey was Wren's short eting with Bernini, the greatest architect of the day, who was in ris to design the new Palace of the Louvre, and to make a bust and equestrian statue of Louis XIV. He was accorded almost royal nours (but most of his projects were quietly sabotaged by the French ists); and it is not impossible that this brief interview convinced en that architecture was an occupation fit for genius, and by no ans lacking in material rewards. The status of the architect in gland was still far below that attained in Italy and France, and it eded a great intellect, such as Wren's, to make possible the whole nosphere of the eighteenth century when architecture took its place ong the professions.

Immediately after his return Wren began to prepare a design for the building of Old St Paul's, since the church was then in a very decrepit ndition. It is not surprising that the new design was based on the at domed church of the Sorbonne, which Wren had seen on his trip Paris. His design was accepted on August 27, 1666: on September 2 Great Fire of London began. The events of those days are best scribed by John Evelyn in his *Diary*:

7 *August*. I went to S. Paul's church, where, with Dr Wren, Mr Pratt, Mr May, Mr Thomas Chicheley, Mr Slingsby, the Bishop of London, the Dean of S. Paul's and several expert workmen, we went about to survey he general decays of that ancient and venerable church . . . the shape of what stood was very mean, and we had a mind to build it with a noble upola, a form of churchbuilding not as yet known in England, but of wonderful grace.

September. This fatal night, about ten, began the deplorable fire, near Fish-street, in London.

September. The fire . . . was now taking hold of S. Paul's church, to which he scaffolds contributed exceedingly. . . .

September. . . . the stones of Paul's flew like grenadoes, the melting lead unning down the streets in a stream, and the very pavements glowing with fiery redness, so as no horse, nor man, was able to tread on them. . . .

> *7 September.* At my return, I was infinitely concerned to find that goo church, S. Paul's—now a sad ruin, and that beautiful portico (for struct comparable to any in Europe, as not long before repaired by the l King)[1] now rent in pieces, flakes of large stones split asunder and nothi remaining entire but the inscription in the architrave, showing by wh it was built, which had not one letter of it defaced! It was astonishing see what immense stones the heat had in a manner calcined, so that all ornaments, columns, friezes, capitals, and projectures of massy Portla stone, flew off, even to the very roof, where a sheet of lead covering a gr space (no less than six acres by measure) was totally melted.

It has been calculated that more than thirteen thousand houses w destroyed in the fire, as well as more than one hundred churches a the cathedral itself. Evelyn estimated the homeless at 200,000, and was this that made the Great Fire so much worse than the second f of 1940. Fortunately, the Government, headed by Charles II hims took effective steps to feed the refugees, and to start work on rebuilding: once again, Evelyn's *Diary* tells us how the work of rebui ing was taken in hand:

> *10 September.* I went again to the ruins; for it was now no longer a city.
> *13 September.* I presented his Majesty with a survey of the ruins and a p [plan] for a new City, with a discourse on it. . . .

Quick as Evelyn was, Wren was even quicker, for his plan for new City had been presented to the King a few days earlier. Char at once appointed a Commission for the rebuilding of the City, no nating Hugh May, of the Office of Works, Sir Roger Pratt, and Wren; the City appointed three more of its own nominees. The Co mission had three main problems to face. They had to provide for rebuilding, as quickly as possible, of thousands of houses and sho of sufficient parish churches for the needs of the large population of City, and for the rebuilding of St Paul's; next, they had to try improve the planning of the City, since before the fire it had consis of a noisome huddle of medieval alleys and mean houses, permanen jammed with traffic, and intermittently swept by contagion or fi Finally, they had to reconcile the claims of thousands of freeh owners with the need for much wider streets and large open spac and it was this which made Wren's plan impracticable. The essence his plan derives from the best contemporary models in France a Italy, and consists of long straight streets, intersecting mostly at ri angles, but with a few main vistas centred on large public buildin such as St Paul's or the Royal Exchange. This rectilinear plan

[1] The great portico was the work of Inigo Jones, in the 1630's.

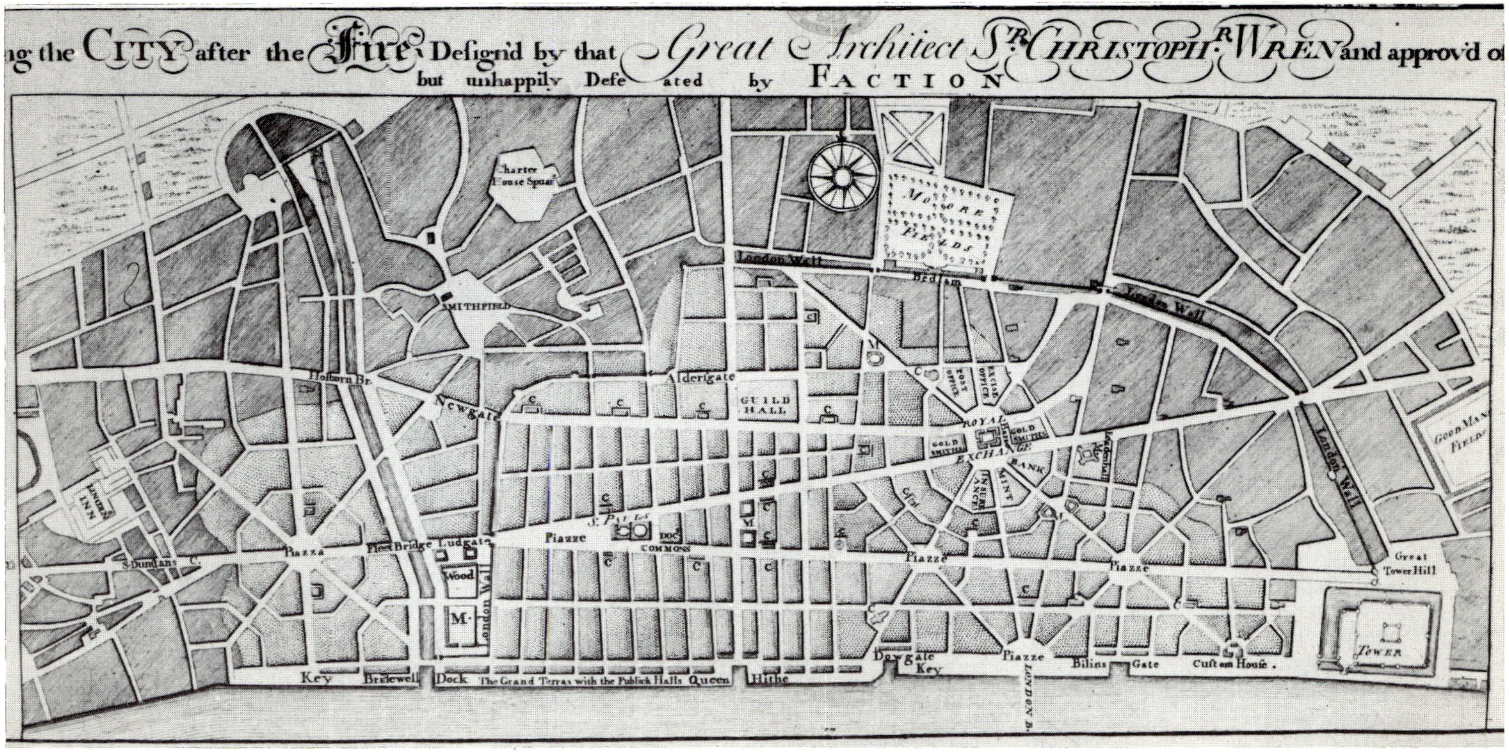

66. WREN'S PLAN FOR THE NEW CITY OF LONDON

complemented by a scheme of piazzas—the very word is derived fro Italian practice—which form the centres of rings of streets. The pla shows how easy it would have been to cross London from north south or east to west, with an extra diagonal link from the focal poin of the Cathedral and the Royal Exchange; further, the main stree were to be 90 feet wide; far wider than their medieval predecessor The snag lay in the fact that Wren's plan took little account of th ownership of land, and would have needed extensive powers of con pulsory purchase, while in many cases the remains of the burned-o buildings and their cellars would also have had to be cleared at grea expense. In the event the owners of the original buildings were allowe to return to their old sites, subject to the restrictions imposed by th Act of 1667, which made it impossible to return to the most insanita aspects of the medieval City. All the houses and shops were rebuilt the owners' expense, but the public buildings were paid for by the Ci and the Companies, and the churches were built out of the procee of a tax on coal. Wren's plan may not have had much effect on th aspect of the City, but it was probably one of the reasons for his appoin ment as Royal Surveyor in 1669, Webb being passed over once agai Under Wren's general supervision work was begun on the new church in 1670, but it is important to remember that, of the fifty-five Wre Churches, only a handful were designed in detail by Wren himse since the majority were very largely carried out by the craftsmen each parish. In most cases Wren provided the plan and, at a later stag the steeple. The plans are particularly important since they were a adaptations of the older parish-church sites to suit the new, Protestan liturgy, a point which he developed at some length in his memorandu on church-building of 1711, insisting on the need for a "convenie auditory" in which "everyone should hear the Service and both he and see the Preacher."

Among the most important survivors of the City churches are S Bride, Fleet Street (1671–78; steeple 1701–3); St Mary-le-Bow Cheapside (1670–73; steeple completed 1680); St Stephen, Walbroo (1672–79), and St Vedast, Foster Lane (1670–73; steeple 1694–97 All of these churches were badly damaged in the Second World Wa but St Bride[1] and St Stephen have been restored, St Mary-le-Bow now (1962) in course of restoration, and St Vedast has been repaire and its tower—its most important feature—survives. Two other church are usually counted among the City churches, although, in fact, outsic the City boundary: St Clement Danes, Strand (1680–82) and St Jame Piccadilly (1682–84).

[1] The St Bride restoration is not in accordance with Wren's design.

Basically the City churches are rectangular in plan, but the cramped l awkward sites meant that the shapes were often very odd, and it :ded all Wren's ingenuity to adapt them to some more or less ımetrical arrangement. The new Protestant type of parish church not need a choir, and it was not usually necessary to have any kind ransept, so the type evolved by Wren is that of a hall, with or with- aisles, but having galleries to contain extra seats, and make it sible to hear the sermon. This type had been evolved in Holland for Calvinists, but it was also a type used by the Jesuits; like them, but ike the Calvinists, Wren had to provide an altar—normally against

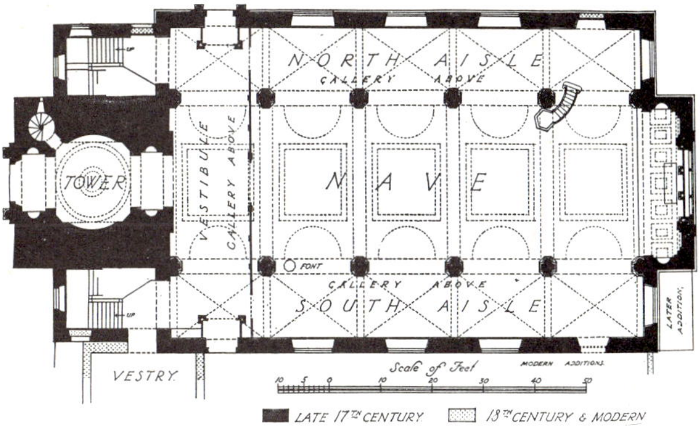

67. Plan of St Bride, Fleet Street

east wall—and his interiors were also intended to be much more ıly decorated than the Calvinists would have allowed. Three plans the surviving churches will show his ingenuity. In the first, St de, he was able to use a pure rectangle since the site was clear; the ırch is therefore a traditional parish type of nave-and-aisles, with east end a mere salient (since there were fewer clergy to fill the ir), and the emphasis on the entrance tower and spire. Wren attached at importance to the steeples, since they were the landmarks and andsome Spires or Lanterns, rising in good proportion above the ghbouring houses . . . may be of sufficient Ornament to the Town." second plan, that of St Mary-le-Bow, is a variation on the same me, but we happen to know that it was based on the Basilica of Con- ıtine, in Rome (which Wren would have known from the engraving erlio), as well as the general idea of the classical basilica, as described Vitruvius,[1] which underlies most of his City churches. The plan ks like an ordinary nave-and-aisles type, with the entrance set at the

e most important architectural writer of ancient times. He lived in the first century B.C.

side under the tower, but the interior shows the great central bar vault supported on the side piers, which are themselves supported flat longitudinal arches and smaller transverse ones—precisely

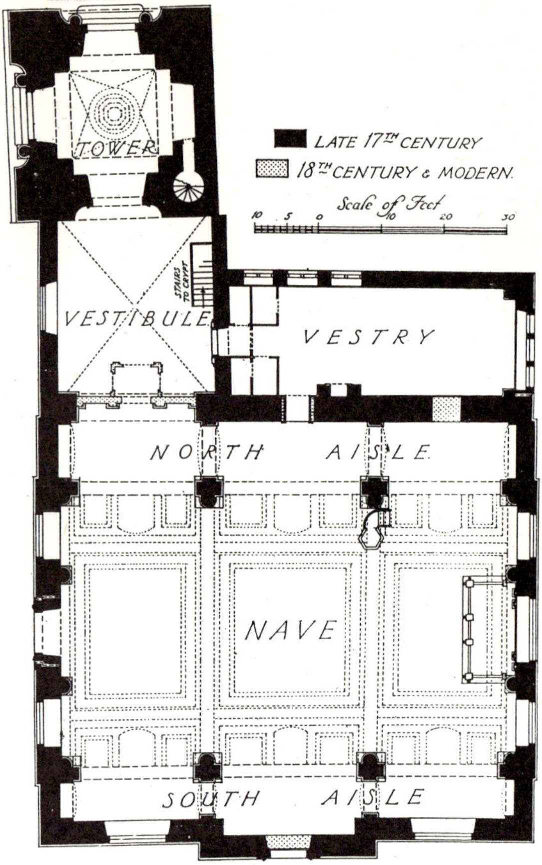

68. Plan of St Mary-le-Bow

constructional system of the great Roman Baths, and the kind exercise needed by the future architect of St Paul's.

St Stephen, Walbrook, is perhaps the finest of all the City church and is generally regarded as a trial run for St Paul's; certainly it i different type of plan, based on the idea of a dominant dome, then s an innovation in English churches. Several of the City churches w based on the centralized type of plan—a square containing a cr (St Martin, Ludgate; St Anne and St Agnes, Gresham Street; St M

69. St Vedast

70. St Bride

71. St Mary-le-Bow

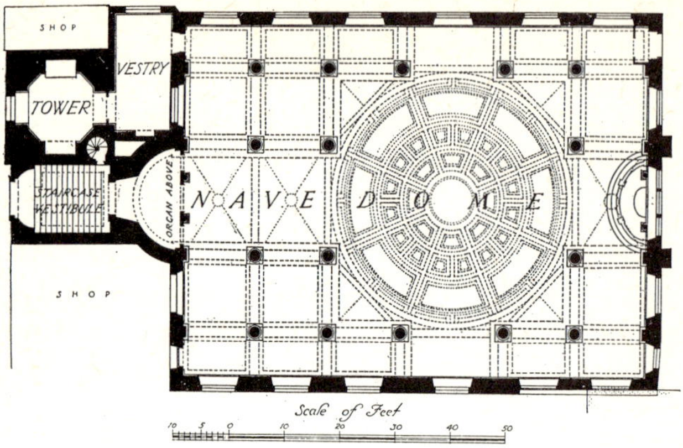

72. PLAN OF ST STEPHEN WALBROOK

73. ST STEPHEN WALBROOK

Hill, Lower Thames Street), or an octagon or similar figure treated an oval (St Antholin,[1] Watling Street; St Benet Fink,[1] Threadneedle reet) or a square covered by a dome (St Mary Abchurch; St Mildred,[1] read Street; St Swithin,[1] Cannon Street), but St Stephen is a particurly subtle combination of a nave and four aisles with a great central omical space. This gives great variety to the internal spaces, and makes e voids between the architectural solids as important as the solids emselves. The dome is carried on a series of arches which spring from ght Corinthian columns set on high bases (originally the pews came to the tops of the bases); but the columns also carry straight entablares running in different planes from the arches, linking the central r domed) church with the long nave-and-aisles one, and giving a nstantly shifting series of spatial effects as one moves round the terior. This use of varying ceiling-levels in the angles owes much to utch Calvinist churches, which Wren can have known only at second nd, but St Stephen differs fundamentally from them in having an tar at the east end, in its much richer furnishing and plasterwork, d in its complexity of spatial treatment—in fact, it is the architectural uivalent of the Anglican compromise between the austerities of alvinism and the splendours of Baroque Rome. This was precisely hat was needed at St Paul's, the first cathedral to be built for the nglican liturgy, and for a Dean and Chapter anxious to maintain the igh Church tradition, and to avoid the Puritanism which was so cent a memory.

The rebuilding of St Paul's began in 1675, and was finished in 1710. is extremely rare for a building of such size and importance to be mpleted in the lifetime of its architect, and it was particularly rtunate that Wren lived to a great old age, for he seems to have odified the design at almost every stage. After the fire the choir of Old Paul's was unusable, but services were held in the nave until, in 68, some masonry fell, and it became clear that the building was ngerous. Wren was then asked to prepare a design for a new choir a preliminary to a complete rebuilding when more money should available. In the event the Coal Tax was almost all spent on the rish churches up to 1675, when the new cathedral was begun on the creased funds available. Between 1668 and 1675 at least three fullale projects were put forward, none of them bearing very much semblance to the executed building, but all of them playing a part its long genesis. By 1670 the first model had been prepared and proved. It still exists in a fragmentary state, but we can say with rtainty of it that it was not really adequate as a cathedral, and that

[1] Destroyed.

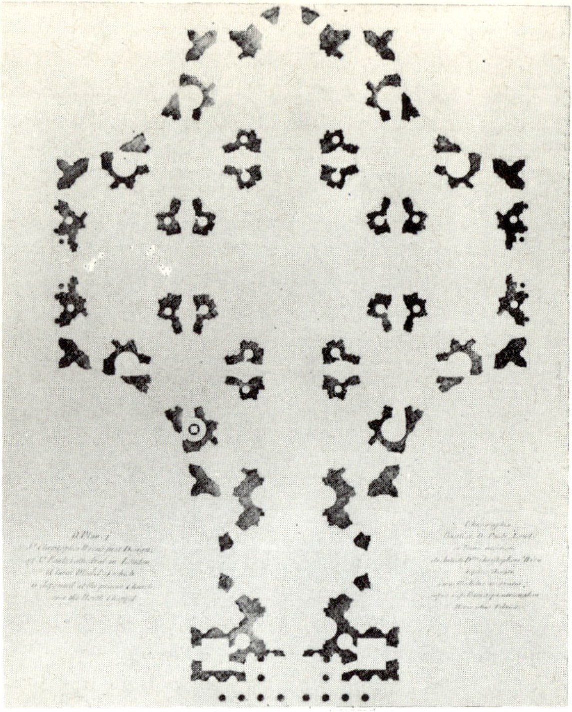

74. ST PAUL'S CATHEDRAL
PLAN OF THE GREAT MODEL DESIGN

75. THE GREAT MODEL: I

had a dome, thus proving Wren's desire to build a domed church omparable to those he had seen in Paris. Certainly he wanted to rovide London with a great landmark, as the spire of Old St Paul's ad once been, and his basic conception was therefore a compact lock building up to a climax in the dome. This idea reached splendid xpression in the Great Model of 1673, 18 feet long, and preserved in

76. The Great Model: II

he cathedral itself. This is supposed to have been Sir Christopher's wn favourite (he was knighted in this year, 1673), and it is easy to see vhy, for it is great architecture which comes from the antique tradition y way of the great Italians—and in particular it is very reminiscent f the plan which Michelangelo had made for St Peter's, and had been revented from carrying out. The most striking features about the Great Model are the clean sweep of the interior under the dome and he use of deep re-entrant curves for the external walls, contrasting with he dome above, as well as with the portico of giant columns which was learly intended to recall Inigo Jones's. The Great Model is not quite fully centralized plan since it has a small dome over the vestibule at he west end—*i.e.*, it has an east-west orientation. Nevertheless it did

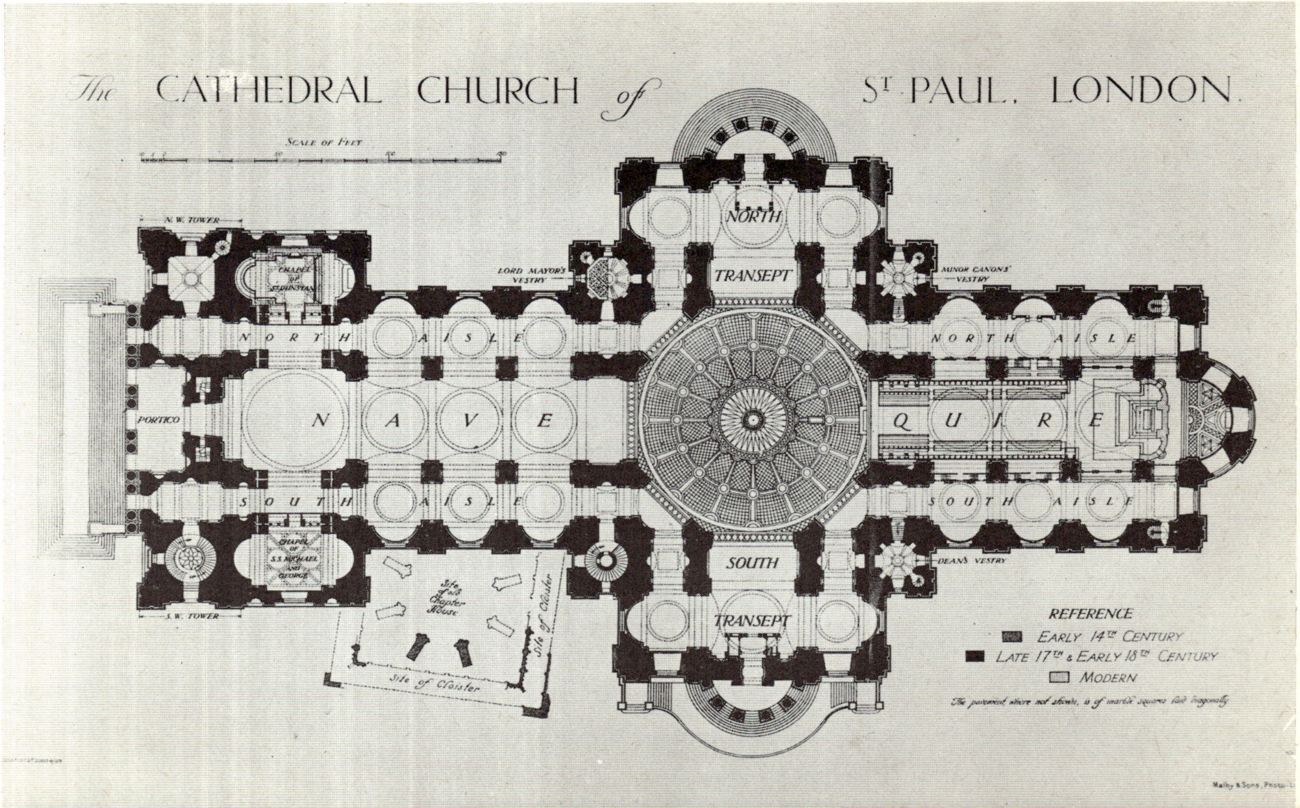
The CATHEDRAL CHURCH of St PAUL, LONDON
Scale of Feet
N. W. TOWER
S. W. TOWER
PORTICO
NORTH AISLE
SOUTH AISLE
NAVE
QUIRE
NORTH TRANSEPT
SOUTH TRANSEPT
LORD MAYOR'S VESTRY
MINOR CANONS' VESTRY
DEAN'S VESTRY
Site of Old Chapter House
Site of Cloister
Site of Cloister
REFERENCE
Early 14th Century
Late 17th & Early 18th Century
Modern
The pavement where not shown, is of marble squares laid diagonally
Malby & Sons, Photo-L

78. The Nave of St Paul's Cathedral

79. St Paul's Cathedral from the East

t look much like a church to most laymen, and the clergy "thought : model not enough of a cathedral-fashion." This probably meant at it did not look like a medieval cathedral, and therefore did not pport their efforts to maintain the theory that the Anglican Church ıs the natural successor to Rome. The model also had the practical awback that it could not be built in stages, as the money came in. was therefore rejected, and Wren drew up another plan, known as : Warrant Design, in 1675. It received the royal approval, although : elevation is almost grotesque, and work began at last. The plan of : Warrant Design is very close to the executed building in that it is a tin cross—"a cathedral form, as they called it, but so rectified as to :oncile the Gothick to a better manner of architecture," while the :erior is a combination of Old St Paul's and Inigo Jones, with an :raordinary dome-cum-spire on the top. Very possibly he did not :e the Warrant Design very seriously, for there is a clause in the rrant allowing him "the liberty . . . to make some variations, rather ıamental than essential, as from time to time he should see proper," d he took advantage of this almost at once. It is true that he never ered the essential Latin-cross plan, but he certainly changed the :erior almost immediately, and he modified the plan to make it

80. ST PAUL'S CATHEDRAL
Aquatint by T. Malton, 1797

approach as nearly as possible to the central type, with the dome the middle as the focus, rather than the east end. The dominance the dome must always have been his concern, for early in the 1680's designed the present upper storey, and shortened the nave. The up storey is particularly important, for, as an air view shows, the up ırt is simply a wall decorated with blind windows, and concealing the ıttresses of the roof; nevertheless, the screen-wall serves the double ırpose of stiffening the supports of the dome (it has the same static nction as pinnacles in a medieval flying-buttress system), while it so makes a far better build-up to the dome itself from all points of ew at ground-level, most particularly from the east, where something the effect of the Great Model can be realized. All the decorative tail of this work is much influenced by Roman Baroque architecture, ıd the best example of this is the use of motives taken from Pietro da ɔrtona's Santa Maria della Pace, in Rome, for the semicircular ›rches of the transepts. This too was decided early in the eighties, so at the years 1675–85 saw a critical period in the evolution of the thedral; these were also the years of some of his most Baroque periments in the City steeples. The west front, except for the towers, ıs perhaps also designed in the 1680's, but here Wren was severely .ndicapped by being unable to get stones large enough for a Giant rder. This is the reason for the double order of coupled columns in e portico, always regarded as one of the weakest parts of the design, ıt largely offset by the triumphant Baroque of the great west towers, ntrasting with, and yet subserving, the glorious curve of the dome ing above them. They were executed between 1705 and 1708, after e dome itself was largely settled, and they owe a great deal to Borro- ini's towers at Sant' Agnese in Agone, in Rome.[1]

In 1697 the dome itself was taken in hand, but there had been ojects before that date, and the final design evolved only in stages. In e same year Wren's salary was halved by order of Parliament because had not adhered to the warrant, which had provided for the com- etion of the choir before anything else was undertaken. There can be tle doubt that Wren realized perfectly well that, if he did as he was ld, the nave, dome, and west end would never get built, or at least t in his lifetime, and so he began the western parts before completing e choir. In December 1697 the choir was opened, but it was not until 11, when an Act of Parliament declared the building complete, that ren received the arrears of his salary.

From the very beginning Wren had intended to provide a dome, to ar over the roofs of the houses, and make a landmark comparable to e spire of Old St Paul's, and his experiment at St Stephen was to give m practice in setting a dome on eight arches. The great difficulty ıich faced him is simply that a dome high enough to serve as a ndmark—indeed, to be visible at all from the ground outside—is

[1] The influence of Borromini is also very marked in the tower of St Vedast, Foster Lane, 1694–97.

81. The Dome of St Paul's Cathedral
Detail from a drawing by R. B. Brook-Greaves and W. Godfrey Allen

cessarily set on a high drum, which gives the effect from inside the ilding of standing at the foot of a factory chimney; on the other hand, dome which looks right from the inside is scarcely more than a allow saucer. The solution to the problem had been found at St ter's more than a century earlier, where Michelangelo provided two)arate shells, not concentric. Wren's practical genius took the ution a stage farther, for he designed a semicircular dome with a ge 'eye' to close the vista upward, lit by a flood of light from the tern far above, and he supported the lantern on a great cone of ck and masonry, which is invisible from inside and outside the thedral. The actual outer dome is a mere skin of lead on a timber mework, and could therefore be designed to satisfy purely aesthetic mands, since the whole of the 850 tons of the lantern was supported the invisible cone, and buttressed by the colonnade of the drum. The onnade is interrupted at every fourth bay by a solid pier with a niche, that the monotony of an unbroken peristyle is avoided, additional ttressing is achieved, and a slight feeling of direction is obtained and ghtened by the very definite orientation of the lantern itself. In ween is the perfect curve of the dome, Wren's masterpiece, and the est of its kind.

Not the least astonishing thing about St Paul's is the fact that it was y one of the commissions Wren had in hand in the last quarter of the enteenth century and the first few years of the next. Apart from the y churches, he was responsible for several public buildings ranging m the Library of Trinity College, Cambridge (1676–84) and Tom wer, at Christ Church, Oxford (1681–82), to Hampton Court lace (1689–1700; south and east wings) and the two hospitals in itation of the Hôtel des Invalides, for Army and Navy pensioners at elsea (1682–91) and Greenwich respectively. Greenwich Hospital is finest work, apart from St Paul's, and is particularly splendid in its ting, rising from the Thames, and leading up the slight slope to the een's House. The Queen's House is, in fact, too small and too far ay to form a true central feature, but Wren had to retain it, and ve the view from it unobstructed; this he did by setting it at the end two splendid colonnades crowned by domes, but although it is tain that this splendid vista is entirely Wren's, it is at Greenwich that come up against the Wren–Hawksmoor–Vanbrugh problem. holas Hawksmoor (1661–1736) went to Wren in 1679 as a boy of hteen, and worked as his clerk on all the important buildings from out 1684. After Wren's death he became a major architect in his own ht, but his style is only now being distinguished from that of his life-g friend and collaborator, Sir John Vanbrugh (1664–1726), and it is quite certain that all three men, with Wren as leader, were respo sible for Greenwich. Greenwich Hospital was begun in 1696 in pla of a projected palace, for which Webb had already built the wing n called King Charles's Block, and Wren was in charge of the n building. The design was altered in 1699, the year after Hawksmo was made Clerk of the Works, and the year in which Vanbrugh bu into architecture. Captain Vanbrugh had been a regular soldier w was arrested in France as a spy, and imprisoned in the Bastille; next became a playwright, producing his best comedy, *The Provok'd Wife*, 1697; equally suddenly he became an architect, in 1699, when Earl of Carlisle commissioned him to design Castle Howard, in Yo shire. It seems that he had no practical experience, and he theref collaborated with Hawksmoor, but the design may well have been l for in 1702 the Earl of Carlisle got him the Comptrollership of Works, which made him Wren's principal colleague. From 1703 he v a director at Greenwich, and in 1716 he succeeded Wren as surve there; it is perhaps not unfair, therefore, to call Greenwich Hospital, the Royal Naval College as it now is, the principal work of the W School. Another similar work is the Orangery, at Kensington Pala

82. Greenwich Hospital

83. St Mary Woolnoth

84. North Front of Seaton Delaval Hall

of 1704, but here there is even less evidence to connect it with Vanbrug and present opinion tends to ascribe the new features here to Wren 'late manner' or to Hawksmoor.[1] Vanbrugh's main contribution English architecture lies in the dramatic power of his imaginatio which gives a personal stamp to all his works, even though the detai may be by Hawksmoor. Vanbrugh had an intuitive sympathy for th ruggedness of medieval buildings—for what he called 'the Castle Ai —which no other architect of his day had; Hawksmoor had a simila feeling for the grandeur of ancient Rome, but his architecture is mo sophisticated, one might almost say introverted, than the expansiv theatricality of Vanbrugh at his best—compare, for example, St Ma Woolnoth, Lombard Street, with the main front of Seaton Delav Hall in Northumberland, since here the two artists are using almo identical forms. Castle Howard, Blenheim Palace, Oxfordshire- where the dramatic setting is Vanbrugh's but many of the fine touches are Hawksmoor's—and the gaunt, romantic ruin of Seatc Delaval are Vanbrugh's major works, and it was at Blenheim that h was able to build on a titanic scale, since he conceived it "much mo

85. Blenheim Palace

[1] Dr K. Downes in his *Hawksmoor* (Zwemmer, 1959), definitely attributes it to Hawksmoor

86. St George's Church, Bloomsbury

an intended Monument of the Queen's glory than a private Habita-
on for the Duke of Marlborough"—this was because the Crown paid
r some of the palace, but not as much as the Duchess thought was
ght. The palace was begun in 1705, and the quarrel between Van-
ugh and the Duchess grew to such a point that in 1725 he was
fused admittance to his own building.

If Vanbrugh was an inspired and slightly flamboyant amateu Hawksmoor was a dedicated professional, supremely competent but once diffident and aloof; his friend Vanbrugh spoke no more than t truth when he wrote, in 1721: "Poor Hawksmoor, what a Barbaro Age have his fine, ingenious, parts fallen into. What wou'd Mons Colbert in France have given for such a man?"

Perhaps his best-known work is his completion of the western towe of Westminster Abbey, in the Gothic style he used for the outside All Souls College, Oxford (1715–40); but there the interiors are in t classic manner he loved and truly understood, as may be seen in t Clarendon Building (1712–15), also in Oxford. His finest works, hov ever, are undoubtedly the London churches built for the Commissi of 1711: St Alphege, Greenwich; St Anne, Limehouse; St George the East, Stepney[1]; St Mary Woolnoth, Lombard Street; Christchurc Spitalfields; and St George, Bloomsbury. This last was built betwe 1720 and 1730 and has a noble portico which challenges comparis with that of St Martin-in-the-Fields. It is, indeed, the contemporary St Martin's, and we have left the Age of Wren, and moved into a ne century, a new reign, and an entirely new conception of architecture

[1] Severely damaged in the Second World War.

CHAPTER 4

Gibbs and the Palladians

'OWARDS the end of Wren's very long lifetime there was a sharp :action against much of what he stood for; and when he died, in 1723, iere was a new and alien dynasty on the throne, and a new approach) architecture which he may well have found distasteful. The archi- :cture of James Gibbs, who built one of the most famous of all English hurches—St Martin-in-the-Fields—formed a link between Wren and ie eighteenth century, and it was Gibbs who helped to spread Wren's leas all over Britain, and indeed all over America as well. While Gibbs 'as building his church the new school of dogmatic followers of the talian architect Palladio (1508–80) claimed to be following in the ootsteps of Inigo Jones, and, with the powerful support of the Earl of urlington, they established what was practically an architectural ictatorship. Before we turn to their ideas and works it will be easier, ith Wren fresh in our minds, to consider the life and achievement of ames Gibbs. He was born in Aberdeen, in 1682, and he died in London, ı 1754; unlike his fellow-Scot and bitter rival, Colen Campbell, Gibbs 'as certainly a Tory (and probably a Jacobite), and a Catholic into the argain. All this, on top of being a Scot in London at the time of the Ianoverian Succession and the Jacobite Rising of 1715, was not alculated to advance any man's career, and it was perhaps fortunate)r Gibbs that Campbell died in 1729.

We now know that Gibbs went to Rome as a young man, in 1703, to udy for the priesthood at the Scots College there; after about two ears, however, he abandoned his studies and finally began to work nder Carlo Fontana (1638–1714), one of the leading exponents of ate Baroque architecture, and a notable teacher. His Italian training 'as Gibbs's greatest asset when he set up in London early in 1709, for e was almost the only architect then working in England who had ot only been to Rome and studied both ancient and modern build- ıgs there, but had also had a regular academic training under a distinguished master. This training, of course, made him sympathetic the English Baroque practised by Wren, and he was thus well qualifie to carry on the Wren tradition. His first great work was the church St Mary-le-Strand, only a few yards west of Wren's St Clement Dane and clearly showing the influence both of Rome and of Wren.

St Mary-le-Strand was built under the Act of 1711 which provide for fifty new churches—the Act responsible for the Hawksmo churches—although in fact only twelve were actually built. Wren w appointed one of the commissioners under the Act, and it was for h fellow-commissioners that he wrote his famous memorandum c church-building. Hawksmoor and Gibbs were architects to the Com mission, but Gibbs did not keep his post for long. He was appointed i 1713 and sacked in December 1715, on the return of a Whig Govern ment under the Hanoverians. Gibbs's first patrons had been the Ear of Oxford and of Mar—and it was Mar who led the 1715 Rising, an was defeated by John Campbell, Duke of Argyll, at Sheriffmuir. A Argyll was Colen Campbell's patron it soon became clear to Gibbs th he could survive in a Hanoverian and Whig world only by trimmin and from about 1720 onward he came to terms with the Whigs, wi the Church of England, and with the architectural principles Palladianism. He managed to live at first by private practice for To patrons, and he also wrote two books—*A Book of Architecture* (1728) an *Rules for Drawing the Several Parts of Architecture* (1732)—both of whic were widely read and copied in England and America, and the brought him in, according to his own account, nearly £2000—a ver considerable sum in those days.

St Mary-le-Strand was built between 1714 and 1717, and looks i many ways like a Roman palace or a Baroque church in Rome, suc as Fontana's San Marcello. The windows were set high up to keep o the noises of the Strand, and the lower range of blind niches was ther fore introduced to balance the composition, and to allow for a doub order of columns both outside and inside, although the building is on one storey high. A double range of columns had been used by S Christopher Wren in the portico of St Paul's, and both churches we implicitly criticized by Campbell when he published a *Design for Church, of my Invention* (1717) with the remarks:

> In those admirable Pieces of Antiquity, we find none of the triflin licentious, and insignificant Ornaments, so much affected by some of o Moderns . . . nor have we one Precedent either from the *Greeks* or *Roman* that they practised two Orders, one over another, in the same Temple i the Outside . . . and whereas the Ancients were contented with o

87. St Mary-le-Strand and Somerset House

Aquatint by T. Malton, 1796

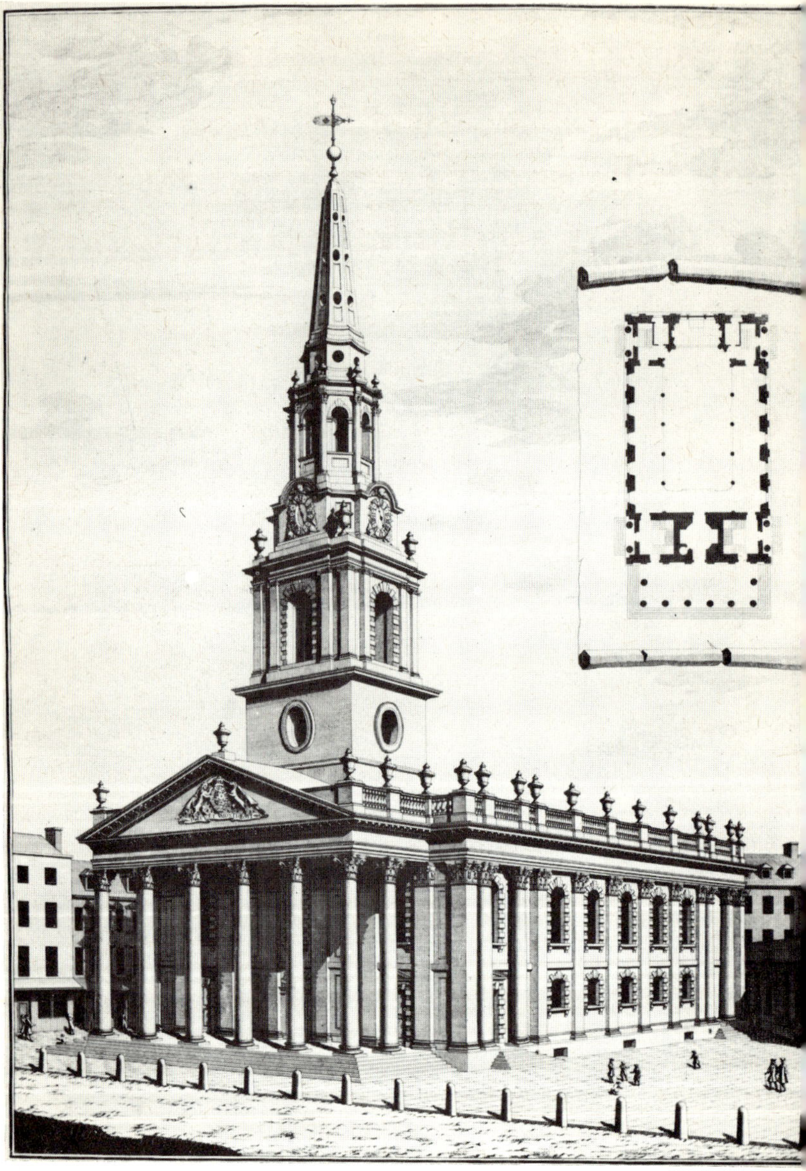

88. A Perspective View of St Martin-in-the-Fields

:ontinued Pediment . . . we now have no less than three in one Side, where .he Ancients never admitted any. This Practice must be imputed either to ın entire Ignorance of Antiquity, or a Vanity to expose their absurd Novelties. . . .

mpbell's design of his own invention is, in fact, little more than a ɔy of the Roman Temple at Nîmes. The richness of texture in bbs's design would be welcome to those people who were accustomed Wren's City churches, and the semicircular portico at the entrance St Mary-le-Strand may be taken as typical of Gibbs at this date; for s clearly reminiscent of the famous Roman church of Santa Maria la Pace, but the same idea had been used by Wren, and, as it were, turalized, in the half-domes over the side entrances of St Paul's. e beautiful little bell-turret over the main portico of St Mary is also arly inspired by Wren's City churches, but it has a rather curious tory behind it. The original design did not provide for a steeple, but re was to be a great column, 250 feet high (Nelson's Column is 184 t), with a statue of Queen Anne on the top, standing in front of the ırch. When the Queen died the idea was dropped, and Gibbs had provide a steeple on a structure which had not been designed to ry a great weight, and on top of a pediment, an architectural ecism that he was to repeat at St Martin-in-the-Fields.

In 1720 Gibbs took a party of Whig generals on a conducted tour of en's City churches, after which they accepted his designs for the uilding of the old church of St Martin-in-the-Fields (1722–26). The ırch as built differs from the early designs, and also from the model served there, but the essentials—the internal planning and the nbination of a steeple with a portico—remain unchanged.

In plan the church is a long rectangle with a big portico at the west l, the entrance front being divided into three equal bays, the central giving access to the church under the steeple, and those at the sides ng provided with staircases and separate entrances on the north and ıth sides, each expressed by deeply recessed giant columns set ween giant pilasters. These recesses are repeated at the east end, ere there are also stairs and entrances to the Royal Pews (St Martin's he Royal Parish Church). On the outside there are two rows of ıdows set between the giant pilasters, and framed with a characteris- series of heavy blocks round the openings; unlike St Mary-le-Strand, two ranges of windows here serve the purpose of lighting two levels ide, the upper ones giving on to the galleries which run round three es of the church. The use of galleries to increase the seating accom- dation was an idea taken over from Wren's churches—in this case,

St James's, Piccadilly, and St Bride's—with the central columns div ing the nave from the aisles, and carrying the galleries at the same tir The most unusual feature is the narrowing of the church at the east e to form the chancel, the incurved diagonals providing opera-b openings for the Royal Pews. The splendidly ornate plasterwork of interior is by the Italians Artari and Bagutti, who worked for most the leading architects of the time; another example of their work Gibbs can be seen in the little church of St Peter, Vere Street (Oxford Street), built in 1723–24, and to some extent a trial run St Martin's.

Externally, the best-known feature of St Martin-in-the-Fields is combination of steeple and portico, which has always pained arc tectural purists, since no classical building ever had a steeple, and very idea of a vertical element riding over a portico is fundamenta unclassical. Gibbs himself said:

> Steeples are indeed of a Gothick Extraction; but they have their Beaut when their Parts are well disposed, and when the Plans of the seve Degrees and Orders of which they are compos'd gradually diminish, a pass from one Form to another without confusion. . . .

and he seems to have seen no reason why he should not combine th beauties with the different ones inherent in the fashionable hu porticoes six columns wide.[1] The first hexastyle portico (to give it proper name) was built by Campbell at Wanstead House, in Ess before 1720, but, at the time when St Martin's was going up, oth were being applied to churches by Hawksmoor at St George's, Bloo bury, and by John James at St George's, Hanover Square. Gibbs ga considerable thought to the problem of combining such a portico w a steeple, as may be seen in the side bays, where the two recess columns marking the side entrance also seem to support the steeple o them. In the choice of forms for the actual steeple he was clea working in Wren's manner, not only in the steeple as it now exists, also in the alternative designs engraved in his *Book of Architecture*. T beauty of its subtle transitions, from the square base, rising out of body of the church and proportioned to the pediment in front of it, to the final concave-sided obelisk spire, has made it one of the be known and most imitated of buildings. One of the earliest and m faithful copies was by Henry Flitcroft—officially a Palladian, and ni named 'Burlington Harry'—in his St Giles-in-the-Fields (1731–34), the other end of Charing Cross Road. Derby Cathedral (1723–25), Gibbs himself, is based on the same idea.

[1] Wren's Memorandum advocates both steeples and porticoes.

Outside London Gibbs's most important work was for the Univer-ies of Oxford and Cambridge, although one of his last works was to ovide a free design for the West Church of St Nicholas, in his native berdeen. At Oxford he took over from Hawksmoor, and built the adcliffe Camera, or Library, between 1737 and 1749. He was very oud of this splendid building for the Tory University, and he ıblished a book of engravings to commemorate it, in 1747.

89. THE RADCLIFFE CAMERA, OXFORD

The Camera consists of two concentric cylinders, the inner of which ses above the outer, and is covered by a dome reminiscent simul-neously of St Peter's, in Rome, and St Paul's, in London. In fact, the rcular design had been projected by Hawksmoor in 1715, and he in rn was drawing on a design by Wren for a circular building near . Paul's and another for a projected Mausoleum in memory of harles I, which Wren had designed in 1678, before Gibbs was born. ı spite of this, and in spite of the air of Ancient Rome which Hawks-oor imparted to the whole scheme, Gibbs can take the credit for the adcliffe Camera as it stands, beautifully sited on an open piazza ehind St Mary's Church, and with University buildings on the other three sides. In a largely Gothic area it combines something of Ancie Rome with still more of the Rome of the Renaissance and the Baroq —which Gibbs had known at first hand—and it adds to this an i debtedness to Wren that never lapses into servile imitation; th perhaps, is no bad epitaph on Gibbs himself.

The architectural equivalent of the victory of the Hanoveri dynasty and of Whig principles is provided by the almost total domir tion of Lord Burlington's circle over the whole field of English arcl tecture. In literature and in the common-sense philosophy of Jo Locke and his disciples there was a marked impulse towards the virtu of moderation and harmony, and a tendency to play down the mc dramatic style of artists like Wren and Vanbrugh—the differen between Milton's *Paradise Lost* and Pope's *Essay on Man* is essentia the same difference as that between St Paul's and Chiswick Villa: bo are perfect of their kind. Pope was to become a friend of Lord Burlir ton, who was only seventeen when the *Essay on Criticism* was publish in 1711, but it contains the lines:

> Learn hence for ancient rules a just esteem;
> To copy Nature is to copy them

and this equation of classical antiquity with the very laws of Natu was later part of Burlington's own creed. In 1731 Pope dedicat Epistle IV of his *Moral Essays* to Burlington, now his friend, and in he addresses Burlington directly:

> You too proceed! make falling arts your care,
> Erect new wonders, and the old repair;
> Jones and Palladio to themselves restore,
> And be whate'er Vitruvius was before . . .

Inigo Jones, Palladio, and Vitruvius—the seventeenth-century Englis man, the sixteenth-century Italian, and the ancient Roman were to the tutelary deities of the new movement, and when we see why Po specified these three names we can understand what Lord Burlingto life-work was, and the nature of the architectural revolution acco plished by him and his two closest associates, Colen Campbell a William Kent.

The great victories won by British troops under Marlborough Blenheim, Ramillies, Oudenarde, and Malplaquet—were all gain between 1704 and 1709, and culminated in the Peace of Utrecht

13; the peace had two interesting consequences, for it meant that the ntinent was once more open to travellers, and it confirmed the eady high opinion of themselves held by Englishmen in the early hteenth century. The Grand Tour had already begun to form an portant part of the education of a rich young Englishman, and for : rest of the century it was to remain the most important single tor in the process of civilizing him. Usually he went to France, and n on to Venice, where he might stay several months, and so on to rence and Rome, where a year was not exceptionally long to stay, d so to Naples, and then home. Travelling was difficult and expensive, that this one long trip was all he ever undertook; but it broadened mind, and brought him into contact with the remains of classical tiquity—and he had been brought up on a diet of little else but Latin d Greek literature. The new feeling of national pride in the place n by British arms in European affairs easily combined with his ssical upbringing to form the idea that Vitruvius, the only architect the ancient world about whom anything much was known, should the guide of the British architect, the more so since Inigo Jones had ought the classic tradition back to England, and had interpreted it ording to Palladio. Palladio's book *I Quattro Libri dell'Architettura* was t published in 1570, and was based on the treatise by Vitruvius, so t he naturally fell into place beside the other two, and one of the st important English translations of his Four Books began to appear 1715.

In the same year the then unknown Scottish architect Colen Camp- l published the first volume of his *Vitruvius Britannicus*—the title is nificant—a collection of large engravings of British buildings of the enteenth and eighteenth centuries. The last volume he supervised nself came out in 1725, so that the eighteenth-century buildings are earlier than that date, and quite a number of them are designs of mpbell's own which were never executed. The Preface to Volume I manifesto of the new Palladian movement, and has a familiar ring. says that foreign things are often praised more than English, hough it is fair to admit that architecture owes much to Italians:

. . above all the great *Palladio*, who has exceeded all that were gone before im and surpassed his Contemporaries; whose ingenious Labours will clipse many, and rival most of the Ancients. . . . With him the great Manner and exquisite Taste of Building is lost; for the *Italians* can now no nore relish the Antique Simplicity, but are entirely employed in capricious Ornaments, which must at last end in the *Gothick*. . . .

It is then with the renowned *Palladio* we enter the Lists, to whom we oppose the famous *Inigo Jones*. Let the *Banqueting-House*, those excell pieces at *Greenwich*, with many other Things of the great Master, be ca fully examined; and I doubt not, but an impartial Judge will find in th all the Regularity of the former, with an Addition of Beauty and Maje in which our *Architect* is esteemed to have outdone all that went before. And here I cannot but reflect on the Happiness of the *British* Nation, t at present abounds with so many learned and ingenious Gentlemen. .

The three people who created and carried on the new movem were Colen Campbell (*d.* 1729), Richard Boyle, third Earl of Burling and fourth Earl of Cork (1694–1753), and William Kent (1685–174 There can be little doubt that the actual creation was the work Campbell, for there are several designs of his in *Vitruvius Britannicus* 1715 which are expressly stated to be in the manner of Inigo Jones Palladio (*Designs for the Duke of Argyll and Lord Islay*, both of th Campbells); and in 1715 Lord Burlington was making his Gra Tour in Italy, and Kent was living in Rome, working as a painter a as a guide to the English visitors. Campbell's first big work was W stead House, near London, begun in 1715 but demolished a cent later, which was chiefly important for its great hexastyle porti claimed to be the first in England. This was copied from the fronts antique temples, since Palladio had thought—quite wrongly—t ancient houses must also have had such porticoes.

Lord Burlington seems to have taken a great interest in the n movement from the moment he returned from Italy in 1715; and helped with the publication of the second volume of *Vitruvius Britann* (1717), employed Campbell to remodel Burlington House, in Piccad (parts survive as the Royal Academy), and finally became his pupil architecture. In 1719 Burlington returned to Italy to visit Palladi buildings in Vicenza, and to buy many of Palladio's drawings (th are now in the Royal Institute of British Architects). When he returr to London he brought Kent back with him, and the two men beca lifelong friends and partners, with Burlington acting as the gene designer, and Kent concentrating on interior decoration, furnitu design, and the layout of gardens.

The first two important buildings were both Campbell's, and w both designed before 1723, when they were well advanced in buildi They were Houghton Hall, in Norfolk, for the Prime Minister, Robert Walpole, and Mereworth Castle, in Kent. Houghton v designed as a house of great state and magnificence for the m important politician of the day, but it was completed by others, a Campbell's original ideas were considerably modified. He intended ıse to be very like Wilton—that is, very like Inigo Jones—and the ɜst remaining part of his design is undoubtedly the Stone Hall, a ɔe of 40 feet, which recalls the Queen's House, but has a cold and ique magnificence of its own. Much of the decoration at Houghton s actually due to Kent, and to the great sculptor, John Michael sbrack.

Campbell's masterpiece is the strangely named Mereworth Castle, ich is a very close copy of the famous Villa Rotonda outside Vicenza, gun by Palladio in the 1550's, and one of the most famous of all his rks. Campbell published his own design, and invited connoisseurs to npare it with the Palladian original, so there can be no question of copying another man's work, and hoping nobody would notice. In t, the differences between the two are quite considerable, the most ɔortant being that, to Palladio, exact symmetry was of supreme ue, and he therefore made all four sides of the house exactly the ıe, repeating the great entrance portico on all sides, and arranging rooms identically in each quarter of the square plan. Campbell ɔt the square plan, with a central dome, but only two of his porticoes e main entrance and the garden one) have steps up to them, the e pair being purely decorative. The house was originally intended, one of Palladio's villas, to be used only for short periods, and so re were not many rooms. The two principal ones are the central, cular hall, which is superbly decorated in the Italian manner by gutti with swags and statues, and the Long Gallery which runs the ole length of the house on the garden front. The hall is very like the l of any of Palladio's villas; but they were designed to keep out the t of the Italian sun, and Campbell provided no chimneys (since ladio's villas obviously did not need any); but he arranged for the ɔke to escape from the top of the lantern of the dome by means of an enious arrangement of flues between the two shells of the dome. The lery is more traditionally an English type of room for receiving npany, and here Campbell kept closer to the model provided by es, but the detailing and the general richness of effect are Campbell's n contribution, and make Mereworth unmistakably an eighteenth-tury English house, and not just a copy of a sixteenth-century Italian .

Palladio's Villa Rotonda and Campbell's Mereworth inspired ɔther and finer imitation at the hands of Lord Burlington himself, in own villa at Chiswick, then just outside London. This was begun ore 1726, by which time Burlington and Campbell seem to have ırrelled, and was the work of Burlington himself, except for the help received from Kent in the interior decoration, and in the layout of the garden; and it is the first example of their happy collaboratio Chiswick Villa is a more subtle and sophisticated version of the Vi Rotonda than Mereworth, partly because Burlington had actually se the villas of Palladio, and also the remains of ancient Rome, a Campbell had not; partly because Burlington used Palladio, not mer as a model to copy, but as a guide to understanding the achieveme of Roman architecture. The plan of Chiswick Villa is complicat

90. Chiswick Villa

more complicated than either Mereworth or Palladio's villa; and two reasons, for the plan of Chiswick is fundamentally different fr that of the Villa Rotonda in that it is not symmetrical and has a vari of room-shapes. The important difference is in the abandonment Palladio's guiding principle of symmetry, for the Villa Rotonda biaxially symmetrical—that is, strictly symmetrical about the nor south axis and also the east–west one. The villa at Chiswick, m sensibly if less mathematically, has one main or entrance front, c garden front, and two identical side fronts, and each façade is trea

[1] It has recently been superbly restored by the Ministry of Works, which is now respon for its upkeep.

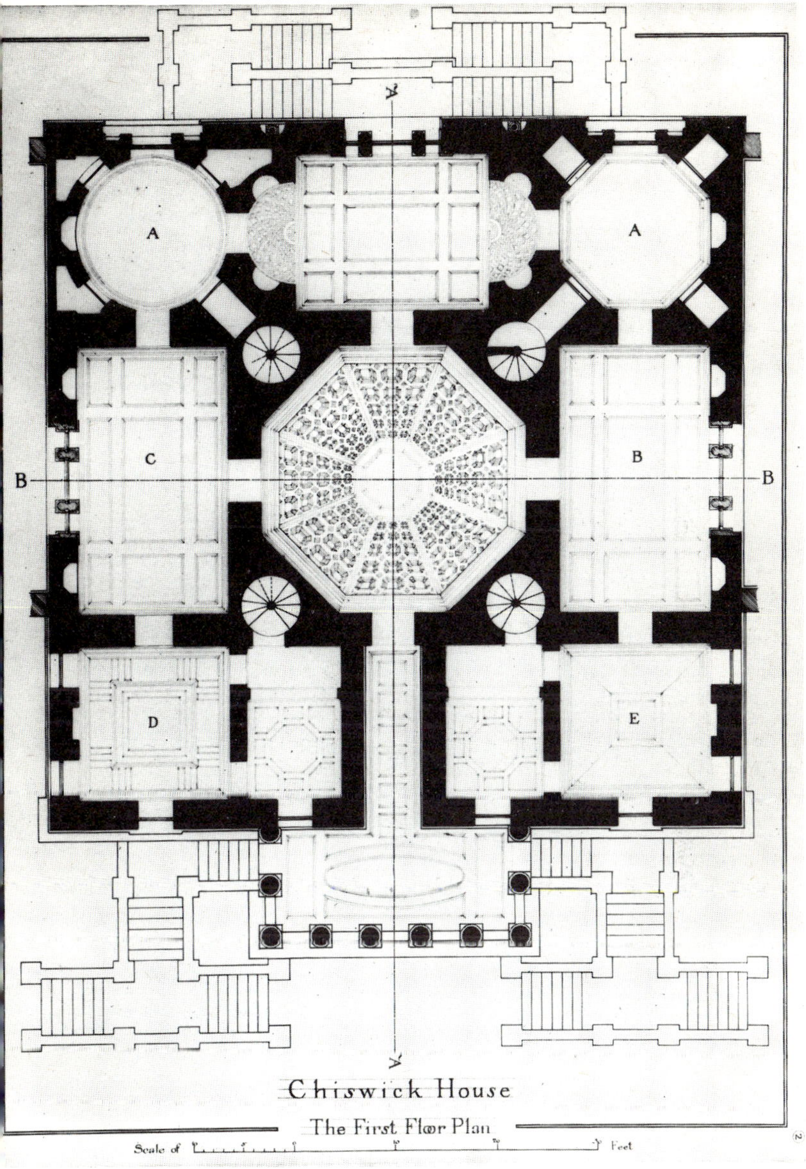

91. Plan of Chiswick Villa

according to its function. Thus, only the entrance front has a portic but it is a grand hexastyle one, flanked by imposing double stairs. Tl garden front also has a stair, but the façade is more decoratively treat with three large windows looking out on to the garden. The plan al shows that the design of the house is strictly symmetrical about tl main axis—which runs through the house from the portico to tl garden—but there is also a variety of room-shapes, some rectangula some round, and one—the main room on the garden side—a lo rectangle with apses at each end. Finally, the great central hall octagonal. This variety of spatial treatment does not derive fro Palladio's example but from classical antiquity, for the Romans bui many of their great baths with such shapes, and Lord Burlington kne this from the drawings of the ruins made by Palladio himself; the were the drawings purchased by Burlington in Italy in 1719, some which he published in 1730.

For all its grandeur Chiswick is quite small, since it was intended be no more than a *villa suburbana* in the Roman sense, and in accordan with this classical ideal it has only one main storey, and was nev intended to have suites of bedrooms for guests. The interior is both ric and classical, and is mainly the work of Kent, as is also the garden wi its temples, statues, and canal in imitation of the Brenta canal whic runs by so many of Palladio's villas. This particular piece of Italianis must surely have been the work of Kent, the history-painter from Hu whose Roman years had left such an impression that he could write in letter:

> I am still at work here the days being so short and cold to an Itali constitution that I keep my little room, only twice a week that I go to tl Operas where I am highly entertain'd, and then think myself out of th Gothick countery. Engagements I have for more work makes all the power-spirited [*i.e.*, poor-spirited] English daubers raile, and make part against me . . . [Hogarth and Thornhill certainly railed against him- see, for example, Hogarth's engraving *Burlington Gate*].

Soon after this, in 1730–32, Lord Burlington was able to buil another rigidly classical reconstruction of an antique basilica as tl Assembly Rooms at York, but the last of the great works produced l Burlington and Kent in partnership was the huge house for Thom Coke, later Earl of Leicester—Holkham Hall, in Norfolk. This is n far from Houghton, and was intended to be even grander and mo classical, and some of the design may be attributed to Coke himse who had made a Grand Tour, met Kent in Rome, and returned fille

92. Holkham Hall

with an ambition to collect editions of Livy, classical sculpture, and have a suitably antique house to put them in. Building did not beg until 1734, and went on for nearly thirty years, after both Kent a Burlington were dead, but the house is their monument. Several desig by Kent for the main façades are known, but none was executed wit out modification; it seems that Kent would propose some rich a imaginative design, which would then be pared down, and made mc austere, by Coke or Burlington or both. An example of their passion f antiquity is the fact that the house is built of brick; Coke, in Rome, h picked up a piece of ancient brick, which is tawny in colour, a different in size and texture from modern English brick, and h brought it home as a souvenir. He found that it could be reproduced a near-by brickworks, and so the 'classical' brick was used for the hou instead of stone (which would admittedly also be dearer). Nowada the vast expanse of this rather dreary brick, made much barer by t fact that all the windows have had their glazing-bars[1] removed a plate-glass inserted—thus ruining the careful balance of void and soli and the feeling for the texture of the wall as a whole, that are among t principal subtleties of good eighteenth-century building—inevitab makes one think of barracks; but the contrast with the interior is the stronger. It must always be remembered that the eighteent century Whig liked a contrast between an austere exterior (which would have equated with the Roman virtue of *gravitas*) and pomp a magnificence in the interior. When the architects were Burlington a Kent it happened all the more that the two aspects should be so co trasted, and, for sheer state, there is hardly another room in England rival the hall at Holkham; and it is a highly informative sidelight the great Whigs that such a room should be built in a country house f the reception of antique statues. Three points about the design serve give an idea of its richness and complexity: first, the change of lev from the main floor to the saloon at the end is used to provide the ma element in the design—the rise of the stair and the vista through t colonnade beyond. The change of level provides a high base on whi to set a colonnade—that is, an antique basilica type which has internal colonnade and a richly coffered roof: the elaborate frieze taken from the Temple of Fortuna Virilis, in Rome. The apsidal e and the coffering above are also antique, but the idea of a vista throu a colonnade is taken from one of Palladio's churches, for Burlingt himself wrote of San Giorgio Maggiore, Venice: "an open int columniation discovers the choir, it ends in a semicircle—most beau ful." The ceiling owes much to Inigo Jones, being based on one of

[1] The glazing-bars were originally gilt.

93. The Circus, Bath

rawings owned by Burlington; and thus it is possible to see, at Iolkham, the combination of Vitruvius, Palladio, and Jones which ope recommended in the passage quoted earlier.

Kent died in 1748 and Burlington in 1753, and the stricter forms of alladianism died with them; but their ideas were to remain pro-oundly influential for at least the rest of the century. Sir William hambers is sometimes called "the last of the Palladians," and he ertainly remained true to ideals of Roman classicism; his work is iscussed in the next chapter. Perhaps even more important was the nfluence exerted by the Palladians on much less exalted architects, on peculative builders, and country gentlemen building with the help of ocal craftsmen. Their work still exists in large quantities in almost very old town, and the traditions they started were often carried on or generations. The most famous of them were architects of national nportance such as John Carr (1723–1807) of York, and, perhaps the nost famous of all, the two Woods of Bath. John Wood the Elder 1704–54) and his son John (1728–81) were responsible between them or most of the building of Bath; and above all they were responsible or the development of the town in an orderly way as the finest piece of

large-scale town-planning then attempted in Britain. The layout o
such schemes as Queen Square, the Circus, and the Royal Crescen
assure their fame more than any single building, fine as are Prior Par
or the New Assembly Rooms, for these street-designs established th
standard type of town-layout in Britain.

CHAPTER 5

Chambers and the Adam Brothers; the Greek, the Gothick, and the Picturesque

AFTER Lord Burlington died in 1753 the rest of the century was dominated by two architects who had just enough in common to dislike each other heartily: they were Sir William Chambers and Robert Adam. Nowadays there are people who would claim that Robert Adam was the greatest of British architects, greater even than Wren, but this would certainly not have been the case in the eighteenth century, except in the Adam family circle, for two of his brothers spent their whole careers in fostering Robert's genius, and in making sure that the rest of the world was aware of it and of the Adam Revolution.

Both Chambers and Robert Adam were ambitious Scots who settled in London at almost the same moment with the intention of becoming the leader of what was gradually developing into the architectural profession; without the other one, either of them could have done this, but, in fact, the two rivals had to share the distinction between them, Chambers getting most of the official honours and Adam most of the publicity. The situation was not unlike the rivalry between their contemporaries, Sir Joshua Reynolds and Thomas Gainsborough, and this professional rivalry alone would have made them antagonists, but their antagonism was much sharpened by their disagreement over what constituted good architecture; for, as we might guess, Sir William Chambers, R.A., was an upholder of tradition as well as one of the principal Founder Members of the Royal Academy and its first Treasurer, and Robert Adam was an innovator who was never elected to the Academy.

William Chambers was born in 1723 in Gothenburg, Sweden, the son of a Scottish merchant who had settled there. While he was still very young he was sent to England to be educated, and then, as a young man, he sailed to China in the service of the Swedish East India Company; not until he was twenty-six did he take up architecture, and then he spent a year studying in Paris and another five years in Italy.

In 1755 he returned to England and set up in practice. The fact that h had been to China was useful to him when he was first making himse known, for he wrote a book about Chinese buildings which caught th public taste, and as a result he was commissioned to lay out Kew Gardens and to build some ornamental and exotic temples there including the Pagoda, which still stands in the Gardens, now rathe forlorn. He also had the good fortune to be appointed architectura tutor to the Prince of Wales (who became George III in 1760) and wa thus soon well established. In 1761 he was made one of the two Archi tects of the Works—but the other one was Robert Adam. His years i France and Italy had given him great prestige in his profession (prestige also possessed by Robert Adam), and they also meant that h was in touch with the latest developments in Paris and Rome, wher most of the leading architects were his personal friends; he was able therefore, to supply a cosmopolitan touch which enlivened the Palla dian tradition he inherited from Kent and Burlington, a traditio which was beginning to wear thin by the time George III came to th throne. Chambers, like Reynolds, was able to give fresh intellectua authority to the classical tradition they inherited, and the Roya Academy was important in the lives of both men. It was founded b George III in 1768, with Chambers playing a leading part in th negotiations which preceded the actual foundation. Reynolds wa knighted and made the first President, but Chambers was mad Treasurer, a position which gave him great power, greater in som ways than Reynolds enjoyed, since he was responsible to the King Although he was not knighted the King allowed him, in 1770, to use Swedish knighthood that had been conferred upon him as if it were a English one.

In spite of all this, if Chambers had died then he would have bee forgotten now, for his masterpiece was not begun until 1776 and too ten years to build; indeed, a good deal of it was not built for man years after that. This is Somerset House, in the Strand, intended fror the beginning to be a grand public building, housing part of the Civi Service, and also some of the learned societies under royal patronage including the Royal Academy itself. There had been no great publi building of this kind in England since Greenwich Hospital, and one c the first things Chambers did was to revisit Paris to study Frenc Government buildings at first hand. Detailed analysis of Somerse House reveals how much he learned from his renewed study of Frencl work, but it also shows how much he had learned from the whol European tradition, for his masterpiece is a wonderfully comple arrangement of ideas and details taken from the entire range of archi

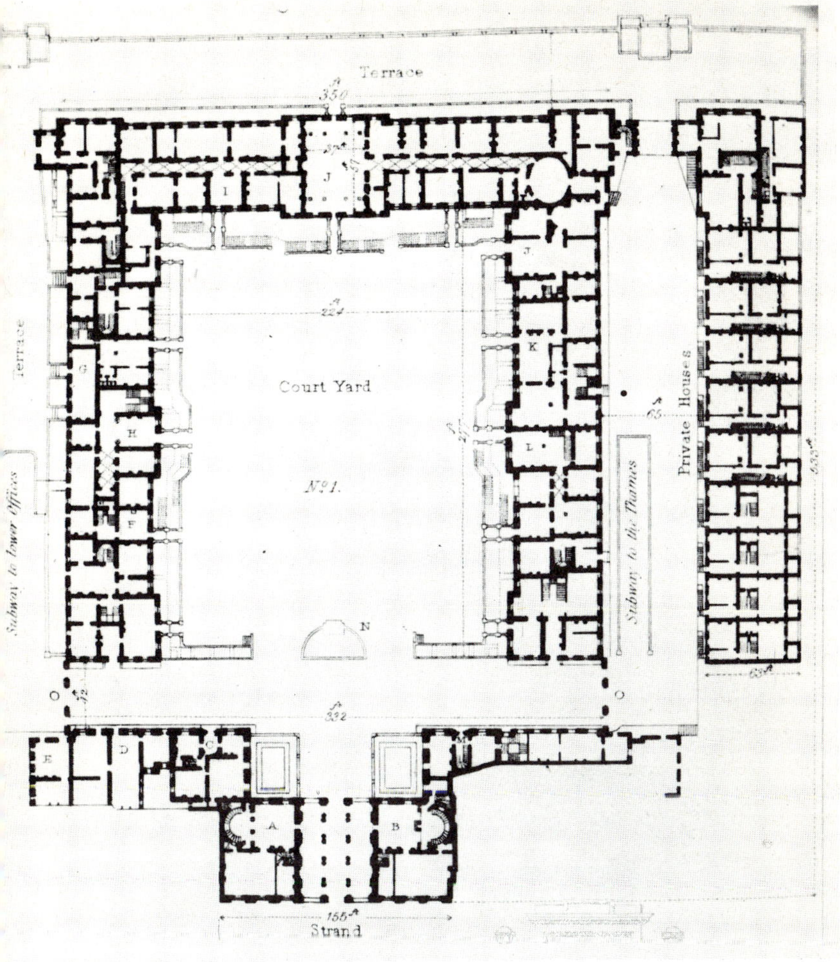

94. Plan of Somerset House

:ctural history as it was then understood—that is to say, Roman and ·alian Renaissance and French seventeenth- and eighteenth-century ·ork, but certainly not Greek or Gothic, both of which Chambers ·athed. Somerset House is learned, it is rich but sober, grand but ·strained: it is a great building but not an original one.

Nowadays it is difficult to see the building as Chambers designed it, ·xcept from inside the main quadrangle. This is because the east and ·est sides were built in the nineteenth century on space which Cham- ·ers left for expansion (the east wing, by Sir R. Smirke, is now King's

College, in the University of London); the south front, facing the rive has had its effect entirely altered by the construction of the Emban ment; while the north front, facing the Strand, though untouched, h had its scale and importance totally disrupted by the towering cliff Bush House opposite. Almost all the interior is inaccessible, and is, any case, now divided up into the dreariest kind of Government office

The plan is governed by two factors: the need to house the Gover ment offices and, separately, the learned societies, including space f the Academy exhibitions and schools; and, secondly, the difficult sit The ground slopes steeply downward from the Strand to the river, ar at the same time the river frontage is much longer than the Strand on For this reason the Strand front[1] is a separate block containing t learned societies, and is rather more elaborately treated than the rest the composition or, as Chambers himself put it:

> The vestibule opens to the most frequented street in London, is a gener passage to every part of the whole design, and the apartments are intende for the reception of useful learning and the polite arts, where, it is humb presumed, specimens of elegance should at least be attempted.

This sedate eighteenth-century prose exactly reflects the character the architecture, which is a splendid restatement of an Italian pala theme, with references to the parts of Old Somerset House the believed to be by Inigo Jones, and to contemporary French designs well. All the details are beautifully executed, and the rich decorativ sculpture was commissioned from Chambers's fellow-R.A.'s; th surviving interior details show the same conscientious craftsmanship.

The Government offices proper lay on three sides of the central cou with the south block as the principal one, much longer on the river sic than the court side. It has a small dome over a central pediment, b these are hardly big enough in scale to go with the court side, and fa too small to go with the long river-front. This is enormously long (abou 350 feet), and Chambers has done his best to break the monotony b subtle alternations of smooth and rusticated stonework, by the ver dramatic river-arches which originally served as a base for the whol but are now stranded on the Embankment, and above all by th 'bridges' with open screens of columns which punctuate the ends of th façade. It is in details like the ranging of columns over the arches o the court side or the alternation of rusticated and smooth wall, colum and window, on the river side that Chambers shows his mastery c classical design. Somerset House makes no grand gestures, but it beautifully modulated, and it was its builder's answer to the sel

[1] See page 189.

lvertisement of the Adams' river-side scheme at the Adelphi, a few undred yards to the west.

Chambers died in 1796. Robert Adam was born in 1728, and died in 792. He was the second son of William Adam, perhaps the best cottish architect of his day, and a man of some substance, for his dest son, John, became a landowner, and both Robert and James ıade their Italian journeys in considerably more state than young chitects could normally afford. Robert matriculated at Edinburgh niversity in 1743, but his architectural career did not really begin ntil 1754 when he went to France, and then on to Rome, where he ayed until 1757. There he met many of the English lords and gentleen who were making the Grand Tour and who were later of great elp to him in his career. In 1757 he went to Spalatro (now called plit) in Dalmatia, and in five weeks he and his assistants measured and ew the ruins of the Palace of the Emperor Diocletian (284–305), ıblishing the drawings as a book in 1764. His object in doing this was vofold; he wanted to produce a book which would make his name ıown when he set up in practice, since this was the usual way for an nbitious young architect to get himself talked about, and, at the same me, he wanted to break away from the usual type of such books. He anted to study the remains of ancient domestic architecture, rather ıan the baths and temples which had been studied so often before, and e also wanted to publish the ruins of a palace outside Rome itself, for ıis was the time when discoveries were being made in places as far way as Asia Minor and Greece. In fact, Robert Adam was himself sentially a domestic architect—a builder of town or country houses— ıd he was able thus to justify some of his new ideas on the grounds that ey had classical authority. He succeeded in making his name known, r he set up in practice in London in 1758, although the book was not tually published until six years later. Almost at once he broke away om the rigidity of Lord Burlington's followers, and introduced a whole ries of new, elegant, decorative motives, some based on Pompeian emes (Pompeii and Herculaneum were discovered in mid-eighteenth ntury), and some based on Italian Renaissance forms (which, in rn, were based on classical ones). This was the greater part of the dam Revolution, and it very soon became the common property of ost London architects and builders: indeed, it has lasted almost to is day. The remainder of the revolution consisted of ideas connected ith what the brothers called Movement, which in itself had close ıks with the theory of the Picturesque. The first volume of the *Works Architecture of Robert and James Adam*, published in 1773, explains hat they set out to do: "We flatter ourselves, we have been able to seize, with some degree of success, the beautiful spirit of antiquity, and transpose it, with novelty and variety, through all our numerous works They pride themselves on having brought about "a greater moveme and variety in the outside composition and in the decoration of t inside an almost total change"; they have banished "the massi entablature, the ponderous compartment ceiling, the tabernac frame," and in their place they have "adopted a beautiful variety light mouldings, gracefully formed, delicately enriched and arrang with propriety and skill." The book was published when they we meeting with difficulties, and it is easy to detect the note of se advertisement, yet it is none the less true that most of these qualiti were theirs; above all, that of movement in the outside compositi which is more fully defined in connexion with the south front Kedleston Hall, Derbyshire (*c.* 1765–70, but never completed):

> Movement is . . . the rise and fall, the advance and recess with oth diversity of form, in the different parts of a building, so as to add great to the Picturesque of the composition. For the rising and falling, advanci and receding, with the convexity and concavity, and other forms of t great parts, have the same effect in architecture, that hill and dale, for ground and distance, swelling and sinking, have in landscape. That they serve to produce an agreeable and diversified contour, that grou and contrasts like a picture, which gives great spirit, beauty, and effect the composition.

The fully developed Adam style may be studied in a number houses, for they were very busy architects, but two of the best a Osterley Park House, Middlesex, and Syon House, Brentford, Middlesex, both near London, and both begun quite soon after Robe set up in practice. Osterley was begun in 1761, and was worked on f more than eighteen years, while Syon was begun in 1762, and finish in 1769. Both were old houses which were more or less drastica remodelled to bring them up to the much higher standards of comfo and luxury demanded by the eighteenth century. Syon was an Eliz bethan house, a hollow square in plan, and therefore containing series of rooms, each of them long and narrow, and opening one in the other. Adam proposed to fill the square internal courtyard with great rotunda for the reception of guests, but this idea was dropped, ar his executed work consists of a series of rooms beginning with t entrance hall, and continuing through an anteroom, dining-room, ar drawing-room to the Long Gallery, which takes up the whole of t back of the house. The hall is very large and formal, almost entire white, with a black-and-white marble floor and a high ceiling, since

95. Kedleston Hall

96. Syon House, the Anteroom

runs the whole height of the house. Because of uneven floor-levels th are short flights of steps at either end, one of which leads to the ar room. This was intended as a waiting-room for liveried servants, an forms the strongest possible contrast to the severe hall, for it is qu small, nearly square in plan, and lavish in gilt and coloured decorat to the point of vulgarity (Adam also worked for the same family at C Northumberland House, in London, and a fragment now in Victoria and Albert Museum shows that the decoration used there, gilt lead and metal foil under plate-glass, was vulgar in the extrem The anteroom at Syon contains twelve columns of antique mar dredged from the Tiber and ranged round the walls; this is purely decorative effect, but the arrangement of one side, with the colun standing well away from the wall instead of against it, allowed Ad to make the room appear square although it is actually 30 × 36½ fe After the highly coloured anteroom comes the dining-room, followed the Red Drawing-room, which is little more than an anteroom to Long Gallery, and was intended to keep out the smell of food and noise of the gentlemen drinking after dinner. The Long Gallery was course, part of the Tudor house, and was adapted by Adam a drawing-room 136 feet long, but only 14 feet wide and 14 feet high. met this difficulty by splitting the room up into five main bays oppo eleven windows, so that the apparent length is reduced. The decorat is also kept very low in relief, but at the same time intricate, so that c looks at it piece by piece.

In 1761 Adam began work at Osterley (now a department of Victoria and Albert Museum), not far from Syon, and, like it, a Tu house which was now to be modernized. A large part of one side o was knocked down to make the splendid double portico, or propyl which gives entrance to the central court, and stands opposite the fr door. It is derived partly from the Propylaea, at Athens, and pa from the Temple of the Sun, at Palmyra, both of which were known Adam from books published a few years earlier. This choice of n Roman models shows a breadth of taste that Chambers disliked; bu is also part of the movement known as Neoclassicism, which was be formulated in Italy and France in the middle years of the century, a of which Adam was one of the leading British exponents. The so-cal Etruscan Room at Osterley, designed about 1775–79, is a good exam of this style, which was also very much in vogue during the 1770's wh several Etruscan rooms were decorated, but almost all have perish They were called Etruscan because they were based on the colo schemes of early Greek vases, which were then thought to be the w of the Etruscan forerunners of Roman civilization; the vases themsel

97. The Etruscan Room, Osterley Park House

·e copied, and the new style spread, by the great potter, Josiah dgwood, who called his new works Etruria (a name they still bear). : flat decoration with strong colours, based on reddish-brown, black, l yellow, and the more or less Greek motives employed in the uscan Room at Osterley, are not only important as an example of a c fashionable style; they are also evidence of the truly international ition occupied by Robert Adam in the Neoclassic movement which ninated the architecture of the whole of Europe in the second half of eighteenth century.

n 1768 the brothers began a great scheme for the building of lium-sized houses for professional people on top of warehouses and lts beside the Thames and running up to the Strand. This was ed the Adelphi (Greek for 'the brothers'), and was a most ambitious lertaking, but unfortunately it was dogged by bad luck, and nearly ıed the Adam family. Most of it was pulled down in 1936. In the o's Robert designed a number of large and splendid town houses, a l in which he was unsurpassed, and which helped to regain some of r losses. The finest surviving house of this group is Home House,

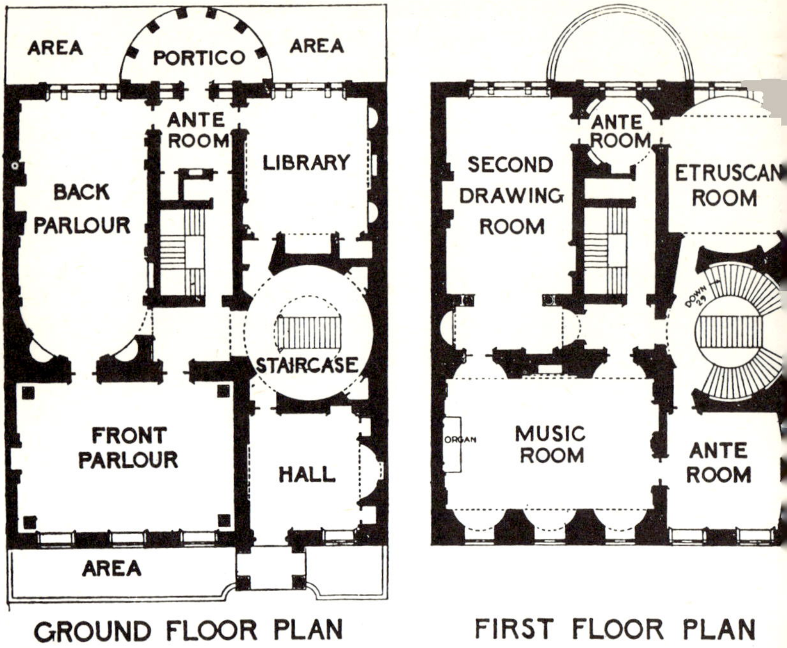

98. Plan of Home House, London

20 Portman Square, London, built for the Dowager Countess of Ho in 1773–77, and now the Courtauld Institute of Art in the Universit London.

The plan is splendidly adapted to the purpose of the house—that the provision of a suitably dignified setting for the formal lives led the wealthy people who inhabited these great houses. Home Hous not very big—it was built for a childless widow in her seventie although it has a wide frontage. The ground floor is divided up int hall, which leads into the centre of the house, occupied by the stairw and from this point the house opens out into parlour, dining-room, library, with a small service stair tucked away inconspicuously, centrally placed. The stairwell is most important since it is the o means of lighting the centre of the house, and the dome at the to used to flood the grand staircase with light. The need to gain li dictated the placing of the stairwell, and that in turn meant that front door was placed off-centre, an abandonment of the symmetri façade that would have been unthinkable to a Palladian thirty ye earlier. The three large windows to the left of the front door can n be used to light a single room, which, since it faces south and looks ı to the square, was the general living-room. The arrangement of the ning-room and the library shows equal care for planning, coupled ith subtle variations of shape in the rooms themselves, making for ıriety, or 'movement,' as Robert Adam called it.

On the first floor there is a sequence of rooms leading from the

99. The Staircase, Home House

ɔuntess's boudoir, through a very highly coloured music-room with a ost elaborate ceiling into a ballroom, and so through a tiny anteroom to the Etruscan bedroom, now restored to its original colour-scheme, ɛe the one at Osterley. These were all state rooms, and so they present with the Adam style at its most decorative. They show the greatest tention to detail, such as the ormoulu door-handles, and even the doors emselves, which are inlaid with satinwood, holly, and ebony on a ahogany framework. A set of very highly finished drawings for Home ouse is in the Soane Museum, London, among the collection of some ght thousand Adam drawings there, and they give a very good idea the meticulous way in which Robert Adam designed everything ɔwn to door-knobs and candlesticks. This tireless attention to detail is good part of the secret of the unity of style, the feeling that every part fits every other part, so that no change could be made without spoili the whole effect, which is what made Robert Adam famous, and w continue to keep him so.

Towards the end of his life Adam had a chance to realize his desi to build on a grand scale, to show that he could do more than bui admirable houses. His work in Fitzroy Square, London, and, above a in Edinburgh, shows what he could do, but unfortunately it was con pleted and altered by others: the General Register House of Scotla (1774–92), at Edinburgh, was his answer to Chambers's Somers House, although it was actually begun a little earlier. Adam's work the university was begun in 1789, but was drastically altered in 181 and again later, and finally his splendid layout of a whole group houses and a church, Charlotte Square, was also altered but enough it remains to serve as an example of large-scale planning.

So eminently successful an artist was bound to be imitated, and t first man who caused him some trouble was James Wyatt (1746–181 whose Pantheon in Oxford Street, now demolished, was a nine day wonder in 1772, when it was opened as a place of entertainment. H name was made overnight—Horace Walpole, in one of his bursts enthusiasm, called it "the most beautiful building in England"—b Wyatt was little more than an imitator of Robert Adam, and h reputation suffered later because of his haphazard conduct of h business affairs, and later still because of his incursions into the Goth style. Heaton Hall, now part of Manchester City Art Gallery, is good example of his 'Adam' style, and even has an Etruscan Room, b he is better remembered as the architect of Fonthill Abbey, Wiltshir and the restorer of Salisbury, Durham, and other cathedrals where h activities gained him the nickname of 'Wyatt the Destroyer' from lat generations of antiquaries. In fact, the eighteenth century regard Gothic architecture as rude and barbarous until, about the middle the century, Horace Walpole and others began to build in the 'Gothi Taste,' just as Chippendale, for example, was designing Gothick chai All through the second half of the century the Gothick was an amusi style for small and unimportant buildings, and was never intended challenge the absolute supremacy of the Roman classical style. It w simply a new thrill, like the Gothick novels of Walpole, Beckfor 'Monk' Lewis, and others; indeed Horace Walpole's Strawberry Hi Twickenham, begun in 1753, and William Beckford's Fonthill Abb were the two great monuments of the style, and it has nothing common with the passionate revivalism and religious enthusiasm of t nineteenth-century Gothic Revival, which would have seemed ridiculo and ill-bred to the eighteenth. Wyatt's work on the cathedrals was,

:t, necessary to stop them falling down, but he seems to have been
ite insensitive to their beauty although his own Fonthill was plainly
sed on Salisbury. This architectural fantasy was built for the eccentric
llionaire, William Beckford, between 1796 and 1807. It soon became

100. STRAWBERRY HILL

legend in the Wiltshire countryside, and when, in 1825, its 276-foot-
gh tower fell down nobody can have been very surprised. Nothing
ɔw remains of the Abbey.

The two great revivals of the nineteenth century were the Greek and
e Gothic, and oddly enough both of them originated as eighteenth-
ntury fashions within a few years of each other. The 1750's saw the
st Gothick experiments, and also a few Chinese buildings, but in the
's the Greek style began to make itself felt. This was rather less of a
shion and more of a serious attempt to widen the accepted range of
chitectural motives, and that was why Sir William Chambers was so
tterly opposed to it. In fact, it soon became accepted on the Con-
ıent as more correctly antique than Roman architecture itself,
though a few people continued to claim that it was no more than a
d imitation of Roman work. The Greek style was introduced into

England by James 'Athenian' Stuart (1713–88) and Nicholas Reve (1720–1804), whose book *The Antiquities of Athens* was announced being prepared as early as 1748, although the first volume did n appear until 1762 and the second, more important one was publish just after Stuart's death in 1788. The impact of this important public tion did not really make itself felt until early in the nineteenth centur partly because neither Stuart nor Revett was sufficiently active ambitious to change the course of architectural history; indeed Stua was extremely dilatory over the commissions he was given, ar frequently went off drinking with the workmen, as one exasperat employer complained. When the great Greek Revival of the nineteen century got under way it was said, quite wrongly, that:

> the chasteness and purity which Stuart and Revett had, with some succe endeavoured to introduce into their buildings in England, and in whi their zeal had enlisted many artists, had to contend against the opposi and vicious taste of Robert Adam, a fashionable architect, whose eye h been ruined by the corruptions of the worst period of Roman Art.[1]

Finally, the Picturesque. This was not strictly an architectural mov ment, but it had a great effect on architecture because of its clo connexion with landscape-gardening. In reaction against the form layout of the French garden a new style was evolved (still called *le jarc anglais* on the Continent), which was claimed to represent a new ki of beauty, the wildness of Nature tamed a little by the order impos by the artist—the ordered wildness of such great seventeenth-centu painters as Claude and Gaspar Poussin. To the eighteenth century picturesque landscape was one which looked as though it might ha come out of a picture, and not, as it usually means nowadays, a lan scape fit to put into a picture.

As a result of this desire to make Nature imitate Art dead trees we planted in gardens and sham ruins built to close a vista and oth amiable absurdities committed; some were Gothic and some Greek ar some even Chinese, but from the point of view of architectural histo what matters about the Picturesque is that it taught people to look at building and its setting, and it encouraged visual sensibility.

[1] J. Gwilt, *An Encyclopaedia of Architecture*, 1842.

CHAPTER 6

Holland, Soane, and Nash: the Regency

'HE last years of the eighteenth century saw a variety of experiments ı different styles, culminating in the style we usually call Regency; dmittedly an amalgam, but possessing a distinct character of its own, nd quite different in intention from the deliberate revivalism of the ireek and Gothic men of the early and middle years of Victoria's eign. One of the most important architects of the later eighteenth entury was Henry Holland (1745–1806), whose style was very largely ased on contemporary French work, thus distinguishing him from the dam brothers and Wyatt, and recalling rather the practice of Sir Villiam Chambers. Unfortunately little of Holland's work survives, so hat he tends to be overlooked, but his position as architect to the Whig ligarchy surrounding the Prince of Wales before he became Prince legent means that Holland must be considered as helping to form the legency style. He began as a speculative builder, and became the on-in-law of 'Capability' Brown, the most important landscape-ardener of the late eighteenth century. In 1776 he was commissioned o design Brooks's Club, which still stands almost unaltered in St ames's Street, and because this was the headquarters of Whiggery, he ained a strong connexion which was to culminate in the commission or Carlton House. At that moment there was a French fashion among he Whigs, and Holland's own tastes coincided with it. He must have tudied the latest French architectural books he did not go to France ntil the eve of the Revolution—and we know that he employed many rench craftsmen, who may have had a considerable share in his uildings. Between 1783 and 1785 he was employed by the Prince of Vales to enlarge and alter Carlton House. Although it was demolished n 1826, we know what it looked like, and the plan shows that Holland lisposed his interiors very skilfully. The Corinthian portico survives, vith some alteration, as the portico of the National Gallery, but it was riginally set back from the street with a screen of Ionic columns in front of it, which must also have added to the French appearance Another work by Holland which has connexions with the Prince Regen was the original house at Brighton (1786–87), later to be expanded int the Brighton Pavilion, and which, in fact, is still the core of that other wise very different building.

Properly speaking, the Regency lasted only ten years (1811–20), bu it is usual to think of it as beginning in the architectural sense rathe earlier, at about the beginning of the new century, and lasting unti the end of George IV's reign, in 1830. This is probably because of th two great figures who dominated the architectural scene during thos years—Sir John Soane and John Nash. John Soane was born in 1753 the year Lord Burlington died, and he died a few months befor Victoria came to the throne, in 1837. His very long life thus covers th whole course of English architecture from the decline of strict Palla dianism to the rise of equally strict dogmas, whether Greek or Gothic but he himself combined motives—sometimes Greek, sometime Adamitic—with a freedom and eclecticism hardly equalled even by th Adams themselves. His approach was at least partly due to the fact tha he was one of the first architectural students of the Royal Academy where eclectic methods were taught, and partly also to the publication which made Greek and Gothic architecture better known. He was on of the earliest professional architects and did much for that sense c professionalism which so greatly raised the status of architects durin the nineteenth century. His professionalism was no doubt partly becaus he was born plain John Soan, the son of a bricklayer, near Reading. I 1768 he came to London as the pupil of George Dance the younger, th City architect. Dance built relatively little, but his masterpiece wa Newgate Prison, begun in 1770, and the dramatic imagination displaye in it explains his influence on Soane and other advanced youn architects. Dance had been in Rome, and was much influenced by th etchings of Piranesi, whose scrupulously accurate plates of the grea Roman ruins are also imbued with a brooding sense of decayec grandeur which was very much in harmony with Neoclassic ideals, anc which recurs in the most unexpected places in eighteenth-century architecture. These romantic overtones to apparently purely classica works are among the principal elements in the very sophisticatec attractions of the architecture of both George Dance and his greate pupil, Soane. In 1772 Soane went to widen his experience by workin for Holland, and in the same year he entered the Royal Academy Schools, and won the Silver Medal. He followed this up by winning th Gold Medal in 1776, and was awarded a travelling scholarship to Italy in 1778. In Rome he made exact measured drawings of the majo ntiquities, thus satisfying the requirements of the new, more accurate, rchitectural scholarship, and at the same time he satisfied some of his wn inner needs by drafting grandiose projects, such as that for a British Senate House, which continued to haunt his imagination. Soane ot as far as Paestum, where he saw the Greek temples, but he was prevented from going on to Greece itself by an offer of employment rom the eccentric Bishop of Derry (later Earl of Bristol). He returned o England in 1780, thus losing a year of his scholarship, only to find he offer was not serious. After this bitter disappointment he had a hard truggle for some years until the turning-point of his career came in 788 with the Surveyorship of the Bank of England. He held this post or forty-five years, and rebuilt the whole Bank, an undertaking even nore complicated than Wren's rebuilding of St Paul's. The Bank gave im an income and status as one of the leading architects of the day, nd in return he created a masterpiece that even now has not been otally destroyed, in spite of the efforts made since 1930.

As soon as he was appointed he made a thorough survey, discovering xtensive rot and damage, and a rebuilding programme was put in and which lasted from 1792 to 1800 when a second, larger programme vas begun. The size of the Bank was nearly doubled when this second tage was completed in 1827, but the problems facing the architect vere more complicated than a mere expansion. The mob had tried to et fire to the Bank in the Gordon Riots of 1780, so the first consideration vas security; this meant that the new building had to be carried on iecemeal, behind strong walls, and it also meant that fireproof construction had to be employed, and, above all, no windows could give n to the street. On top of this was the very awkward site, roughly riangular, which made an adequate wall-treatment difficult—the ongest wall was 451 feet long, windowless, and lacking any kind of natural climax such as a portico.

The structural problem was solved by the most ingenious use of Roman constructional methods based very closely on the great baths, using very light shell domes with top lighting in a dynamic system that owed a great deal to such Gothic cathedrals as Ely, which he knew and admired. The decorative motives, on the other hand, are freely adapted rom the Greek as well as from more usual Roman sources. The resulting halls were superbly personal architectural expressions of their unction, but they were hardly ever accessible, and most of them have been destroyed. Sir John Summerson has described their soaring quality as "the Gothic miracle rediscovered at the heart of the Roman tradition," but most of Soane's contemporaries were shocked by his free treatment of classical detail, and would probably have agreed with

101. The Bank of England, Tivoli Corner

the anonymous author of an imaginary epitaph on Sir William Cham bers, who said:

> A Fabric . . . in a barbarous style,
> Of which, though pretending to originality,
> The peculiarities are borrowed
> From the example of the Dark Ages. . . .

Another critic more pithily described his pilasters decorated wi incised ornament in an austerely Greek manner as "scored like loins pork."

On the outside Soane's worst problem was probably the very acu angle made by the junction of Princes Street and Lothbury, which also one of the most prominent parts of the whole façade. He exper mented with various angle-treatments from 1804 until he evolved tl highly sophisticated construction known as Tivoli Corner, complete in 1807. This, which has suffered badly in recent years, can still be see Its name comes from the fact that Soane decided to use the mc ornate form of the Corinthian Order, that found in the Temple

:sta, at Tivoli, in order to give the maximum effect of richness to the tual angle covered by the segment of the temple in a way which ows that he had not been blind to the Rome of the seventeenth ıtury. Inside his 'temple' there are two unfluted columns for contrast d to get the maximum effect of shadow, while the movement of the sign as a whole is completed by the curious semi-Greek sarcophagus ıich serves as a finial, and is based on a concave rectangular form posing the curved and convex shapes below; in short, the extreme ıte angle of the corner seems as though it were deliberate, and not a ficulty to overcome.

The Soane of this period, from the 1790's to about 1815, was the most ginal genius in architecture then alive. Unfortunately, much of his rk has been lost, but there are still three buildings by him, all in ndon, which are easily accessible. They are Pitzhanger Manor, ling; the Picture Gallery and Mausoleum of Dulwich College; and ane's own house in Lincoln's Inn Fields.

Pitzhanger Manor (now Ealing Public Library) was built about 70 by George Dance for himself, and was bought by Soane in 1800 a country house for his own family. He retained two of the rooms

102. Pitzhanger Manor

built by his master, but between 1800 and 1803 he made seve important alterations, the most important being the main front. T he treated as a revised version of Robert Adam's south front of Ked ston, but he went back to Adam's original model, the Arch of Cc stantine in Rome, and set free-standing columns in front of the wa supporting nothing but statues. In spite of his apparent closeness to t classical prototype Soane's effect is much less Roman than Adam's; other words, the Soane revolution was more fundamental than t Adam one. The tiny entrance hall at Pitzhanger has a ceiling whi also affords the strongest possible contrast with Adam, for it is a sub essay in the enclosure of space, like the inside of a sarcophagus hollow out and seen from below, and it has none of the ornament or colc that Adam used to give accent to his ceilings.

The Picture Gallery at Dulwich was built between 1811 and 18 much altered in the nineteenth century, destroyed by a flying-bon and rebuilt in 1953 from the original designs. It was one of the fi 'modern' picture-galleries with top lighting, and is still one of the m satisfactory. In his later years Soane was much occupied with what called the Poetry of Architecture, and a good deal of this seems to ha been due to the Picturesque movement. Part of his poetry lay spectacular effects of light, sometimes filtered through coloured gl and sometimes reflected by small pieces of mirror-glass set in odd plac At its worst this has a rather tawdry mock-Romanticism, as in Monk's Parlour in his own house; at its best it can have a wonder sense of lightness and space, as in the 'hanging ceilings' lit from sides so that they appear like tents suspended in space. Again there examples in his own house, now the Soane Museum. Originally Soa lived at No. 13 Lincoln's Inn Fields, but he spread into parts of N 12 and 14, and from 1812 he designed and altered his house to fit it a museum for future generations of architectural students. It is cramm with every possible object that could interest a romantic yet aust architect in the early nineteenth century—an Egyptian sarcophagus a Hogarth paintings, the drawings of John Thorpe as well as those Robert Adam, and, of course, all his own drawings and models.

Soane was an architect of genius, a scholar using the classi tradition who yet evolved an intensely personal style in the last years the eighteenth century. John Nash (1752–1835), the favourite archit of George IV, is perhaps best described as an architectural impresar a creator of townscape, and an organizer of genius who knew little, a cared less, about the finer points of architectural scholarship. Na though an exact contemporary of Soane, was a nineteenth-century ma and it is a curious fact that he achieved nothing until he was abc

103. The Quadrant and Part of Regent Street

fifty-five. He set up as a speculative builder on a legacy of £1000, a went bankrupt; then he met the landscape-gardener Humphr Repton, and became his architectural partner, learning from him t principles of picturesque disposition that he was to apply in so revol tionary a way to houses in towns. He made a mysterious marriage 1798—it was said to a lady that the Prince of Wales was anxious to s married—and from then on he had money and the patronage of t Prince.

At the beginning of the nineteenth century there were numero schemes described generically as 'Metropolitan Improvements' whi were part of the 'Neatness and Elegance' of the Age of Jane Auste Such an opportunity arose with the falling-in of the Crown leases Marylebone, and the decision to redevelop the park. The first schem for what we now know as Regent's Park were formulated in 1810–1 and with them—it was Nash's stroke of genius—a scheme to drive great north-south road up from the Houses of Parliament and t Carlton House area to the new park where the Prince could have *guinguette*[1] and a Triumphal Way to link it with Carlton House. T new park was to be dotted with neat villas which could be let Members of Parliament, lawyers, and similar prosperous folk w would need a direct road to Westminster. Thus Regent Street came in existence. Nash was also responsible for further improvements, in James's Park for example—and projected even more, for the Regen Park that we still possess is much less than he planned. In 1811 laid out a group of nine cottages, all different, to form the artifici Blaise Hamlet, near Bristol, and this truly Picturesque adaptation Repton's principles of irregularity and apparent extent were tried o in it, and then in Regent's Park. The beauty of Nash's scheme was th it consisted of maintaining the park as an open space but dotting with forty-odd villas, so disposed that, according to Repton's princip of apparent extent, each was invisible to its neighbours and appear to possess the whole park; the genius of the scheme lies in the way t garden-city was to join on to London (which ended at Marylebo Road) by means of the formal links of the terraces, and above all t square and half-circus at the top of Portland Place. Behind the n quarter was a canal and a barracks, and a whole service district w planned near Albany Street.

To the south the existing Portland Place was incorporated bodil and the link with Carlton House was made by means of Regent Stre This swerves alongside the "narrow Streets and meaner Hous occupied by mechanics and the trading part of the community" to t

[1] A country cottage.

st of the Hanover Square district, marking its changes of axis by eye-tchers—All Souls', at Langham Place; Oxford Circus; the splendid eep of the Quadrant at the junction with Piccadilly Circus, and then

104. THE PAVILION, BRIGHTON

formal straight stretch down to Waterloo Place and Carlton House rrace. It is sad that the scheme was no sooner finished than Carlton ouse was demolished, and Nash was involved in the building of ckingham Palace. This caused great scandal over costs, and he was lled before a Select Committee. Almost all that survives of his palace the Marble Arch, intended as an entrance. As a palace-builder it is rhaps fairer to him to enjoy his more imaginative flights, such as mberland Terrace, Regent's Park, or Brighton Pavilion. In the first se he has contrived a perfect stage-setting, with a whole terrace of ious houses dressed up with a pediment, and made to pretend, for the nefit of the Royal Villa opposite (which was never built), that they e one big palace. Much the same air of make-believe surrounds the vilion, at Brighton, which began life as an ordinary villa by Holland. bout 1805 Sezincote House, in Gloucestershire, had been built in the Hindoo' style, and Repton seems to have proposed something similar for the Royal Pavilion. The Regent approved, and Nash was co missioned to execute the work in a vaguely Oriental style. In 18 Coleridge's Kubla Khan "a stately pleasure-dome decreed," and so time afterwards the bulbous dome appeared on the sea-front Brighton.

With the death of George IV, in 1830, Nash disappeared. He died his own East Cowes Castle five years later.

Most of the houses in and around Regent's Park were not design by Nash, whose talents were absorbed in laying out the whole, and complicated financial transactions connected with it. Among the arc tects responsible for the houses was Decimus Burton (1800–81), w later built the Athenaeum Club and the open screen of Ionic colum at Hyde Park Corner. He was, however, only one of the many talen men then working in a style influenced by Soane and Nash, and th were hundreds of builders all over the country who put up houses a whole streets, many of which still survive. John Buonarotti Papwo (1775–1847) was responsible for much of the splendour of Cheltenh in the years 1824–32, and scores of streets and houses in Lond Clifton, Tunbridge Wells, and, above all, Brighton and Hove, s remain as testimony to the vitality of the Regency style.

CHAPTER 7

Victorian and Modern Architecture

ɪs final chapter must cover a very large amount of ground in a very rt space. One reason for this is that in almost every town or village Britain the great majority of the buildings date from Victorian or r times, so that there is no room here for more than a sketch of the in developments of the last hundred years; years that have seen nendous changes in the actual materials used by the building les, so that the architect's job nowadays is very different from what as a century ago (and probably also much more exciting). The sheer ntity of nineteenth- and twentieth-century architecture which vives means that much of it must necessarily be bad, since bad work always been done; yet even at its best it is often inferior to the work he seventeenth and eighteenth centuries. This is partly because much he best work of the Victorian Age was then considered to be civil ineering rather than architecture, for it was in the railways, docks, lges, and other feats of engineering that the new challenge presented the Industrial Revolution was met. Another reason is to be found in attitude of many architects, whose efforts were devoted to the cise copying of details from earlier styles, archaeology rather than hitecture, and this attitude is reflected in the Battle of the Styles.

his was fought between the Greek men and the Gothic men, and it a battle nearly as much moral and ecclesiological as architectural, the classical styles, based on Roman and Greek architecture, still l almost undisputed sway. The Greek Revival could trace itself back tuart and Revett, and was sure of itself because of the link between ek and Roman art—they could (and did) claim to be practising a rer' style of Roman art. The Gothic men could also claim to go k to the Gothick experiments of the eighteenth century, like Straw-ry Hill or Fonthill, but these were felt to be rather frivolous, and the hic movement was given the seriousness it needed by two factors. first of these was the major architect of the style, Augustus Welby

Pugin (1812–52), in whose mind Gothic buildings had a specifica moral quality—"Pointed, or Christian Architecture," as he called i but Pugin was a fervent Catholic, and the hand of Rome was frequen discerned in the design of Gothic buildings; this was, however, par offset by the connexion between the Gothic style and patriotism wh was often made by partisans, for the historical and archaeologi researches of the late eighteenth and early nineteenth centuries w held to prove that Gothic was really the national English style. T success of these ideas is best gauged from the fact that when the Hou of Parliament were burnt down in 1834 it was decided that the n building should be in the Tudor style—that is, in a style felt to refl the moment of England's greatest glory. Much as we may regret Houses of Parliament that Soane could have built, the new build brought both Barry and Pugin on to the scene. Their sons were conduct a long warfare over the respective shares of the two mer Pugin junior claiming that his father was responsible for everyth good in the design—but it is now clear that Barry was responsible the general layout, the detailed planning, and the conduct of the wh He spent most of his life on it, and there are eight thousand surviv drawings for it by him. It was opened in 1852, when Barry was knight but it was not completed until after his death in 1860. Apart from knighthood he was a Royal Academician, a Fellow of the Ro Society, and Vice-President of the Royal Institute of British Archite (he refused the Presidency); in short, he was a successful Victor professional. He was born in 1795, and spent six years as a surveyo pupil before he inherited some money and was able to travel mu more widely than the average architect. He left England in 1817, a went to France, Italy, Greece, and Turkey, and then on to Egypt a Syria. His first important building after his return was the Ro Institution (now the City Art Gallery), Manchester (1824–35, in classic manner), but his great success came with his astylar, or Itali manner, developed first at the Travellers' Club (1829–31), and th on a larger scale in the Reform Club (1837–41) next door to Travellers', in Pall Mall. Both these buildings are very closely based Italian prototypes of the sixteenth century, in particular the Pala Farnese, in Rome, and it was this which appealed to contemporar since the Italian Renaissance was sufficiently old, and sufficien classical, to be acceptable to eyes which still regarded Gothic forms either frivolous or barbarous; on the other hand, the Greek and Rom Orders had become dulled by pointless repetition (as Soane h realized) and the new astylar—that is, Orderless—façades, depend on careful fenestration and on a judicious use of rustication, were bou

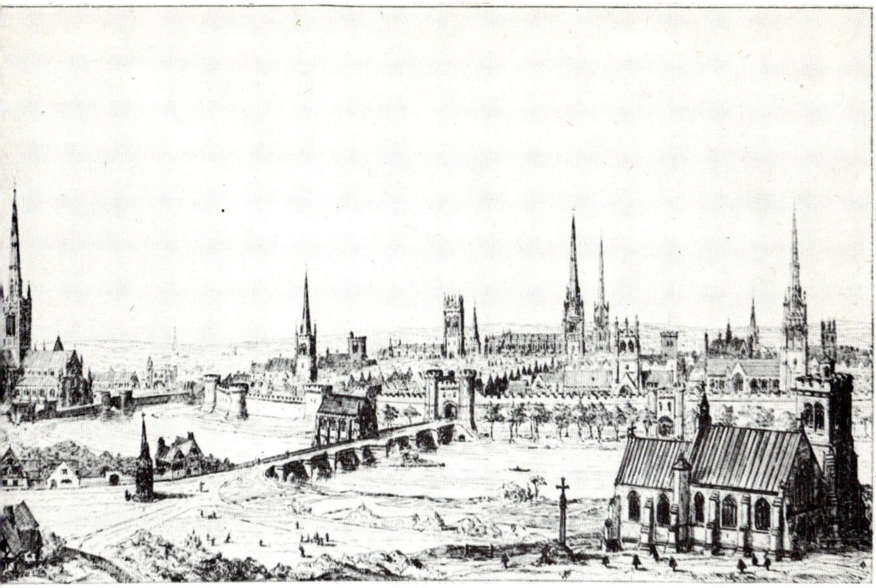

105(*a*). CATHOLIC TOWN IN 1440

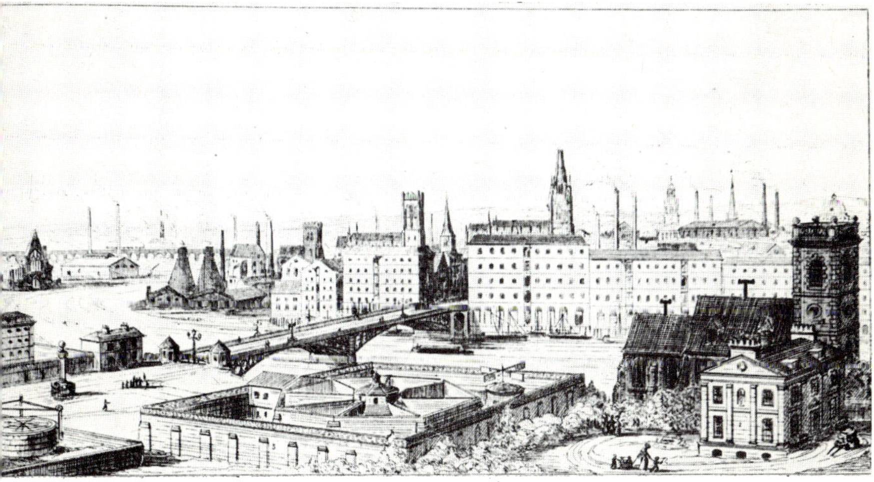

105(*b*). THE SAME TOWN IN 1840
From Pugin's "Contrasts"

to please. Huge tracts of South Kensington and other residential are in most of the larger cities bear witness to its popularity as well as to i ability to survive the attentions of the speculative builder.

It is hard to imagine a more different architect than Pugin, yet tl two men did in fact work quite well together on the Houses of Parli ment, and although many people felt that Pugin did the 'architecture yet he himself would have been the first to admit that he could nev have handled the vast and complicated administrative work involve Pugin became a Catholic in 1834, and at once adopted the position th Gothic architecture and Catholicism went together; in 1836 he pul lished his *Contrasts*, a satire which compares nineteenth-centu civilization with that of the fifteenth. In 1841 he stated his position ve clearly in *The True Principles of Pointed or Christian Architecture*, in whic he says that architectural style is not a matter of choice but an expressic of society, and a good society can hardly help having good architectur His first principle of design is the one from which all modern archite ture springs—to admit nothing which is not essential for convenienc construction, or propriety—that is, the doctrine of functionalisn Further, ornament must be an enrichment of this essential constructic and no more. This is the theory which was to be expressed by Violle le-Duc in France a few years later, and which is still one of the mo powerful battle-cries of modern art, but unfortunately Pugin could n resist attacks on all other architectural ideas: "One of the greate defects of St Paul's, London, is its fictitious dome. *The dome that is se is not the dome of the church*, but a mere construction for effect . . . co structed at a vast expense without any legitimate reason." Perhaps eve more unwisely he allowed himself to express his passion for ritual an symbolism in a famous passage (not from *True Principles*):

> The stoups are filled to the brim; the rood is raised on high; the scre glows with sacred imagery and rich devices . . . the lamps of the sanctua burn bright; the saintly portraitures in the glass windows shine a gloriously; and the albs hang in the oaken ambries, and the cope ches are filled with orphreyed baudekins; and pix and pax, and chrismato are there, and thurible and cross.

This was too much. Ruskin (1819–1900) found it necessary to "put tl movement on a Protestant basis" in two ways—first, by denying th he himself owed anything at all to Pugin; and second, by advocatir the use of Venetian Gothic forms. The first he did easily: "One mig have put this man under a pix, and left him, one should have thoug . . . he is not a great architect, but one of the smallest possible or co ceivable architects. . . ." In fact, Ruskin's advocacy of the high oured Venetian Gothic was not universally accepted, and most glish architects, for patriotic reasons, preferred to work in the Early glish or Pointed styles (indeed, there are cases where their confidence s such that they restored genuine Gothic buildings in 'a purer style' *.e.*, an earlier one). Ruskin's great personal influence assured the :eptance of the Gothic Revival, and as Pugin died at forty, in 1852, : movement was put upon a Protestant basis, and a great wave of ırch-building began. Gothic was also very popular for the new town ls that were called into existence under the Municipal Corporation ts (1835–82) and for schools, one of the finest being the now de-lished King Edward's High School, in Birmingham, the earliest nt work of Pugin and Barry (1833–36).

The next generation of Gothic men can be summed up in the names Scott, Street, and Butterfield. Sir Gilbert Scott (1811–78) claimed to no more than the humble pupil of Pugin, but his career shows a ɔacity for tenacious self-advertisement quite different from Pugin, d he is generally regarded as the typical Victorian architect on :ount of the Albert Memorial (1863–72), in Kensington, which he cribed himself as having called forth his "highest and most enthusias- efforts." There is hardly a town in the country which cannot display ne example of his work, either in the town hall, or the workhouse, or, st often, in one or more churches put up or restored by his very cient organization. Only once did he meet his match, and even then contrived to erect a building which "is often spoken of to me as the est building in London." The words are his own, and the building St Pancras Station. The story connected with it is a curious one, for ɔtt made some designs for two Government offices in Whitehall, in 57; they were unsuccessful in the public competition, but he then :ceeded in obtaining the appointment, only to find that Lord lmerston had become Prime Minister, and "told me, in a jaunty y, that he could have nothing to do with this Gothic style and . . . ıst insist on my making a design in the Italian style." Even after :uperating at the seaside Scott found himself still forced to design in : Italian manner, but the drawings made for his original Gothic ɔject, with suitable modifications, became St Pancras Station and tel. It is this apparent interchangeability which gives the game away, King's Cross Station, next door to St Pancras, is a splendid piece of gineering, obviously designed as a railway terminus, and far more :cessful, for that very reason, than the Foreign Office-St Pancras, :n though, as has been pointed out, Scott's revision took account of :h things as the entrance ramps for cabs, and the circulation of the ffic.

William Butterfield (1814–1900) and G. E. Street (1824–81) w
less successful as businessmen but are perhaps more interesting
architects, in that Butterfield at least seems positively to have gloried
ugliness where Scott was no more than Philistine. Butterfield was mu
influenced by Ruskin's theories and made great play with polych
matic brickwork and mosaic; his two major works are All Sair
Margaret Street, in London (1849–59), and Keble College Chap
Oxford, mostly built between 1868 and 1870.

Street defeated Scott in the competition for the Law Courts held
1866, but building was not even begun until 1874, and Street di
before the courts were completed in 1882; they are said to be the l
major public building to be put up in a pure Gothic style, in this c
a French thirteenth-century one. The next phase was to be larg
associated with a pupil of Street's, William Morris, but before
consider the developments which lead into the twentieth century
must turn back to the earlier part of the century and the Greek Reviv

At least two of the great architects of the reign of George III, Soa
and Nash, have been called Greek Revival men, but this is not true

106. St Pancras Station Hotel

107. KEBLE COLLEGE CHAPEL, OXFORD

ioane's elaborated eclecticism, and even less so of Nash's rather slap-lash approach to detail. The principal exponents of the true Greek Revival were to be found almost equally in London: Smirke, the nwoods, Wilkins, and outside: Playfair and Hamilton, in Edinburgh, Greek' Thomson in Glasgow, Dobson in Newcastle, Simpson in Aberdeen. It would not be true to say that all were equally Greek, but hey were by no stretch of the imagination Gothic, and their finest work an well claim to be among the best architecture of the century, particularly in the New Town of Edinburgh, the planning of which oes back to the eighteenth century. Two buildings may serve as xamples of the scholarship and sense of style which were their inheri-ance—the Royal High School, Edinburgh, by Thomas Hamilton 1785–1858), and St George's Hall, Liverpool, by Harvey Elmes (1814–7). Hamilton's building was begun in 1825 and finished in 1829, and s fortunate in having one of the finest imaginable sites. The massing is uperb, and the detail of the pure Doric Order precise, but the secret of the effect lies in the combination of the passionless Greek with the pirit of the Romantic Movement typified by Sir Walter Scott, and in

108. The Royal High School, Edinburgh

109. St George's Hall, Liverpool

this the High School is no more than the finest example of the ideas that found expression in the Athens of the North. Elmes's St George's Hall is a true Victorian work, in the sense that the High School was not, for it began as the winning design of the competition held in 1839, when Elmes was twenty-five. In 1840 Elmes also won a competition for a new Assize Court, and the two buildings were then amalgamated. The planning owes much to the Baths of Caracalla, in Rome, while the main front at least owes something to the work of Schinkel in Germany, where Elmes went to study recent work before settling down to carry out his own design. It will be seen that this is not really a Greek building at all, although it was finished after Elmes's premature death by C. R. Cockerell (1788–1863), who had spent four years in Greece and was an acknowledged authority on Greek archaeology.

Among the many other practitioners of a more or less Greek style, sometimes crossed with Barry's Italianate ideas, Philip Hardwick (1792–1870) is well known for his gigantic Doric portico[1] at Euston Station and for the splendid Great Hall, based on Italian palaces. Behind the Great Hall were the railway sheds, and in a sense this is typical of much Victorian architecture, which would lovingly cull details from the Palazzo Massimi for a ticket-office, and leave the platforms to the engineers. To modern eyes, accustomed to rank function and construction high among the architectural virtues, much of the Victorians' civil engineering seems preferable to their architecture, and indeed for sheer scale and grandeur of conception it is necessary to go back to Imperial Rome to find anything comparable with some of the great feats of the engineers, such as the Forth or Menai Strait bridges, or a piece of virtuosity like the Clifton Suspension Bridge.

Among the great names in civil engineering are those of Telford, Brunel, Stephenson, and Captain Fowke, of the Royal Engineers, who built the Albert Hall (1867–71), once again with a clear reference to Rome. At the end of the century Sir John Fowler, Bart., and Sir Benjamin Baker built the Forth Bridge (1882–90): their titles sufficiently indicate the new status of the civil engineer. At the beginning of the Victorian Age the greatest opportunities were offered by the railways, which had virtually covered the country by 1845. Many of the buildings needed by the railways were entirely new—viaducts, tunnels, engine-sheds, even stations and bridges were not quite like anything known previously, and the engineers at once rose to the challenge. Thomas Telford (1757–1834) was the son of a Dumfries shepherd, and much of his finest work was done in Scotland on roads and harbours, but three of his masterpieces are the aqueduct at Chirk (1796–1801), in Wales,

[1] Now (1961) about to be demolished.

110. CLIFTON SUSPENSION BRIDGE, BRISTOL

the Dean Bridge (1829–31), at Edinburgh, and the Menai Bridge ove the Strait, begun in 1819 and completed in 1824. The grandeur of th Chirk aqueduct was recognized as early as about 1803, when John Sel Cotman made a watercolour of it (now in the Victoria and Alber Museum). The Menai Bridge was one of the first to be built in thi country on the suspension principle, and the beauty of its rectilinea lines clearly influenced the other great bridge over the Menai Strait the Britannia Bridge (1845–50) by Robert Stephenson and Franci Thompson, in which architect and engineer collaborated to produce monumentally grand effect by combining Stephenson's severe iron tubes for the trains to run in with rusticated pylons and grand Egyptia entrances to the tunnels. Perhaps even more impressive, on account o the splendour of its setting, is the suspension bridge over Clifton Gorge near Bristol. This was derived from Telford's Menai Bridge, and wa designed by Isambard Kingdom Brunel (1806–59), who won th competition held in 1830. Work was not actually begun until 1837, an the bridge was completed in 1864, after Brunel's death. He himsel wrote of it:

> A work of art thus thrown across such grand and imposing scenery should be as simple and unobtrusive as possible, that it should fix the observer rather by the grandeur of the ideas that it gave rise to than attract his attention by anything inconsistent with the surrounding objects.

In other words, he was thinking of his job as a work of art, and not ·lely as an engineering problem, great and fascinating as that was. runel later became engineer to the Great Western Railway, and had hand in most of its great works, including the 100-foot spans used at addington Station (Brunel and M. D. Wyatt, 1852–54), where cast-on columns and ribs are used to carry the glass vault in a way that ould have been impossible without the stimulus of the Gothic Revival nd the attendant interest in construction.

Even more to the point is the parallel with the Crystal Palace, uilt in the space of nine months for the Great Exhibition of 1851. 'he original designs were not very satisfactory, and the projected uilding in brick and stone with a 200-foot dome was properly criticized s being too solid for a temporary exhibition. Joseph Paxton's design ›lved the commissioners' difficulties. He had begun life as a gardener › the Duke of Devonshire, and had built two notable greenhouses in ıst iron and glass. The original jotting which he made on June 11, 850, was based on the greenhouse principle, enlarged to more than athedral proportions. His design was published in the *Illustrated London 'ews* on July 6, and caught the imagination of the public. The founda-ons were laid in August, and the Queen opened the Great Exhibition n May 1, 1851. In at least one sense, Paxton (1801–65) founded ıodern architecture at the Crystal Palace, for the whole gigantic :heme depended on two things—the possibility of getting cast-iron olumns and girders prefabricated and delivered ready for use, and the ossibility of obtaining an almost limitless supply of panes of glass, each xactly 49 × 10 inches, the largest size then available in sheets. The esign was thus conditioned by mass-produced materials, and equally :rictly related to function; and these were really revolutionary changes ı the whole conception of architecture and the building crafts, for reviously everything needed for a building was made on the site. The uge building was an enormous success. It had a central nave 72 feet ·ide, with 48-foot avenues on either side, and the original idea was ıodified by a transept, barrel-vaulted and carried on timber arches, ·hich allowed whole trees to be enclosed (there had been violent pposition to the whole scheme, and particularly to the use of Hyde 'ark, and the cutting down of some elm-trees), so that when the sun ıone through the thousands of panes of glass high above tree-top level ıe effect was that of fairyland, as Queen Victoria observed.

111. The Crystal Palace

112. THE TRANSEPT, CRYSTAL PALACE

After the exhibition closed the whole building was taken down and -erected, with some alterations, at Sydenham, where it survived for ɔre than eighty years before its destruction by fire.

The next two stages in the development of modern architecture were ain technological: the invention (1855) of the Bessemer process for e production of mild steel in quantity, and the exploitation, in France the nineties, of reinforced concrete. This is probably the most portant new building material since Roman times, since it enables ıds and stresses to be carried easily which no other material could ar. The principle is simple, for it consists of a grid of steel rods encased in concrete. Ordinary concrete will bear tremendous loads, long as they are dead weight, or 'crushing,' as engineers call it, b concrete cast into bars or beams is easily snapped, since its tens strength is very low; the enclosure of quite a small quantity of steel me or rods at once increases the tensile strength enormously, so that it possible to use reinforced concrete as beams and supports as well as f columns and floors. The invention of mild steel meant not only th steel was available for reinforcing concrete but it was also now possil to develop the steel-framed building. The Crystal Palace was made cast iron, which is very brittle, but the new steel joists could car enormous weights on the frame, and, with reinforced concrete, became possible to attempt constructional feats that would previou have been quite unthinkable. In fact, architects were rather slow realize the potentialities of the new materials—even now there are s experiments being made—and the Ritz Hotel, which is said to ha been the first building in London with a steel frame (1905), certair shows no trace of a revolution. Almost any modern building will sh how a steel frame means that the outside walls, which previously had carry the entire weight of the building and the roof, can now be made sheets of glass, since the main piers inside the building carry the weig on the frame, and the outside walls can be cantilevered out from t frame as far as necessary. A further development of the same princi is to support the building on stilts, so that the ground floor is open the street.

One reason, however, for the comparative slowness of Brit architects to seize upon the possibilities inherent in mass-produc and prefabricated elements was undoubtedly the influence of Willi Morris (1834–96). His hatred for the squalors of nineteenth-centu industrialism led him to combat the whole idea of mechanical p duction, and thus to counter the ideas which Paxton or Brunel h propagated. He founded the Arts and Crafts Movement with t intention of ensuring sound design by making the individual craftsm conscious of his own responsibilities. In 1859 Morris married, and commissioned Philip Webb (1831–1915), who had been his fello pupil in Street's office, to design him a house at Bexley Heath, in Ke This was the famous Red House, built between 1859 and 1860, a often regarded as one of the landmarks in nineteenth-century arc tecture because it was built of brick, and in a style which approximat closely to that of the local Kentish farmhouses—in other words, it w 'vernacular' architecture. Certainly it was designed to be a comforta house to live in, and the architect did not bother about symmetry the elevations, in which respect its progeny are still with us. When ne to furnishing the interior Morris found that it was simply not sible to obtain good materials at any price, and, as a result, he nded the firm of Morris, Marshall, Faulkner and Company in 1861 produce wallpapers, furniture, tapestries, and even stained-glass

113. THE RED HOUSE, BEXLEY HEATH

ndows; it is, however, perhaps ironical that the most famous of his erprises was the Kelmscott Press, printing being the most essentially chanical of the arts. The new freedom from both stucco and symtry that Webb found in his design for the Red House was of profound portance for the design of houses in the next few decades, especially the hands of Webb himself, C. F. A. Voysey (1857–1941), Norman aw (1831–1912), and even Sir Edwin Lutyens (1869–1944). For ne reason, perhaps the use of red brick, the houses built by Webb l Shaw in the seventies were often called Queen Anne although in the jority of cases they can hardly be said to have much in common with actual buildings of that date; later, however, there was a tendency evive early eighteenth-century features. Norman Shaw subsequently rked in a variety of manners, building many large country houses l the first Garden Suburb (Bedford Park, at Hammersmith), and

114. THE SCHOOL OF ART, GLASGOW

concluding with what is sometimes called a Neo-Baroque style, v seen in his Piccadilly Hotel (1905 and later), in London. Perhaps best-known work, however, is entirely different in style: New Scotl Yard (1887–90) is a highly coloured pile in red brick and stone, an has been suggested that the Scottish Baronial style is deliberate, an reference to its name.

Shaw's career extended into the present century, and indeed his l works are considered Edwardian rather than Victorian, but the r century saw several new ideas and new men, of whom the one r regarded as the most influential was Charles Rennie Mackintosh (18 1928), a Glasgow man whose works were at first much influenced by contemporary 'Art nouveau' then being developed in Belgium France. Mackintosh was one of the leaders away from the exaggerate floral ornaments associated with the style, and his design for Glas School of Art (1897–99) had great influence outside Britain, especi in Vienna and Munich. Mackintosh's career rather petered out, Sir Edwin Lutyens, who was a year younger and lived until 1944, s established himself as the leading English architect and garden desig

115. Design for Coventry Cathedral

working in a highly personal form of Georgian until 1912, when he commissioned to lay out New Delhi as the capital of the Indian Emp This enormous work was finished in 1931, but it lies outside the sc of this book. In this decade Maxwell Fry (born 1899) built Ker House as a working-class housing scheme in London, while the Tec group built a similar block, much taller and for middle-class tenants Highgate (Highpoint Flats, 1933–35). The Congrès Internationa d'Architecture Moderne (C.I.A.M.) and the work of individ French, German, American, and Scandinavian architects all began be felt in England, and after 1945 the huge housing programmes bodies like the L.C.C. or the schools built in Hertfordshire gave enormous impetus to young architects, and a new idea of architect to many thousands of people who had not previously thought abou at all. This impetus is still continuing, but this book may fitly concl with two examples of post-war design—the Royal Festival Hall (cc pleted in 1951), by R. H. Matthew and J. L. Martin, which i brilliant solution to the problem of so isolating a concert hall that it be built inside a concrete shell which stands next to a railway-brid The floating of the auditorium inside its enveloping shell allows most ingenious arrangement of levels and foyers so that the wh building can be emptied in a very few minutes; and since the ear part of this book was of necessity concerned with cathedrals it appropriate that the last illustration should be of the imaginative des for the new Coventry Cathedral, the only one built in Britain in century with the materials made possible by nineteenth- and twentie century engineering.

A Note on Books

here is a very considerable literature on English architecture, and perhaps .e most important books are those published by or on behalf of the archi-cts themselves and intended as more or less genteel self-advertisements. hese include such important source-books as Colen Campbell's *Vitruvius ritannicus*, and the *Works in Architecture* of Robert Adam and his brothers, ıt they are not always easy to get hold of, nor are they very useful to the eneral reader. The following books are nearly all modern, authoritative, and irly easy to come by: all of them ought to be in every Public Library of any ze.

Part One

. S. R. Boase: *Oxford History of English Art*, Volume 3, 1100–1216 (O.U.P., 1953).

Brieger: *Oxford History of English Art*, Volume 4, 1215–1307 (O.U.P., 1957).

. W. Clapham: *English Romanesque Architecture before the Conquest* (O.U.P., 1930).

— *English Romanesque Architecture after the Conquest* (O.U.P., 1934).

)an Evans: *Oxford History of English Art*, Volume 5, 1307–1461 (O.U.P., 1949).

)hn Harvey: *Gothic England* (Batsford, 1948).

— *Henry Yevele* (Batsford, 1946).

. Rickman: *An Attempt to Discriminate Styles of English Architecture* (5th Ed., J. H. Parker, 1848).

. F. Salzman: *A Documentary History of Medieval Buildings* (O.U.P., 1952).

. Hamilton Thompson: *Military Architecture in England* (O.U.P., 1912).

. F. Webb: *Architecture in Britain: The Middle Ages* (Penguin Books Ltd., 1956).

Part Two

. M. Colvin: *A Biographical Dictionary of English Architects, 1660–1840* (John Murray, Ltd, 1954). Not a history but with very full details of the lives and works of every British architect of the period.

. Pevsner: *The Buildings of England* (Penguin Books, Ltd). A series, now nearly half finished, of critical inventories of the architectural heritage of England, arranged by counties.

SIR J. SUMMERSON: *Architecture in Britain, 1530–1830* (Penguin Books, Lt third edition, 1958). The most complete and up-to-date historical surv of the whole field. English architecture of the period from 1830 to t present is treated as a part of another volume in the same series (*T Pelican History of Art*).

H.-R. HITCHCOCK: *Architecture: Nineteenth and Twentieth Centuries* (Pengu Books, Ltd, 1958), which deals with the whole development of mode architecture.

Two volumes in *The Oxford History of English Art* have so far appeare dealing with the period since 1550:

M. WHINNEY AND O. MILLAR: *English Art, 1625–1714* (O.U.P., 1957).

T. S. R. BOASE: *English Art, 1800–70* (O.U.P., 1959).

The intervening period has been covered by three volumes by:

C. HUSSEY: *English Country Houses.* (i) *Early Georgian, 1715–60*, (ii) *Mi Georgian, 1760–1800*, (iii) *Late Georgian, 1800–40* (Country Life, Ltd, 195 58).

Glossary

anthus capital: capital decorated with the fleshy acanthus foliage used on antique Corinthian capitals.

sle: lateral division flanking the main body of the church.

nbulatory: an aisle which enabled processions to pass round and behind the high altar.

se: polygonal or rounded termination of the sanctuary in a church.

silica: originally a term applied to an assembly hall, but in medieval architecture it can apply to any large church with prominent nave, aisles, and clerestory.

llet-moulding: moulding made up of short cylindrical or rectangular blocks spaced at regular intervals.

ttress: mass of masonry erected against a wall to counter the thrust of an arch or vault.

pital: crowning member of a column which unites the round column to the square abacus it supports.

ancel: eastern arm of the church usually divided from the main body of the church by a screen.

apter-house: assembly hall for the execution of the administrative work of the clergy.

evet: eastern complex of the church usually comprising the main apse with its high altar, ambulatory, and chapels.

evron ornament: the ubiquitous zig-zag ornament in Anglo-Norman architecture.

oir: see Chancel.

erestory: the upper part of the nave wall which contains a range of windows.

oister: name given to the covered walks around an open quadrangle which connect the domestic quarters of the monastery to the church.

nfessio: chapel or altar erected over the body of a saint or the place of a martyrdom.

rbel: projecting block, often carved, to support roofs, beams, and floors, etc.

ypt: vaulted substructure usually beneath the choir, but occasionally extending beyond the main body of the church.

aper pattern: a simple geometric decoration repeated over the surface of a wall.

Drum-pier: a cylindrical support made up of rubble and masonry. The dru of a dome is the cylindrical support below the dome proper.

Entablature: the horizontal element above a column, consisting of architra frieze, and cornice. With the appropriate column it forms an Order.

Fenestration: the arrangement of windows in a façade, particularly wi reference to their spacing and proportion.

Fluting: decorative channelling in vertical parallel lines on the surface o column or pilaster.

Flying-buttress: an arch attached to a free-standing pier of masonry to abso the thrust of a vault.

Gable: upper section of the wall between the enclosing lines of the roof.

Galilee: covered porch at the entrance to a church, often used as a chapel penitents.

Giant Order: one which continues through two or more storeys (*see* Order).

Grisaille: monochrome painting that gives the effect of a piece of sculptu

Hammer-beam: a projecting sole-piece in timber roofs, supported by, a supporting, arched braces. This made it possible to dispense with the t beam, and allowed further decoration.

Hexastyle portico: a portico with six free-standing columns. Tetra-, octa-, a decastyle porticoes have four, eight, and ten columns respectively.

Lady chapel: chapel dedicated to the Virgin, and usually situated at t extreme east end of the church.

Lancet: slender window with an acutely pointed arch at the top.

Lantern: a turret which crowns a roof or a dome and is pierced with windo or arcading.

Lierne: a short intermediate rib connecting bosses and intersections vaulting-ribs.

Lintel: horizontal beam or block of stone spanning an opening and supporti the wall above.

Motte and bailey: a type of castle consisting of a mound (motte), with su rounding ditch, and a fortified enclosure (bailey), surrounding or co verging on the mound.

Mullion: upright shaft dividing a window into a number of "lights."

Nave: central aisle in the western arm of a cruciform church.

Octagon: eight-sided drum usually covering the crossing.

Order: denotes a column, generally with base, shaft, capital, and the enta lature it supports.

Oriel: bay window projecting from the surface of the wall and supported corbels.

Pattern-book: a sketchbook which contained architectural drawings and w mainly responsible for the spread of architectural ideas; also a collecti of engravings.

Pele: a fortified tower which was found in the north of England in t fourteenth and fifteenth centuries, dominating a palisaded enclosu from which the name was derived.

iano nobile: in an Italian palace always the first floor, the ground floor being let off as shops and the upper floors used for bedrooms and servants' rooms.

ier: a support of solid masonry more often compound or square in section than round.

eliquary: a portable casket containing sacred relics.

etrochoir: area that lies behind the high altar.

idge-rib: rib in the vaulting system which runs horizontally along the apex of the roof.

oll-moulding: a simple rounded moulding.

otunda: building constructed on a circular ground plan.

ustication: rough-cut stonework with recessed joints, often used for the base of a building on account of its strong appearance.

haft: part of the column between capital and base, and also a single member in a compound pier.

olar: the private chamber in a residential suite, usually adjacent to the hall of a medieval castle or palace.

tring-course: horizontal moulding projecting from the surface of the wall.

ie-rod: a link, usually of wood or metal, between masonry subject to outward pressures, which it was intended to counteract.

racery: ornamental ribwork of stone used as a frame for stained glass or as a purely decorative feature on the surface of the wall.

ribune: storey above the aisles with an arcaded opening on to the nave.

riforium: space in the eaves of the aisle roof, with an arcade opening on to the nave.

illa suburbana: a country house, distinguished in classical times, and later, as one near enough to the city to be used for short visits only; thus it often had no bedrooms.

Vall-passage: gallery in the thickness of the wall, enabling communication between one part of the building and another above ground-level.

Index

Figures in bold type refer to the numbers of the illustrations